AF602038

CONGREGATION FOR INSTITUTES OF CONSECRATED LIFE
AND SOCIETIES OF APOSTOLIC LIFE

THE MANAGEMENT OF THE ECCLESIASTICAL GOODS OF INSTITUTES OF CONSECRATED LIFE AND SOCIETIES OF APOSTOLIC LIFE

At the Service of *humanum* and the Mission in the Church

Proceedings of the International Symposium
Rome, March 8-9, 2014

Presentation by
Cardinal João Braz de Aviz

Original title:

*La gestione dei beni ecclesiastici degli Istituti di vita consacrata e delle Società di vita apostolica. A servizio dell'*humanum *e della missione nella Chiesa*

1st Edition *2014*
Print on demand Edition *2021*

English translation by CAROL GLATZ

On the cover:

The Multiplication of Loaves – The Last Supper, sculpted ivory, 11th-12th century
© Courtesy of the Department of BSAE of Salerno and Avellino
Diocesan Museum of Salerno

00120 Città del Vaticano
Tel. +39 06 698 45780 - Email: commerciale.lev@spc.va
www.libreriaeditricevaticana.va
www.vatican.va

ISBN 978-88-266-0500-5

MESSAGE OF POPE FRANCIS TO THE PARTICIPANTS IN THE INTERNATIONAL SYMPOSIUM

To the Venerable Brother
Cardinal João Braz de Aviz
Prefect of the Congregation for Institutes of Consecrated Life and Societies of Apostolic Life

I cordially greet you and all the participants attending the International Symposium on the theme: "The Management of the Ecclesiastical Goods of Institutes of Consecrated Life and Societies of Apostolic Life, at the service of the *humanum* and the mission in the Church."

Our age is characterized by significant changes and developments in various fields, with important consequences for the life of mankind. Despite having reduced poverty, the goals attained have oftentimes contributed to building an *economy of exclusion and inequality*: "Today everything is regulated by the laws of competition and the survival of the fittest, where the powerful feed upon the powerless" (cf. Apostolic Exhortation *Evangelii Gaudium*, n. 53). In the face of the uncertainty in which most of the men and women of our time live, as well as the spiritual and moral frailty of so many people, especially young people, we feel challenged as a Christian community.

The institutes of consecrated life and societies of apostolic life can and must be active protagonists in living and testifying that the *principle of gratuitousness and the logic of gift* find their place in economic activity. The founding charism of each institute is fully inscribed in this "logic": of *being gift*, as consecrated people, you can make a true contribution to economic, social and political development. *Fidelity to the founding charism* and to the subsequent spiritual heritage, together with the finality proper to each

Institute, remain the first criterion for evaluating the administration, management and all of the work carried out in the institutes at every level: "The nature of the charism... directs their energies, sustains their fidelity and directs the apostolic work of all towards the one mission" (Post-Synodal Apostolic Exhortation *Vita Consecrata*, n. 45).

Attentive vigilance is needed in order to ensure that the goods of the Institutes are administered with prudence and transparency, that they are protected and preserved, combining the primary charismatic-spiritual dimension with the economic dimension and with efficiency, which has its own *humus* in the administrative tradition of the institutes which does not tolerate waste and which is attentive to using resources properly.

The day after the closing of the Second Vatican Council, the Servant of God Paul VI called for "a new and authentic Christian mentality" and for a "new style of ecclesial life": "We note with watchful attention that, in this period of ours, which is all absorbed in gaining, possessing, enjoying economic goods, a desire is apparent in public opinion both inside and outside the Church, to see evangelical poverty practiced. It is almost a need. People want to see it most where the Gospel is preached and represented" (*General Audience*, June 24, 1970; *L'Osservatore Romano*, English Edition, July 2, 1970, p. 3).

I wished to recall this need also in this year's Lenten Message. The institutes of consecrated life and societies of apostolic life have always been a prophetic voice and living witness to the newness which is Christ, of conformation to the One who made himself poor so that we might become rich by his poverty. This loving poverty is solidarity, sharing and charity and is expressed in moderation, in the quest for justice and in taking joy in the essential, so as to guard against the material idols which blur the authentic meaning of life. Theoretical poverty is not needed, but rather the poverty that we learn by touching the flesh of the poor Christ, in the humble, in the poor, in the sick, in children. Still, today may you be for the Church and for the world, the outposts of care for all of the poor and for all material, moral and spiritual poverty, and examples in overcoming every form of egoism through the logic of the Gospel which teaches us to trust in the providence of God.

As I express my gratitude to the Congregation for Institutes of Consecrated Life and Societies of Apostolic Life who have promoted and prepared this Symposium, I also wish to express my hope that it will produce the desired results. For this I invoke the intercession of the Blessed Virgin Mary and I bless you all.

From the Vatican, March 8, 2014

FRANCIS

SPEECH BY CARDINAL PIETRO PAROLIN

Secretary of State of His Holiness

Eminences, Excellencies,
Dear Brothers and Sisters,

The antiphon to the *Magnificat* of these Vespers of the First Sunday of Lent reminds us that "One does not live by bread alone, but by every word that comes forth from the mouth of God" (*Mt* 4:4). On the other hand, it is beyond doubt that man also needs bread, and so many other things in order to live. Your symposium during these days is an important occasion to reflect together on the criteria and method required for the correct management of the goods of institutes of consecrated life and the societies of apostolic life.

The available resources are a gift of providence, to receive and manage wisely. These should be used in fidelity to the founding charism and according to the proper purposes of each institute, with an administration that is as cautious and prudent as is possible. In order to achieve this, there is a need for adequate preparation in order to discern and act responsibly, adopting criteria of frugality and transparency in such a way that the evangelical counsel of poverty may be respected coherently in the management of goods, both generally and in particular choices.

The words of Jesus, cited above, demand the just order of priorities. Material goods and their management cannot be the first things with which we are preoccupied. But this certainly does not mean taking no interest in them or treating them carelessly. Rather, it helps us to understand how, when an economic-management problem worsens, this is often the symptom of some deeper difficulty, the warning sign of a certain tiredness and loss of the charism's vitality and strength. In such a case, the reform of economic management alone does not suffice, rather, it is good to consider what the true weakness may be that ends up also leading to dwindling resources. Otherwise, it is possible that while management is made ever more perfect, one can nevertheless observe an increasing difficulty in having the adequate resources available for one's mission, and thus one enters into a vicious circle.

"Not by bread alone does man live," Jesus replies to the tempter. These words challenge us profoundly and invite us always to keep the Word of God first, to attest with freshness to the charism that each person has received, to experience the Gospel in authenticity and fullness.

Instead, if we are too preoccupied with the little bread available, and we get worked up about the best way to save some crumbs, this bread could "inexplicably" disappear even more. In spite of keeping the management criteria up-to-date according to best practices, we could have difficulty finding the minimum amount of resources adequate for the aim that was proposed to us. One has saved, donation offerings have been diminished, an optimal *spending review* has been made, but instead of multiplying, the loaves and fish have run low. Why?

The Evangelist's comment at the end of the account of the multiplication of the loaves is always striking: "They all ate and were satisfied, and they picked up the fragments left over – twelve wicker baskets full" (*Mt* 14:20). Not only did the crowd get fed, but a great surplus was left over!

It is certainly important to save, to be prudent, to find the best system of management, to identify the most suitable and prepared finance officers and administrators, but this is not the heart and soul of optimal management when it is the Gospel that inspires it. The heart and the soul is the fire of the faith and of charity that gladdens us and holds us responsible and gives impetus to creativity and inventiveness at the service of the founding charism and mission of the Church, and thus also of *humanum.*

If this light shines and warms hearts and minds, it will be easier for the "twelve full baskets" to be left over, and one's obligations in the economic sphere will come with less anxiety. If this light shines and we seek first the Kingdom of God and his justice, the management of ecclesiastical goods, like many other things, will give us less worry and more satisfaction. Let us ask the Lord for this strength, this light and this faith. Providence will provide us the rest, not as a miraculous blessing to one who does not make an effort, but as a gift to the one who, though making the utmost effort, trustingly abandons oneself to the providence of God, and places Him first and foremost in one's thoughts and actions.

May the Lord bless you and your work at this symposium, and reward those who organized it with care. May it mark a step forward for a management of goods that may always be a sign of fraternity, poverty and sharing.

PRESENTATION BY CARDINAL JOÃO BRAZ DE AVIZ

Prefect of the Congregation for Institutes of Consecrated Life and Societies of Apostolic Life

Dear Friends,

As prefect of the Congregation for Institutes of Consecrated Life and Societies of Apostolic Life, it is my task and my pleasure to welcome all the participants to this event of reflection and study, which was wanted by the Holy Father, Francis, – *supreme administrator and dispensator of all ecclesiastical patrimony* (cf. can. 1256); it was organized by this dicastery for consecrated life since part of the institutional competence of consecrated men and women concerns temporal goods as well.

"As the faithful and prudent administrator has a vocation to care attentively for those goods that have been entrusted to him, so the Church is conscious of her call to safeguard and carefully administer her goods in light of her mission of evangelization, with special care for the needy." These are the words of Pope Francis himself, at the beginning of his apostolic letter *Fidelis dispensator et prudens* issued "Motu Proprio" on February 24, 2014 – with which a new structure was set up to coordinate the economic and administrative affairs of the Holy See and of Vatican City State.

The theme which we are called to reflect upon is the management of goods in institutes of consecrated life and societies of apostolic life, which are goods belonging to the Church in the service of *humanum* and the mission of the church. In line with the "*evangelical discernment*" (*Evangelii gaudium*, 50) Pope Francis called for in his apostolic exhortation, the symposium proposes to begin a reflection on "ecclesiastical goods," that is, goods at the service of the Church's proper purposes (cf. can. 1254 § 1), with particular attention to current problems arising from the administration and management of the works of institutes of consecrated life and societies of apostolic life. Through these works, consecrated persons "have emphasized the prophetic nature of their charism and the richness of their spirituality in the Church and in the world" (*Starting Afresh from Christ*, 36).

At the service of humanum: *Caritas in veritate* (21) reminds us that "the complexity and gravity of the present economic situation" require consecrated men and women to make their prophetic witness real as a contribution to a "*new humanistic synthesis.*" This means adopting "a realistic attitude as we take up with confidence and hope the new responsibilities to which we are called in a world that is in need of profound cultural renewal, a world that needs to rediscover fundamental values on which to build a better future" (*ibid*). "Prophecy of the Kingdom [...] is a non-negotiable. [...] religious are men and women who light the way to the future," Pope Francis said November 29, 2014 to the superiors general.

And the mission of the Church: "A proposal of goals without an adequate communal search for the means of achieving them will inevitably prove illusory" (*Evangelii gaudium*, 33). From this perspective, consecrated persons are aware that whenever "we make the effort to return to the source and to recover the original freshness of the Gospel, new avenues arise, new paths of creativity open up, with different forms of expression, more eloquent signs and words with new meaning for today's world. Every form of authentic evangelization is always 'new'" (*Evangelii gaudium*, 11).

The Church follows consecrated life with special care: the universal presence and the evangelical nature of consecrated persons' witness are decisive elements for the mission of the Church and for its vocation of communion and holiness (cf. *Vita Consecrata*, 9). Every single institute of consecrated life and society of apostolic life, like the faithful and prudent administrator of the Gospel, must always take care of what has been entrusted to it. Consecrated persons, as members of the Church, must acquire increasing awareness of the fact that, for the Church, a correct administration of temporal goods is not just a duty of honesty or style, it is, so to speak, a human duty.

The management of ecclesiastical goods is a real genuine mission, as affirmed in *Gaudium et spes*, which must give "witness and voice to the faith of the whole people of God." The proper purposes of the Church itself, therefore, are what give substance and legitimacy to its rights of an economic nature, justifying the existence of ecclesiastical goods. These purposes are principally the following: to order divine worship, which obviously includes the construction and maintenance of sacred buildings and what pertains to them; to provide decent support of the clergy as well as other people who dedicate themselves to serving the Church, providing also for appropriate spiritual, doctrinal and systematic formation; to carry out works of the apostolate and charity, particularly in favor of the poor, which is an essential part of the life of the Church together with preaching the Word and celebrating the sacraments. The need for economic and material means, with the consequences that come from seeking them, asking for them and managing them, must never exceed "the 'ends' to which they should serve and from which they should sense restraining limitations, the generosity of the investment, and the spiritual significance" (Paul VI).

We know the economy often plays a determining role in human history, including religious history, and, particularly in today's culture, often it determines the structure of the social organization and tends to reflect our vision of humanity itself. Within this culture, consecrated men and women, in their particular *sequela Christi*, must stay faithful to the Gospel and humankind. Theirs is not a private service, but an ecclesial one, which hinges not so much and not only on the functionality of the structures and the effectiveness of services, but on their capacity to be close to others and witnesses for Christ's love.

On the one hand, consecrated persons are almost led or compelled to get used to the inner workings of the laws of the modern economy, but they must do so with the simplicity and prudence befitting a disciple of the Lord. On the other hand, they must be aware that they can run the risk of losing their proper identity as a consecrated person, turning into mediocre or bad administrators, without any points of reference, and therefore acting at odds with evangelical requirements and with justice, thus tarnishing the image of the Church itself. The careful and forward-looking management of ecclesiastical goods and works, therefore, takes on an evangelical character. The protection and management of the goods of the Church cannot but happen in the light of its mission of evangelization.

The purposes of ecclesiastical goods are also the guidelines for a correct management of the goods of the Church and, for consecrated persons, they entail the vital safeguarding of the Christian and Catholic identity of every institute of consecrated life or work of charity as a precondition for protecting the charismatic legacy. As consecrated people, we are exhorted to walk the path of communion in the management of temporal goods, too. Indeed, if the development of peoples depends "on a recognition that the human race is a single family working together in true communion, not simply a group of subjects who happen to live side by side" (*Caritas in Veritate*, 53), all the more will we be required to walk in solidarity and synergy with institutes of consecrated life and societies of apostolic life, which by their nature exist as a gift in the Church-communion. Other indispensable guidelines are: intra-ecclesial collaboration, which takes into account the identity and autonomy of the various institutes; respect for the wishes of donors and providers; the principle of financial transparency and respecting legitimate civil legislation on these matters.

We must not forget that economic and financial management is intimately tied to the specific mission of the Church, but also in relation to the common good in the context of the integral development of the human person. Considering the great effort and significant contribution offered by institutes of consecrated life and societies of apostolic life, this particularly difficult moment in history and the need to continue working for the good of everyone require we have this meeting of reflection and study for the Treasurers General and, through them, all institutes of consecrated life and societies of apostolic life. It is necessary to take stock of the situation, which presents lights and shadows, for a renewed awareness of the responsibility of each institute, which must familiarize itself with proper planning in order to engage all of its resources – without wasting them – in its mission, which is the mission of the Church, while being faithful to its own charism.

To be faithful administrators of ecclesiastical goods, it is necessary to be aware of the great responsibility of carefully safeguarding and managing the goods of institutes of consecrated life and societies of apostolic life as ecclesiastical goods, in light of the proper purposes of the goods of the Church in the context of its evangelizing mission. We will be aided in our reflection by reports and papers presented by experts, who have been called – based on their particular skills and experiences – to talk about the various aspects of the management of ecclesiastical goods. They are pastors of the Church, university professors, officials at the Congregation for Institutes of Consecrated Life and Societies for Apostolic Life and members of institutes of consecrated life, who are in a position of authority or are engaged in the daily management of the goods of their institute.

Right from the start, I would like to thank everyone in our dicastery who worked behind the scenes with their most concrete and effective service to plan and prepare this symposium. Furthermore, I want to express my most heartfelt thanks to all those who will take the floor, each making a contribution to our communal reflection. I hope that with this symposium we can start afresh with renewed awareness, commitment and vigor concerning the management of temporal goods, in charismatic faithfulness and in docility to God's Spirit, which entail a change in mentality, behavior and sometimes, we urge, in the structures, too.

PROCEEDINGS
OF THE INTERNATIONAL SYMPOSIUM

Rome, March 8-9, 2014

INTRODUCTION

NICLA SPEZZATI, ASC

On the occasion of the *World Day of Peace* (January 1, 2014), and with evident echoes from the recent Apostolic Exhortation *Evangelii gaudium*, Pope Francis, in his *message*, sees "the succession of economic crises" as events that must "lead to a timely rethinking of our models of economic development and to a change in lifestyles. Today's crisis, even with its serious implications for people's lives, can also provide us with a fruitful opportunity to rediscover the virtues of prudence, temperance, justice and strength. These virtues can help us to overcome difficult moments and to recover the fraternal bonds which join us to one another, with deep confidence that human beings need and are capable of something greater than maximizing their individual interests. Above all, these virtues are necessary for building and preserving a society in accord with human dignity." [1]

At the service of *humanum*

The history of consecrated life – with its extraordinary variety of charisms – has undoubtedly contributed to the elaboration of "models of economic development," thanks also to its ability to change and adapt "proper lifestyles." One thinks, for example, of St. Benedict's "*Ora et labora*", which is not simply the path towards individual holiness, but the foundation of what subsequently will be expressed as a work ethic based on the principle of the nobility of work that Judaism already had expressed in some way. The experience of Benedictine and Cistercian monasticism represents the arrival point of reflection on economic life that the

[1] FRANCIS, Message of the Holy Father for the celebration of the XLVII World Day of Peace, *Fraternity, the Foundation and Pathway to Peace*, 6.

Fathers of the Church, starting in the fourth century, had already begun with acumen by subjecting the human relationship with earthly goods to the close examination of Christian ethics. Therefore, monastic culture was the cradle in which the first economic and commercial lexicon was nurtured, which shaped the Europe of the Early Middle Ages. Abbeys were, in fact, the first complex economic structures that required adequate forms of accounting and management.[2]

Francis of Assisi, choosing voluntary poverty, carried out a cultural revolution that places itself at the heart of the modern market economy, which would not be as we know it without Franciscan works and economic thought. We find the first systematic reflections on the economy, on the value and the price of goods, and on money, in the works of William of Ockham, Peter Olivi and Duns Scotus – all Franciscan thinkers. The Franciscan school of thought developed a doctrine of economics that contains new socioeconomic ideas and gives rise to the first forms of microcredit in history. The Franciscan movement, like the Benedictine, influenced – as is well noted – the religious, cultural and, not least, economic life of Europe.[3] Furthermore, St. Benedict and St. Francis, in their respective Rules, interpret and bear witness to ways and practices of life in which each developed his own vision – becoming an exemplary – as *a way of thinking* about one's relationship with goods even before their *arrangements* for using them (*Report* by Father Santiago González Silva, CMF).

"Model of development" and "ways of life" – on closer inspection – converge toward a *new humanistic synthesis*, a synthesis which saw and indeed sees its most luminous witness in the saints of charity. "Figures of saints such as Francis of Assisi, Ignatius of

[2] Cf. M. Folador, *L'organizzazione perfetta. La Regola di San Benedetto. Una saggezza antica al servizio dell'impresa moderna*, Milan 2006.

[3] Cf. O. Bazzichi, Franciscan paradigm and "Caritas in veritate," in *La Società* 6 (2009) pp. 784-800; cf. A. Cacciotti - M. Melli (edited by) *I Francescani e l'uso del denaro.* Proceedings from the VIII Historic Conference of Greccio (May 7-8, 2010), Milan 2011.

Loyola, John of God, Camillus de Lellis, Vincent de Paul, Louise de Marillac, Joseph Benedict Cottolengo, John Bosco, Luigi Orione, Teresa of Calcutta – to name but a few – stand out as lasting models of social charity for all people of goodwill. The saints are the true bearers of light within history, for they are men and women of faith, hope and love."[4] In this light, we understand the "charitable works" of institutes of consecrated life and societies of apostolic life. These are "works" which have left their mark on history and today confront problems that lead to changes in culture and practices that deal with the reorganization and management of the works themselves. It has been observed that, "sometimes it seems that these historical works not only belong to a past age, but are almost confined there, because they lack the ability to communicate the evangelical character of their witness in the present-day."[5] The "evangelic character" becomes credible in the witness of charity "recognized as an authentic expression of humanity and as an element of fundamental importance in human relations, including those of a public nature."[6] Indeed the "charitable works" carried out by institutes of consecrated life and societies of apostolic life did not limit themselves to responding to the individual's needs, but gathered from them the most profound question of *humanum*: "Christianity, the religion of the 'God who has a human face,' contains this very criterion within itself."[7] Criterion which invites the Church and society of our times "to generous solidarity and to the return of economics and finance to an ethical approach which favors the human being," as Pope Francis affirmed in his Apostolic Exhortation *Evangelii gaudium.*[8]

[4] Benedict XVI, Encycl. Lett. *Deus caritas est*, 40.

[5] Synod of Bishops, XIII Ordinary General Assembly, "*The New Evangelization for the Transmission of the Christian Faith.*" Instrumentum Laboris (2012), 32.

[6] Benedict XVI, Encycl. Lett. *Caritas in veritate*, 3.

[7] *Ibid.*, 55.

[8] Francis, Ap. Exhort. *Evangelii gaudium*, 58.

With an eye towards bearing witness to the Gospel of charity and engaging with the new questions and needs of our time, an *International Symposium* was held in Rome at the Pontifical University "Antonianum" March 8-9, organized by the *Congregation for Institutes of Consecrated Life and Societies of Apostolic Life.* The theme focused, in particular, on "The Management of the Ecclesiastical Goods of Institutes of Consecrated Life and Societies of Apostolic Life" from the complementary visions of approach: "At the service of *humanum*" and "the mission in the Church." From this perspective the ecclesial event intended, furthermore, to "re-plan our journey, to set ourselves new rules and to discover new forms of commitment, to build on positive experiences and to reject negative ones." [9] The ongoing crisis "thus becomes *an opportunity for discernment, in which to shape a new vision for the future.* In this spirit, with confidence rather than resignation, it is appropriate to address the difficulties of the present time" and the sometimes dramatic consequences of the economic behaviors of a society undergoing profound transformations.[10] Today, the great challenge, which is cultural and political at the same time, is to go beyond the traditional model of a capitalist market economy, without, however, rejecting the advantages this model has ensured until now. Indeed, it is not true, as some would like to believe, that in order to preserve and extend the social order founded on the market, one must necessarily accept (or endure) its traditional capitalist form. The belief has spread today to large swaths of public opinion that the so-called *financial turbo-capitalism* model has by now exhausted its propulsive thrust. The precious opportunity to rethink the way we conceptualize the meaning of the market is lying right before us at this very moment. Indeed, in the near future, we will increasingly be asking the market not only to

[9] BENEDICT XVI, Encycl. Lett. *Caritas in veritate*, 21.

[10] Cf. G. MANZONE, Oltre la crisi: il contributo della Caritas in veritate, in *La Società* 23 (2014) 305-315.

produce wealth and ensure sustainable income growth, but also to focus on integral human development, that is, on a development in which material, social-relational and spiritual dimensions may progress in harmony (*Paper* by Professor Stefano Zamagni).

And the mission in the Church

In an essay in 1965, Father Yves Congar, OP, observed that few theologians have examined the issue of the temporal goods of the Church, "and yet this is a reality which also belongs to ecclesiology."[11] The Conciliar Constitution *Gaudium et spes* recalls this perspective and affirms that "the Church herself makes use of temporal things insofar as her own mission requires it."[12] This particular identity and condition find expression in the style and structures that are consistent with her salvific pastoral mission or "purposes." This relationship is echoed in the words of Pope Paul VI: "The necessity of economic and material 'means,' with the consequences that entails – to seek them, to ask for them, to administrate them – should never overpower the concept of the 'purposes' to which they must serve and from which they must feel the restraint of limits, the generosity of their use and the spirituality of meaning."[13] The question of the administration of temporal goods is thus rooted in the same profound truths which form the basis for the identity of the Church and her mission.

This was the common thread running through the symposium: "Ecclesiastical goods" are goods *for* the Church and as such are at the "service of *humanum* and the mission *in* the Church." (*Paper* by Archbishop José Rodríguez Carballo, Secretary of CICLSAL). The ecclesiology of communion remains the context in which it is

[11] Y. CONGAR, *I beni temporali della Chiesa secondo la tradizione teologica e canonica*, in *Chiesa e povertà*, Rome 1968, 257.

[12] SECOND VATICAN ECUMENICAL COUNCIL, Past. Const. *Gaudium et spes*, 76.

[13] PAUL VI, General audience June 24, 1970, in *L'Osservatore Romano*, June 25, 1970 (Editor's translation).

possible to overcome a merely instrumental view of goods and to reinstate them – qualify them – as resources for the communion-mission of the Church within the communion-mission of particular churches. In this perspective, it remains a matter of urgency that all consecrated people, and particularly those responsible for managing the goods of their institution, become aware of the need to search for a radical response to the economic and ethical problems that such management entails. This response must build its foundations on the Gospel and in a reading of the charism truly rooted in an ecclesiology of communion. This is an ecclesiological theme that impacts the daily tasks of many institutes of consecrated life and societies of apostolic life. Particular situations – in different national contexts – cannot be reduced to "case studies," but rather to experiences that open up new avenues of reflection and planning between particular churches and institutes (*Paper* by Archbishop Joseph W. Tobin of Indianapolis, U.S.A.). An awareness has progressively emerged over the years of the importance of not remaining inside "market patterns" and of highlighting the ecclesial meaning of goods.

This same vision is connected to a reflection on the norms of the Code of Canon Law (*Report* by Father Yuji Sugawara, SJ), which refers to a fundamental point of reference for the protection and promotion of this ecclesial nature. The key themes of the *Social Doctrine of the Church* – both its principles and content – receive a detailed reflection, which provides the background of the complex problem of the relationship with the ordering of the state (*Report* by Father Mirolaslav Konštanc Adam, OP).

In institutes of consecrated life and societies of apostolic life, the concept of "administration" is in the process of being in harmony with the concept of "management." Hence the theme that is the focus of our symposium. This is not a superficial change in name, but a substantive change in the actual way activities are conducted and, therefore, a change in the approach to management and, consequently, in the corresponding instruments of managing certain activities. It is a change which involves specific situations of an economic-managerial nature. Just to give a few examples, in particular there is: the underestimation of problems, which turn into insurmountable "crises"; negative growth rates of activities and assets, and the consequent limited investment in innovation; accounts being "in the red," rendering it necessary to cover ordinary needs with extraordinary funding by means of gradual financial dependence on outside entities or funding systems; in some cases, situations of "Band-Aid" management and "putting out fires"; resorting to letting go of assets and works with the illusion of resolving crisis events, which are sometimes irreversible; and finally, the limited capacity to attract and retain people of quality.

Economic-administrative problems also have consequences within the framework of the proper law of institutes of consecrated life and societies of apostolic life. This law finds its "legal framework" in Book V of the Code of Canon Law: *The Temporal Goods of the Church,* which can. 635 § 1 expressly refers to with reference to the ecclesiastical goods of religious institutes. "Ecclesiastical goods" were at the heart of the speakers' reflections. Nonetheless, it would serve little to have new forms of organization (including legal), to have targeted adjustments to rules and norms, and to propose or adopt "alternative" juridic persons, if we were not to switch, at the same time, to a real change of mentality and management culture, which directly affects the way "proper works" are carried out in the world of consecrated men and women. In this light, it is just as important to focus on the relationship between the service of authority and the role of the finance officer (*Paper* by Brother Álvaro Rodríguez Echeverría, FSC). This is an aspect which needs further in-depth study because it is decisive not only for sound management, but above all for making procedures for the vigilance-oversight of administrative acts more concrete. We must therefore strengthen the synergies between roles (of superiors and treasurers) – that is, create "partnerships," as we hear over and over again, by opening up new channels of cooperation while respecting and valuing each other's own separate capabilities and competencies.

It is normal that when the context changes – think, for example, of the legislative changes triggered by the economic-financial crisis – the way we manage our organizations must also change. Many of the problems shown above truly indicate a direct showing of this necessity, that is, of this change. As emerged over the course of the symposium, our institutes of consecrated life and societies of apostolic life have been required: to transition from a mindset of "passive" administration of goods based on the formal respect of regulations to a management logic that is by nature innovative; to valorize their patrimony and safeguard a certain stability for it;[14] to carry out planning projects within a global vision of institutional planning (*Report* by Sister Yvonne Reungoat, FMA); not to be organizations that are "closed," but open to "relationality," which is to say, attentive to their relations with people and towards all critical stakeholders within and outside our entities. It is a change that does not constitute a world being turned upside down, but is an integration, a new point of view, that is currently still at the stage of being implemented (cf. contributions made by the "roundtable").

Today institutes of consecrated life and societies of apostolic life have been called to take up certain challenges, above all, in a *change of mentality*, but in particular:

– not to use one's purpose as a justification for inefficiencies; it is possible to pair up good management and the institute's charismatic mission without making light of the present difficulties;

– not to hold onto past experience as a constant frame of reference that puts at the risk or is used to the detriment of suitable (or required) innovations;

[14] Cf. ITALIAN CONFERENCE OF MAJOR SUPERIORS - ITALIAN UNION OF MAJOR SUPERIORS, *Il Patrimonio stabile. Novità, significato, recezione di un istituto a tutela e garanzia dei beni ecclesiastici*, Rome 2014.

– not to confuse or overlap the concept of the institute's "internal hierarchy" (superiors) with distinct administrative and managerial levels out of fear of "losing control";

– not to presume that staff (lay and religious) can be self-motivated without the support of specific training done ahead of the desired innovation.

The many suggestions that emerged both from the speeches and the respective discussions can be traced back, broadly speaking, to certain areas. The first is already strongly highlighted by Pope Benedict:

– "The great challenge before us, accentuated by the problems of development in this global era and made even more urgent by the economic and financial crisis, is to demonstrate, in thinking and behavior, not only that traditional principles of social ethics like transparency, honesty and responsibility cannot be ignored or attenuated, but also that in *commercial relationships* the *principle of gratuitousness* and the logic of gift as an expression of fraternity can and must *find their place within normal economic activity.*" [15]

– In this light, we should position the desired "new planning vision" that is geared towards better identifying and increasing the *specific features* of services within this view of one's *proper charism* – with the latter seen as the criterion of credibility/reliability inside the communities where they are based.

– The attention and vigilance of those responsible (major superiors and treasurers) cannot be limited to "everyday" operational problems, but must be directed towards an "overall strategy," adopting tools for planning and organization, and not just reporting.

– Alongside initiatives which may result in losses, other supplementary initiatives should be implemented, planned and managed in a way that makes them compensate for the former.

[15] BENEDICT XVI, Encycl. Lett. *Caritas in veritate*, 36.

– One should avoid the erosion of the entity's overall patrimony, which, in the end, constitutes the real guarantee of the continuity of the *non-economic* mission over time.

"By her very nature the Church is missionary," Pope Francis affirms in *Evangelii gaudium*, "she abounds in effective charity and a compassion which understands, assists and promotes." [16] The charisms of consecrated men and women in the mission of the Church spring from this same charity because within them we recognize "the profound connection between evangelization and human advancement, which must necessarily find expression and develop in every work of evangelization," [17] particularly for the poor. Consecrated men and women have never been deaf to their cry (cf. *Ex* 3:7). Today it has to do with re-creating a new mentality because "the option for the poor is primarily a theological category rather than a cultural, sociological, political or philosophical one."[18] Consecrated life has made an option for the poor to be understood as a special form of primacy in the exercise of Christian charity. This symposium did not lack the voices of those who live and witness this closeness on the frontiers of "new fragilities," which produce "new poverties": migrants, victims of human trafficking, women, unborn children.

From this point of view, the *roundtable* compared meaningful experiences of institutes and ecclesial movements, which find themselves engaged in building an economy which is prophetic and lived as communion and solidarity. Finally *quaestiones* of current juridical-canonical affairs were posed, connected with the very broad questions of civil legislation and in particular with the reorganization of works: the responsibility of institutes and of members (can. 639) concerning debts and obligations (Father Jesu Pudumai

[16] FRANCIS, Ap. Exhort. *Evangelii gaudium*, 179.

[17] *Ibid.*, 178.

[18] *Ibid.*, 198.

Doss, SDB); public juridic persons with particular attention paid to the context and experience in the United States, noting the interest in a management option, which deserves consideration (Sister Peggy Ann Martin, OP); an assessment of the "instruments" of foundations, real estate funds and their compatibility with the identity of the institutes of consecrated life (Monsignor Alberto Perlasca). Last but not least, there was the question of the "stable patrimony" of an institute of consecrated life (can. 1295 § 1), which is back in the canonical debate, and we also see before us some entities going through "a patrimonial crisis-situation" (Father Sebastiano Paciolla, O.CIST).

By dealing with the administration and management of ecclesiastical goods, we did not want to end up in a "web of obsessions and procedures,"[19] which limit the scope of the problems and urgencies. Rather, we wanted to draw up a roadmap that addresses the responsibilities of consecrated men and women in the mission of the Church and avoids easy conclusions. Thus, it is an invitation to broaden horizons. Consecrated men and women do not *do* mission, "*I am a mission* [...] of bringing light, blessing, enlivening, raising up, healing and freeing."[20]

The symposium has undoubtedly contributed to delineating a "*status quaestionis,*" which the attention and concern of institutes of consecrated life and societies of apostolic life had been focusing on for a while. From this point of view, the dicastery has expounded upon a problem that has been felt strongly at an international level. At the same time, an exercise of "farseeing imagination"[21] has been set in motion, which is to say, getting institutes of consecrated life and societies of apostolic life to discern their current potential/possibilities; to hasten/reawaken the "innate" creativity generated by charity and to identify guidelines that give

[19] *Ibid*, 49.

[20] *Ibid.*, 273.

[21] PAUL VI, Ap. Lett. *Octogesima adveniens*, 37.

reasons for hope and a vision of the future. Only "through an effort of *community* imagination, it is possible to transform not only institutions but also lifestyles and encourage a better future for all peoples" [22] and for consecrated life itself.

NICLA SPEZZATI, ASC
Undersecretary CICLSAL

[22] PONTIFICAL COUNCIL FOR JUSTICE AND PEACE, *Towards Reforming the International Financial and Monetary Systems in the Context of Global Public Authority*, Conclusions.

FIRST SESSION

Moderator

FATHER SEBASTIANO PACIOLLA, O.CIST.

Under-secretary of the CICLSAL

THE ADMINISTRATION AND MANAGEMENT OF THE ECCLESIASTICAL GOODS OF INSTITUTES OF CONSECRATED LIFE AND SOCIETIES OF APOSTOLIC LIFE AT THE SERVICE OF *HUMANUM* AND THE MISSION IN THE CHURCH

BIBLICAL AND ECCLESIOLOGICAL GUIDELINES

✠ JOSÉ RODRÍGUEZ CARBALLO, OFM

Situating ourselves

The mission, with a contemplative dimension and fraternal life in community, forms what we can call the "backbone" of consecrated life. Consecrated men and women are, in fact, those who are called and summoned to be sent (cf. *Mk* 3:13-14). The mission, which cannot be detached from these two aforementioned elements, requires dealing with material goods. From this requirement stems the need to administer goods with all due diligence, so as not to endanger the mission of the institute and, sometimes, its very survival – something which could happen with bad administration – but to advance it in all of its dimensions: apostolic activity, formation of the institute's members and its collaborators, attention to elderly and sick brothers and sisters, all without forgetting about solidarity with those most in need.

Therefore, the theme of this symposium, "*The management of goods by religious institutes*" is extremely timely, as also can be seen by the large number of participants, not just because this kind of management, even if for different reasons, worries all of us a little, but I would say, above all, because consecrated men and women put their credibility and evangelical significance very much on the line with the way in which they manage goods. In fact, behind the numbers and the way goods are managed also lies a concrete lifestyle that attests to – or not, their words, enough for it to be said that the management of goods indicates whether a consecrated person or an entire institute is travelling along the right path.

And, since the administration of goods is intimately linked with the poor and austere lifestyle of the institute, which is made concrete in the vow of poverty or in the *vivere sine proprio*, it is equally important to look after the lifestyle of the person who took the vow of poverty, creating a style of economic life and administration that, on the one hand, favors the mission of the institute and lived poverty and, on the other hand, constitutes "an administrative and financial policy which can provide an alternative to what is offered by neo-liberalism, and a convincing answer to the needs of the religious institutes at the service of the poor." [1]

It requires, then, a reflection on the administration of goods in religious institutes in general: this is the main objective of this symposium. Something that should be added is the elaboration of *guidelines* for the just and proper management of goods by consecrated men and women,[2] who form the context of such management and administration as they are called to respect other norms such administration must be subject to, such as canon law and the civil laws of the country in which the institute conducts its activities. This is why, let's say it right off, the management of goods on the part of consecrated men and women cannot leave out of consideration the spirituality that animates the life and mission of a particular charism; or, better yet, such management cannot be done as something removed from evangelical values, which every consecrated man and woman is called to make his and her own with the profession of the evangelical counsels and the ecclesiology that is the legacy of the Second Vatican Council.

[1] UNION OF SUPERIORS GENERAL, *Economy and Mission in Consecrated Life Today*, Rome 2002, n. 2.

[2] The Congregation for Institutes of Consecrated Life and Societies of Apostolic Life is at this time developing these said guidelines.

The great challenge: efficiency or effectiveness?

What has been said places consecrated men and women before a great challenge: choosing between efficiency or effectiveness. Consecrated men and women, in particular treasurers or other financial officers since they are managers of the goods entrusted to them, often live a great tension. Paul VI made reference to this in 1974, that is: the tension between having a perfect and qualified organization and, as consecrated men and women, the duty not to let ourselves take on more than what is *necessary* in view of "that *optimam partem* that the Lord praised in Mary of Bethany [...] unlike her far too busy sister (cf. *Lk* 10:42)."[3] A temptation that often attracts us, at the present time, is "to seek first of all for a humanly effective activity,"[4] a technical and organizational *efficiency* of our material resources and of our works, instead of spiritual *efficacy* in our actions. In their management of goods, consecrated men and women cannot totally renounce *efficiency* and obtaining material results that show; however, they also cannot forget or put effectiveness in second place, which guarantees results in people's inner life.[5]

An example to make it clear: An institute that manages a school cannot but offer good intellectual formation to its students (*efficiency*), but it also cannot forget their integral formation, which prepares them to be active creators of a new society, which is more in consonance with the values that give meaning to the life of the members of the institute who manage the school (*effectiveness*).[6]

[3] Cf. PAUL VI, Discorso agli economi delle comunità religiose, in *L'Osservatore Romano*, May 9, 1974. (Editor's translation).

[4] PAUL VI, Ap. Exhort., *Evangelica testificatio*, 30.

[5] In the administration of goods in consecrated life, the necessary tension between being well prepared so that it is done with necessary efficiency and paying attention to efficacy must be managed well. This tension must always be animated by sufficient transparency and conformity and by a large dose of prudence and good sense. Cf. E. ARENAS - F. TORRES, *Vita consacrata ed economia. Manuale per l'amministrazione degli Istituti religiosi*, Milan 2006, 9ff.

[6] Cf. A. BACHELET, *Economia e fede*, Rome 1990, 11ff.

The management of goods by consecrated men or women, whether it is ordinary management or the fundamental planning of an institute's activities, must be, therefore, a *spiritual management*, that is, management animated by the spirit of the charism of the institute, which drives such management forward. We can also call this management, *ecological management*: a management that takes into account the needs of the institute but also the needs of the Church and the needs of the poorest.

Reasons for a *spiritual* or *ecological management* of goods

A discussion on the management of goods by religious and, therefore, a management that I called spiritual and ecological must be based on solid evangelical, theological, charismatic and social foundations. This is what I propose in my presentation, even if for reasons of space and time I need to keep it limited and present it in a very concise way.

We can draw from the texts of the New Testament three important affirmations in order to offer a foundation for a *spiritual* or *ecological* management of goods: Jesus is a poor man who lives in solidarity with the poorest; there is a close link between discipleship and poverty/solidarity; and riches can distance us from God and make us insensitive to the poorest.

Jesus, a poor man, united with the poor

Prior to other considerations, let us look at Jesus. One thing is clear: according to Gospel accounts, Jesus lived poorly.[7] He presents himself as the Son of man who "has no place to lay his head" (*Lk* 9:58). Jesus chose a poor and itinerant life for himself, without human security, but also a life of fraternity. The evangelists' insistence in recounting how much Jesus loves to share meals with others, particularly with the poor and sinners, is significant

[7] Cf. B. MAGGIONI, Gesù e il denaro, in *Parola, spirito e vita* 42 (2000) 111-118.

(cf. *Lk* 14:23). The accounts of healings of the sick show a Jesus profoundly in solidarity with those who suffer, particularly the poorest. For John, the memory of Jesus as poor and in solidarity with others lingers in the communal gesture of the washing of the feet (cf. *Jn* 13:1 ff.). Jesus is poor and is in solidarity with others: this is beyond dispute.

Jesus made this choice to show the true face of God, the face of the God of the poor (cf. *Lk* 1:46-56), in order to belong totally to his mission (He is the true poor man who lives without anything of his own and, therefore, is free from everything) and in order to give witness to his total trust in the Father, just as his enemies could see: "He trusts in God: let God deliver him now, if he desires him" (*Mt* 27:43).[8] In this way, Jesus not only speaks for and represents those who live in a state of oppression, injustice, poverty and violence, but he makes present the kingdom of God among men and women of goodwill.

Discipleship and poverty/solidarity

In this context, we cannot but listen again to the first beatitude: "Blessed are you who are poor, for yours is the kingdom of God" (*Lk* 6:20). "Blessed are the poor in spirit, for theirs is the kingdom of heaven" (*Mt* 5:3). According to Luke's reasoning, it will be necessary to correct unjust structures, to share material goods, to transform the economic order..., so that the poor have what is theirs according to justice. In fact, we find the same demands of social justice in the Gospel of Luke as in the prophets. According to Matthew's reasoning, a new attitude toward having is necessary. The evangelist wants it to be recognized that, before God, everyone is poor; he wants that people accept depending on God and that people be valued for what they are and not for what they have. Neither Luke nor Matthew makes a political or economic point,

[8] G. ROSSÉ, Il denaro e la ricchezza nell'evangelista Luca, in *Parola, spirito e vita* 42 (2000) 119-130.

but their doctrine has enormous consequences on the way to live among humanity, just as Matthew recalls in that well-known Chapter 25. Wealth and poverty are two cultural ways of living. With this beatitude, Jesus unsacramentalizes wealth, removing the nature of a "sacrament of promise" from it; he puts having, riches and money under God's rule, stripping from them their power over people and their status as a measure of people's relationships with each other; he situates humanity on the plane of being, on that which truly matters: the values that stem from the Beatitudes.[9]

Retracing the Gospels as the recollection that the communities passed on about Jesus' proposal and praxis, linked with the reading of the problems and challenges of their time, we note that the poor and poverty are not only the focus of Jesus' attention, but also a fundamental part of the life and choices of the communities. And, in a certain way, the same aspects that determine Jesus' choices are also decisive for the choice of poverty that Jesus will ask of his disciples, as we read in the Gospel of Luke: "Those of you who do not give up everything you have cannot be my disciples" (*Lk* 14:33). For Luke, the relationship between following Jesus and poverty is very clear: the disciple is called to renounce everything that can get in the way of following the poor Christ. And again: "You cannot serve God and mammon" (*Lk* 16:13). The disciple is called to place all his "security" in God and only in God.

Jesus, who chose poverty for himself, now asks his disciples to do the same. To renounce all of one's possessions is the condition for becoming a disciple, and this renunciation is always motivated by love for him and does not make one be harsh on others. On the other hand, with the words: "You cannot serve God and mammon," Luke strikes down the attempt to reconcile the irreconcilable. A slave is someone who belongs to another. Belonging to God out of love is the highest level of freedom. Belonging to riches (*mammon*) is total slavery. Those who become "lovers of money" (cf. *Lk* 16:14; *2 Tm* 3:2) and make it true idolatry

[9] B. LAMBERT, *Las bienaventuranzas y la cultura hoy*, Salamanca 1987, 62ff.

(cf. *Eph* 5:5) cannot be disciples; and because their wealth has "rotted" (cf. *Jas* 5:1 ff.), they will have a difficult time entering the Kingdom (cf. *Lk* 18:24 ff.). The disciple is asked not only to choose poverty on a personal level, but also in the mission. This must be realized in poverty. Disciples need not have anything with them: "No bread, no bag, no money in their belts" (*Mk* 6:8). For the disciple, Jesus is enough; everything else would only obscure their witness. I believe it is important in this context to refer to James. Using an expression of the prophets (cf. *Is* 13:6), the Apostle James tells the rich landowners of their imminent and certain ruin: "Come now, you rich, weep and howl for the miseries that are coming upon you" (*Jas* 5:1). This text recalls, also literarily, the curses against the rich, the satisfied and the pleasure-seekers in the Gospel according to Luke: "But woe to you who are rich... Woe to you who are well-fed now... Woe to you who laugh now..." (*Lk* 6:24-25).

But is it not enough to be poor: the disciple, particularly in the Gospel according to Mark, is born in welcoming the poor and acting with them. It is significant that when Luke presents the ideal of a Christian community (cf. *Acts* 2:42-47; 4:32-35), he places the growth of the community within fraternal communion, in overcoming poverty, and in solidarity, as the fulfillment of *Dt* 15:4: "There will be no poor among you." The Acts of the Apostles always present wealth and the use of goods as not only linked to the theme of discipleship, but especially to the theme of mission, to the point that the detachment from goods is, so to speak, the "business card" of the first Christian communities called to be witnesses of the Gospel. Luke presents the ideal of Jesus realized in a fellowship that shares goods so that there is no one in the community who is poor or in need (cf. *Acts* 2:44-45). It is a community of fraternal communion and sharing, according to the Old Testament promise of Deuteronomy cited above. Only a community of disciples that does not allow itself to be attracted to the trappings of power and money, but maintains its heart oriented towards God the Father, is a credible witness of the Risen Christ and the power of the Holy Spirit.

In this context, it is good to remember that the logic that runs throughout the Gospel is *the logic of gift.* Starting from the contemplation that: *He who gave himself fully to us*, and that *everything*, in a radical sense, *belongs only to him* (St. Francis); the disciple is not permitted to live outside this logic nor to manage goods as if he or she were the real owner and, therefore, marginalize others, especially the most needy. It is a question of justice towards God – He is the only true owner – and of justice towards others; goods belong to everyone. He who does not respect this sense of belonging, St. Francis of Assisi says, is a usurper, a "thief." To round up what has been said, we must remember that the Word of God invites us repeatedly to stick to what is essential – here symbolized in food and clothing: "Life's prime needs are water, bread, and clothing, and also a house for decent privacy" (*Sir* 29:21). Actually, according to Sacred Scripture, the same piety is characterized by soberness (*autárkeia*) (*1 Tm* 6:6).

The danger of riches in one's relationship with God and others

As already mentioned, the disciple, according to Luke, is called to have a "heart" firmly set on God and oriented totally towards the true "treasure" (cf. *Lk* 12:34). For Luke, trust in riches is opposed to trust in God. The account of the rich young man (cf. *Lk* 18:18ff.), whom Jesus asks to let go of his wealth, not only affectively but also effectively and immediately, in order to be able to follow him, as well as the parable of the rich man and the poor Lazarus (cf. *Lk* 16:19-31), where the third Gospel warns of the danger of becoming insensitive to the situation of those who live in need, all indicate that we cannot take lightly Jesus' commandment (in *Lk* 14:33) to renounce all of one's possessions. Luke cautions his readers, telling them that money and wealth can take the place of God in man's heart and separate us from the poor. That is why the third evangelist warns against the accumulation of "treasures" and not becoming rich in what matters to God (cf. *Lk* 12:16ff.). A text that seems to me to be important in this context is found in the Jewish apocrypha, the *Book of Enoch*, preserved in the Ethiopian language: "Woe to you, you rich, for you have trusted in your riches, but from your riches you will depart for you did not remember the Most High in the days of your riches" (*1 Enoch* 94:8). The danger of wealth is losing one's "memory" of God and trust in him.

In addition to what has been said, wealth acts as a shield against the Gospel proclamation or the participation in the kingdom of God: the deceitfulness of wealth prevents the seed from growing (cf. *Mk* 4:19). Also, the metaphor of the eye of the needle recalls how difficult it is for the rich to enter the kingdom (*Mk* 10:25). The denunciation of greed is found also in the Pauline tradition with particular virulence in *Colossians* 3:5: "Put to death, therefore, whatever belongs to your earthly nature: sexual immorality, impurity, lust, evil desires, and greed, which is idolatry" (cf. *Eph* 5:5). The negative consequences of the desire for wealth are listed in the Pastoral Epistles in a gradation of qualifying adjectives that are apt indicators of an obsession that is contrary to the true nature of man, a temptation, a trap that leads to drowning. The list ends with two terms with connotations of eschatological judgment: "destruction" (*òlethros*) and "perdition" (*apoleia*) (cf. *1 Thes* 5:3; *2 Thes* 1:9; *Phil* 1:28; 3:19; *Rm* 9:22; *2 Pt* 2:1.3; 3:16). These are warnings to bear in mind.

Instead, poverty chosen for the kingdom is a *sacrament*, that is, an efficacious and concrete sign of faith in God. Without poverty, there is no faith, except in words. Disciples must lead a life like that of Jesus, like that of the "birds of the sky" and the "lilies of the field" (cf. *Mt* 6:25-35), transparent through and through with the message of faith in God they must bear witness to. Poverty is the royal "staff" of the disciple, who is by now free from the slavery of possessing.

As a synthesis of managing goods in the light of the Gospel, allow me to offer five key perspectives: the idea of sharing what one has (cf. *Jn* 6:1-13); the idea of an alternative that puts the brakes on ambition (cf. *Mk* 9:42-48); the idea of incisive lucidity, as demonstrated in the parable of the rich man (cf. *Lk* 16:19-31); the idea of equality and the idea of equity which lead to generosity (cf. *Mt* 19:30; 20:16). All this speaks of the need for an exodus that heads towards alternatives that lead, in one way or another, to the fight against poverty and to be apostles of new relationships.

Church as *koinonia.* Called to fraternity and solidarity

As the theologian Yves Congar[10] foresaw a few years before the Second Vatican Council, basing the theology of the mystery of the Church on the concept of *koinonia* is perhaps the most significant innovation of the doctrine of the Council for post-Conciliar ecclesiology and for the life of the Church. This idea is intimately tied to another key idea from Vatican II, that of the "people of God." In this "Church of communion," timidly developed in the years after the Council, every baptized person has his or her place: the pope as supreme pastor of the universal Church, as the successor of Peter in the See of Rome; the bishops, as successors of the apostles, shepherds, teachers and priests in communion with the pope;[11] the priests, as "prudent cooperators with the episcopal order," who "sanctify and govern under the bishop's authority, that part of the Lord's flock entrusted to them,"[12] consecrated men and women, as prophets of the values of the Kingdom and witnesses of the same form of life as the obedient, poor and chaste Son of God; lay people as active members within the people of God, who wander as pilgrims in this world. Recognizing the place of every member of the Church and his or her mission in the ecclesial community entails an "ecclesiological conversion" that stems from

[10] Cf. Y. Congar, *Sainte Église. Études et Approches ecclésiologiques*, Paris 1963, 21-24.

[11] Cf. Second Vatican Council, Dog. Const. *Lumen gentium*, 25-27.

[12] *Ibid.*, 28.

the baptismal consecration – upon which the fundamental equality of all the members of the Church is based – and recognizes and respects the vocation and mission of each person.

This new paradigm of Church is nourished by the *spirituality of communion*, a powerful and significant proposal by Pope John Paul II in 2001 at the beginning of the new millennium: a guiding principle of education wherever ministers of the altar, consecrated persons, and pastoral workers must be formed; a "place" and "space" where families and communities are built up.[13] For us consecrated men and women, it is not possible to understand nor to realize authentic relationships with other members of the Church without decisively employing this guiding principle of education of the spirituality of communion. I believe it can be said that this is the indispensable theological and ecclesiological feature of the current moment, which speaks about what the Spirit is asking in order to give the Church a new impulse to spread the Gospel: "To make the Church the home and the school of communion, that is the great challenge facing us in the millennium which is now beginning, if we wish to be faithful to God's plan and respond to the world's deepest yearnings." [14]

This path proposed by the pope is not a personal journey. Precisely because the spirituality of communion is deeply rooted in the mystery of the Most Holy Trinity, it has very concrete consequences. Among these we can underline two of them: feeling profoundly united to all members of the mystical Body, therefore, to perceive others as those who "are a part of me," to share their joys and sufferings and to sense their desires and attend to their needs; and welcoming and valuing the other as a "gift for me," "to make room" for my brother, "to carry each other's burdens" (*Gal* 6:2). After proposing this guiding principle, John Paul II concludes: "Let us have no illusions: unless we follow this spiritual path, external structures of communion will serve very little purpose.

[13] John Paul II, Ap. Lett. *Novo millennio ineunte*, 43.

[14] *Ibid.*

They would become mechanisms without a soul, 'masks' of communion rather than its means of expression and growth." [15] If the entire Church must live within this guiding principle of education, consecrated persons must live by it all the more, for they, because of their life choice, are called to be "specialists" in communion. This is why the Church entrusts to consecrated men and women the particular task of "*spreading the spirituality of communion*, first of all in their internal life and then in the ecclesial community." [16]

What consequences does this theology of a Church of communion have for the administration of goods? The Second Vatican Council, in the Pastoral Constitution on the Church in the Modern World, *Gaudium et spes*, reminds us that the administration of goods must be done in a way that they benefit not only the owners but others, too.[17] In his encyclical letter *Caritas in veritate*, Benedict XVI affirms that a lack of brotherhood is a key cause of poverty, particularly in the area of relationships.[18] In turn, Pope Francis is convinced that the fight against poverty entails a detachment from goods, "a sober and essential lifestyle" and the sharing of one's wealth, so as to be able to "experience fraternal communion with others [...] which constitutes their most precious good." [19] Pope Francis also wrote recently: "As the faithful and prudent administrator has a vocation to care attentively for those goods that have been entrusted to him, so the Church is conscious of her call to safeguard and carefully administer her goods in light of her mission of evangelization, with special care for the needy."[20] Therefore, some criteria that must guide the management of goods by the Church and consecrated persons: thinking of others, which means being less self-referential, having relationships marked by frater-

[15] *Ibid.*

[16] JOHN PAUL II, post-syn. Ap. Exhort. *Vita consecrata*, 51.

[17] Cf. SECOND VATICAN COUNCIL, Past. Const. *Gaudium et spes*, 69.

[18] Cf. BENEDICT XVI, Encycl. Lett. *Caritas in veritate*, 19.

[19] Francis, *Message for the World Day of Peace* (2014) 5.

[20] FRANCIS, Moto prop. *Fidelis dispensator et prudens*, February 24, 2014.

nity, living sober and basic lifestyles, engaging in the evangelical mission and being concerned about the poor.

All of this is opposed to greedily seeking material goods, the impoverishment of interpersonal relationships and the search for profit beyond sound economic reasoning, which is fruit of the "individualism of our postmodern and globalized era that favors a lifestyle which [...] distorts family bonds."[21] It is what Pope Francis calls a "new tyranny, invisible and often virtual" of a "deified market" where "financial speculation," "widespread corruption" and "self-serving tax evasion" reign.[22] These attitudes, or rather we should say this "throwaway culture," in which "the excluded are not the 'exploited,' but the outcast, the 'leftovers,' "[23] lead humanity further from God and neighbor, and therefore lead to a proliferation of poverty.

Speaking about some of the challenges of the world in this context of today, Pope Francis denounces the current economic system as "unjust at its root,"[24] in that it privileges "the survival of the fittest," where "the more powerful feed upon the powerless."[25] And it is for this reason that the current economic system "kills." The economic crisis that we are experiencing should lead us to rethink economic development models and consider a change in lifestyle that is characterized by sobriety and solidarity. Solidarity is the criterion that breaks with the logic of the greedy search for material goods and shows the need to create "a new mindset which thinks in terms of community, fraternity and the priority of the life of all over the appropriation of goods by a few;" a mentality that emerges from the conscience, as the social doctrine of the Church teaches and as then-Cardinal Bergoglio reminded us several years ago when he said the universal destination of goods is a paramount

[21] Pope Francis, Ap. Exhort. *Evangelii gaudium*, 67.

[22] *Ibid.*, 56.

[23] *Ibid.*, 53.

[24] *Ibid.*, 59.

[25] *Ibid.*, 53.

right "antecedent to private property, insofar as it is subordinate to the other." [26] This new mindset "must become the flesh and thinking of our institutions. It must cease being a dead letter so it can turn into a reality that establishes another culture and another society. It is urgent to fight for people's redemption, these sons and daughters of God, but above all against the pretence of an indiscriminate use of the goods of the earth." [27]

Solidarity, then, is not a "feeling" but a way of intending and living one's actions – in this context, actions dealing with finance – and living in society itself. In our case, solidarity must translate into ideas, praxis, feelings, structures and institutions at the service of the poor. In this way, solidarity becomes culture. Solidarity, therefore, is a global attitude that must be translated into our relationships with groups or people, and seek to face social inequalities; but it also puts ways to prevent these inequalities into action. So, as we ask ourselves where among us – in our communities, institutes, in the Church itself – has this solidarity become the culture, we must revise the criteria that guided us in the financial field up until now. These are paths that are not easy to navigate, but they are fitting for consecrated persons, becoming a kind of "trademark" or "certificate of authenticity" of the lifestyle of a consecrated man or woman.

Consecrated men and women are called to overcome "superficial solidarity," characterized by one-off aid, and delve into a "fruitful solidarity" and an "excellent solidarity." This anchors its roots in the Gospel, that is, in the logic of gratuitousness and unconditional gift; it goes hand in hand with intelligence, ability and efficacy; it seeks to manage resources with greater responsibility and seriousness; it puts into action adequate mediation to help those who are in difficulty; and it has as its goal the construction of

[26] Jorge Mario Bergoglio - Pope Francis, in *Riflessioni di un pastore. Misericordia, Missione, Testimonianza, Vita*, Vatican City 2013, 462-463. (Editor's translation).

[27] *Ibid.*, 463. (Editor's translation).

an inclusive and fraternal society.[28] Respecting these principles entails just and ethical management. For consecrated persons, it is not simply about doing charity – which in itself is already very demanding – but about solidarity that is just: giving to each person what belongs to him and her.

"Give, and it will be given to you: A good measure [...] running over, will be put into your lap" (*Lk* 6:38) because "it is in giving that we receive."[29] "It is more blessed to give than to receive" (*Acts* 20:35). The letter and, above all, the spirit of these texts do not consent to a management of goods with a labored, excessive, conditional or exaggerated search for results that are purely financial. In this context, I would like to refer to a text by St. Ambrose. The holy Bishop of Milan says: "You own goods that guarantee you prosperity for many years. Do not limit yourself to preserving them. Make them bear fruit for yourselves and for others. In which way? By putting them in a place that is inaccessible to thieves; safeguarding them in the hearts of the poor. These are your strongboxes: the stomachs of the hungry. These are your granaries: the homes of widows. This is your depository: the mouths of orphans [...]. You have no justification when you use only for yourselves that which, through you, God wanted to give to his people. The prophet Hosea says: 'Sow seeds of justice.' Plant, then, your seeds in the hearts of the poor."[30]

In light of these principles, we are all called to ask ourselves: what must change in the management of goods in the communities, the entities and the institutes of consecrated life, so that they respond to an ecclesiology of communion? It is clear that all consecrated persons are asked to travel a journey in *supportive synergy*, even in the management of goods, in order to demonstrate with concrete gestures their love and service to the poor, a sign of the

[28] *Ibid.*, 465-468.

[29] *Prayer* attributed to St. Francis.

[30] Ambrose of Milan, La viña de Nabot, in *El buen uso del dinero*, Bilbao 1995, 96-97. (Editor's translation).

kingdom of God that Jesus came to establish,[31] and to place their talents and hands at the service of the "program of the Good Samaritan, the program of Jesus."[32]

To conclude: certain urgent matters, considerations and criteria in the management of goods by consecrated persons

I do not pretend to offer the last word on the subject we are looking at. Surely, the presentations that will follow will shed abundant light on this subject, which indubitably is of paramount importance right now. For now, I think what is important is to present some urgent matters, considerations and criteria to keep in mind in the management of goods by religious, in light of what we have said so far. Therefore, here are some requirements that emerge from what I have said:

- It is urgent that all consecrated men and women, particularly those who are responsible for the management of their institute's goods, become aware of the need to seek a radical response to the economic and ethical problems that are involved in such management. The foundations of this response must be deeply rooted in the Gospel, an ecclesiology of communion and each institute's charism.
- It is just as urgent for consecrated men and women to be well aware that their way of proceeding with the management of goods can either give great evangelical meaning to their mission or seriously compromise their witness and their significance in society.
- In the management of goods, it is also urgent to look at the question of poverty and the poor with the eyes of the heart, as it is only with the heart that one can see rightly (Saint-Exupéry). This includes breaking away from "gloomy" or discouraged views of poverty and the poor. It involves questioning oneself about

[31] Cf. FRANCIS, Ap. Exhort. *Evangelii gaudium*, 48.

[32] Cf. BENEDICT XVI, Encycl. Lett. *Deus Caritas est*, 31b.

the causes of poverty, even if this brings with it judgment and condemnation: "When I give food to the poor they call me a saint. When I ask why the poor have no food, they call me a communist" (Hélder Câmara). It entails a vision that does not put the tragedy of poverty and the poor in second or third place, but makes it a top priority. If we look with the eyes of the heart, we will realize that, starting from the Gospel, the big question is not what will be the future of our presence, but what I can do for you. In fact, this is Jesus' big question before the world of poverty (cf. *Mk* 10:51). Giving real priority to the world of poverty would lead consecrated life not so much toward modernizing its economic approaches, as much as putting itself at the service of the need for mercy, compassion, and solidarity with the poor and the needy. It would lead to heading out to the margins of poverty. The meaning of the vow of poverty resides greatly in this. To look with the eyes of the heart involves having a gaze that transforms the elusive question from being: "What can be done or what can I do?" into: "What am I ready and willing to do myself?"

• The management of goods cannot be done apart from some of the challenges that the world of the poor presents to consecrated life: the poverty of so many brothers and sisters must not leave us indifferent; the strong desire to live differently must not diminish; we must not lose that capacity to dream in an different way that is characterized by justice (cf. *Lk* 12:49).

• To respond to these urgent issues it is fundamental that the subject of the management of goods, with all of its implications, be included in programs of formation, both initial and ongoing. These programs must place the person and their integral development at the center of the issue of the management of goods and, more particularly, of the economy as well as pay greater attention to managing goods not just in regards to quantitative growth. This entails dissociating *homo oeconomicus*, who is insatiable in his desire for goods and whose choices are determined above all by the maximization of personal interests, and instead embracing *homo fraternus*, the man in relation to others. The challenge is to create a way of life in which human development and the quality of relationships grow.

Other principles to keep in mind in order to not seriously compromise the evangelical management of goods and to protect what we have called "spiritual management":

• Prior to any decisions being made, clearly and responsibly evaluate the possible consequences on the life and the mission of the members of the institute and on the social context in which they work, without ever forgetting "the fate" of the poor.

• In no case can rectitude, honesty and justice be disregarded. Guiding the management of goods according to these values is already a way of preaching the Gospel and making an alternative way of life present in society.

• Austerity is a criterion to always keep under consideration in the management of goods by consecrated men and women. The desire to follow Jesus Christ demands it, even in the apostolate. All that is superfluous or can be seen as ostentatious must be avoided.

✠ José Rodríguez Carballo, ofm
Secretary CICLSAL

THE CHARISM AND GOODS OF AN INSTITUTE AND THEIR RELATION TO THE LOCAL CHURCH

✠ Joseph W. Tobin, CSsR

Introduction

If asked what I might offer to the rich content of this important symposium, I would confess that I have been not been invited to speak today because of my academic prowess or because I possess a notable record of outstanding administration. Rather, the superiors of the Congregation for Institutes of Consecrated Life and Societies of Apostolic Life (CICLSAL) have extended this kind invitation simply because I have been privileged to serve the Church in different ways: first, in the leadership of my religious family and, most recently, as a diocesan bishop.

These experiences have given me some insight into the theme that has been assigned to me, that is, a reflection on the way members of the consecrated life administer temporal goods within the context of a particular Church. There are a number of loci where the pastoral governance of the diocese and the economic administration of a religious institute intersect, such as fund-raising by religious institutes or the just compensation of their members. I am also aware of how the apparent economic power of an international religious community can engender confusion or ill will, especially in the young Churches of developing countries. However, because of limits both of time as well as the patience of participants in this symposium, this modest contribution will focus on the question of the alienation of temporal goods by a religious community and the sort of consideration that is due to the local Church.

Why is it important to consider this question? When a religious institute decides to abandon a particular work, the decision frequently elicits incomprehension, even active opposition by the local bishop. Such a reaction can be intensified by the manner in which the religious dispose of temporal goods that they have acquired during the time their community was present within the diocese. Circumstances may cloud or complicate the question of alienation and the actions of the bishop and religious superior may bewilder, even scandalize the faithful, harming the *communio* that ought to characterize the Church. Thus, the *modus operandi* is not simply a vindication of rights but also an eloquent expression of the quality of the ecclesial life.

In fact, even at the beginning of this discussion we might ask whether knowledge of a doctrine or the observance of norms is sufficient to bring about the desired harmony in a local Church. There is no doubt that both theology and law illuminate and indicate channels of relationship between bishops and religious superiors. However, even when norms are scrupulously followed, we still can find ourselves overwhelmed by reality! That is to say, by facts or circumstances that hinder relations that, from a theological or canonical standpoint, should be clear. Looking at a few examples of these situations can signal, even indirectly, some solutions.

Examples of conflict caused by the decision to alienate

Since most of the participants in this symposium are superiors or treasurers of their institutes, I presume that you are familiar with the potential for conflict in a decision to alienate a school, church or other institution. I ask your patience if I cite a few examples that I have known, either directly, from experiences during my years as superior general of the Redemptorists, or indirectly, from the testimony of other bishops or religious superiors during my service in the dicastery that accompanies members of the consecrated life.

1. An exempt religious congregation constructed a school and administered it successfully for decades. Eventually, a downturn in vocations meant that there were no more religious to administer

the school, which became too expensive to staff with lay personnel. The property was offered to the local diocese for purchase. When the bishop did not respond, the closing of the school was announced and the property was sold to a supermarket.

In an ill-advised decision, the local bishop seized the property and, with the support of the parents of the students and other benefactors, reopened the school. The civil authorities initially supported the move, citing eminent domain. Of course, the bishop had no title to the property. The religious had not sought canonical permission for the sale. The result was genuine confusion, but eventually, the diocese had to surrender the property to the owner of the supermarket.

2. A congregation of women religious administered a school for many years, but a shortage of vocations led them to decide to close the school, which they intended to sell and apply the proceeds to finance their mission in other countries. The bishop of the place did not give a favorable opinion regarding the proposed alienation, since the property that provided the operating income for the school had been donated years before by a benefactor who had stipulated that the gift be used for the education of the children in surrounding area. The dicastery eventually agreed with the bishop and asked that the intention of the donor be honored.

3. A congregation of religious had established a public juridic person (PJP) to carry on its mission in health care. The PJP decided to sell a small hospital to a secular, for-profit health system, meaning that a small city and surrounding rural district would no longer have a Catholic hospital. The bishop was informed of the decision shortly before it was announced. He protested, saying that the decision would discriminate against the poor of the area, who would not have the means to travel considerable distance to another Catholic hospital. The bishop also questioned whether the PJP could not find another Catholic system that might purchase the hospital.

Because of the bishop's protest, the sale of the hospital was delayed. Eventually the PJP did find a Catholic health care system that was willing to purchase the hospital.

In my experience, a particularly troublesome question concerns instances in which religious institutes actually own a parish church or the land on which a parish is built. There seems to be little uniformity in practice regarding the question of ownership and the right to be compensated. The same ambiguity is present in cases where the diocese holds title to the land on which a religious institute has made significant investments of capital to develop a school, church or orphanage. What sort of compensation is due to them, if they abandon the work, or the bishop invites them to leave?

Relevant norms are useful but insufficient

It is clear that some of the conflictual situations just cited could have been avoided if the bishop and the major superior had followed the norms that govern the process of alienation by religious,[1] as well as the general norms in Book V of the Code.[2] What is more, because the goods of the Church often come from the generosity of the faithful, who wish to express in this way their relationship with God – itself a religious purpose – the will of the faithful is sacred and must be respected by whoever accepts material support from them.[3]

[1] Particularly can. 638 § 3 and § 4

[2] Cf. cann. 1290, 1291, 1292 § 3 and 1293 § 1, 2°.

[3] V. DE PAOLIS, *La Vita Consacrata nella Chiesa*, ed. by V. Mosca, Venice 2010, 405. The intent of the donors must always be respected. For some bishops in the United States, this concerns the sale or donation of property formerly held by religious, especially when it finishes in non-Catholic hands. Frequently the property acquired by religious institutes (building of hospitals, schools, clinics, convents, etc.) came through the charity of the clergy and laity of a diocese because of the service provided on behalf of the local Church. Donating or

In many countries, the sale of Catholic hospitals is a particularly complex issue. Religious institutes are expected to seek to sell an institution to a Catholic system and present documentary evidence of their efforts. Such a sale is not always possible, however, due to the large investment of capital required in order to guarantee the viability of the hospital. While the incident cited above had a felicitous conclusion, there are notable examples to the contrary. If a bishop refuses to submit his opinion in order to signal his objection or writes a very negative letter, insinuating that he knows that a different sale is possible, the delays and eventual publicity can be very damaging to available health care in the region, employment, etc.

It cannot be denied that a reason for conflict around the question of alienation is that often neither major superiors nor bishops are familiar with the canonical norms that govern the process. As a result, property is sold by the religious before the proper steps are followed or the local ordinary may make an inopportune – or even, unjust – intervention. However, as useful as the existing norms are in guiding the process of alienation, their mere observance is not sufficient to remove all ambiguity that may surround the decision to alienate and to guarantee that the process does not result in a counter-testimony to communion within the Body of Christ.

A crucial element in any effort to ensure that the decision to alienate does not become a stumbling block in a particular Church is the relationship between the local bishop and the religious involved, particularly their major superior. The Code does not oblige pontifical institutes of consecrated life to obtain the permission of the local ordinary before alienating property. The praxis of the CICLSAL, however, requires that the religious obtain the opinion (*parere*) of the bishop where the property is located. At times, religious do not seek the opinion of the bishop before concluding

selling such property in a way that no longer supports the mission of the Church is extremely problematic and often a source of scandal.

the transaction; it also happens that the bishop does not respond to such a request, or fails to understand the reasons that the religious present.

In the following section I will attempt to illustrate why this communication is inherently difficult, given the theological and canonical development following the Second Vatican Council, especially regarding the ecclesial significance of the local Church and its bishop.

The enhanced authority of the diocesan bishop

One of the characteristics of the revised Code of Canon Law is the enhanced role given to the diocesan bishop. Canonically, he is the chief pastor and key authority figure in the diocese.[4] The diocesan bishop has all the authority he needs to carry out the mission that has been entrusted to him.[5] His power is *ordinary*, i.e., attached to his office; *proper*, i.e., exercised in his own name; and *immediate*, i.e., exercised directly over all the faithful of the diocese without the need of an intermediary.

The bishop administers the diocese in his own name: not as a representative of the Roman Pontiff, but as a vicar or delegate of Christ. Since the diocesan bishop's power can be regulated by the pope and restricted in certain respects, such as by requirements for consultation and consent in administrative matters, his power is not absolute.[6] In virtue of this power, bishops have the right and duty to issue laws for the faithful, to make judgments and to regulate everything pertaining to the good order of worship and the apostolate.[7] There is an interconnection of the teaching, sanctifying and governing *munera* that focuses the entire ministry of the bishop on serving God and the Christian faithful.

[4] Cf. can. 369.

[5] SECOND VATICAN ECUMENICAL COUNCIL, Dogmatic Const. *Lumen gentium* [henceforward *LG*], 27; can. 381 § 1.

[6] Cf. cann. 131 § 1 and 381 § 1.

[7] Cf. *LG* 27; can. 391 § 1.

A principal service of the bishop is to ensure the good order of the apostolate throughout the diocese. This is an area in which religious and their apostolic works relate most directly to the diocesan bishop for the pastoral welfare of the people of God. Canon 394 calls on the diocesan bishop to promote various forms of the apostolate in the diocese and to coordinate all apostolic works throughout the diocese. The canon goes on to exhort him to urge all the faithful to participate in the works of the apostolate according to their vocation and to make sure that the various needs of the diocese are being met.

The Code also addresses the bishop's authority specifically with regard to apostolates either proper to or entrusted to the care of religious institutes. As sponsors of Catholic institutions, institutional leaders and those who minister with them are subject to the authority of the diocesan bishop in three areas: the *cura animarum*, public worship, and all other works of the apostolate.[8]

It is not hard to see that consultation, coordination, and cooperation among major superiors, leaders of religious institutions and the diocesan bishop are essential for the sake of the mission in the local church. In practice this means, for example, that a religious institute does not decide to close or end sponsorship of a school, college or other apostolic work without communication and consultation with the diocesan bishop. It means that the diocesan bishop exercises oversight responsibility for the teaching of faith and morals in apostolic works of religious institutes. It also means that the diocesan bishop should involve the leadership of religious institutes and their apostolic works in the pastoral planning of the diocese. In other words, the more open the channels of communication and coordination are between the major superiors and leaders of apostolates that have been entrusted to religious and the diocesan bishop, the more effective will be the missionary dynamism of the diocese.

[8] Cf. cann. 678 and 681-682.

The task of coordination is directed toward achieving good order in order to safeguard the unity of the apostolate. Practically speaking, such coordination usually requires the development of channels or structures of communication and collaboration to facilitate and encourage a healthy exchange of information and experience.

Coordination of apostolic works on the part of the diocesan bishop and major superiors requires recognition of the rights and duties of the faithful in building up the Body of Christ. This includes the rights of religious regarding church property.

Religious institutes

With approval of their constitutions, religious institutes[9] are erected as collegial public juridic persons with canonical rights and obligations similar to those of natural persons.[10] One of these rights is the right to acquire, administer and alienate church property. The assets are ecclesiastical property subject to the norms of Book V of the Code of Canon Law.[11] As canonical stewards of the property belonging to the institute, superiors are responsible to fulfill their function with the diligence of a good householder.[12]

When a religious institute determines in accord with its proper law and the canons of Book V that it wishes to dispose of its one or more of its assets, such as the building and property of a school, motherhouse or hospital, the major superior should consult the diocesan bishop in accord with the exhortation of canon 678 § 3, which calls for mutual consultation between bishops and superiors regarding the apostolate, especially if the apostolate of the diocese (which the bishops has the responsibility to coordinate) will be affected. If the property is to be alienated or if it is a transaction

[9] Those of diocesan rite as well as pontifical rite.

[10] Cf. can. 634.

[11] Cf. can. 1257 § 1.

[12] Cf. can. 1284.

that could jeopardize the patrimonial condition of the institute,[13] the major superior must obtain the written consent of the council and any other body determined by proper law.[14] Other requirements regarding a just cause, written estimates or expert appraisals are listed in canon 1293. If the transaction exceeds the ceiling determined by the Holy See for religious institutes of a particular territory, the permission of the Holy See is also required. This applies not only to buildings and land, but also to precious art with historical value and items given to the institute by vow. For diocesan institutes and autonomous monasteries, the diocesan bishop must approve the request.

It is crucial for religious to establish and maintain a relationship with the diocesan bishop, so that the first contact is not motivated by a problem or the need for his opinion regarding a proposed alienation. He should be involved in discussions prior to the request being sent to the Holy See. Not all transactions resulting in the sale of property belonging to religious institutes requires approval by the Holy See. It is often in these situations that communication between bishops and superiors fails.

The new name for charity

Let me try to summarize the principal parts of my argument. First, there are clear norms that govern the process of alienation of property by a religious institute, although these norms may not be known by either the major superior or the bishop. However, the knowledge and observance of norms alone will not guarantee that the bishop and religious express the *communio* that must characterize the Church. Rather, the mission that is entrusted to both bishops and religious requires that they establish a sincere relationship of collaboration through an efficacious dialogue.

[13] Cf. can. 578.

[14] Cf. can. 638 § 3.

In the apostolic exhortation, *Vita Consecrata*, John Paul II stresses the importance of this cooperation so that there might be an "organic development of pastoral programs in the local Church."[15] He recommends a "constant dialogue" between bishops and superiors and judges it as "most valuable" for promoting mutual understanding and a "necessary precondition for effective cooperation."[16] Canon 678 § 3 strongly exhorts bishops and superiors to "proceed through mutual consultation" in organizing the apostolate, and suggests that meaningful consultation will happen only if mutual trust, openness and honesty characterize the dialogue and collaboration that take place between bishops and superiors.

The fact that such dialogue and collaboration does not always characterize a local Church is not attributable simply to clashes of personality or clericalism. Rather, a diocesan bishop and a religious institute may think about the Church in distinct ways. As we have already seen, a theological development of Vatican II has been the enhanced authority attributed to the diocesan bishop. The Council thereby expressed a renewed appreciation for the particular Church and envisioned the bishop as one who is charged with ensuring the good order of the apostolate throughout the diocese.

The service of coordination by the bishop becomes problematic, if he understands the role of religious principally as useful or functional rather than as "sign." A functional appreciation of religious may lead to an expectation that their goods are to be seen finally as funds for the diocese, while making more difficult to accept the reality that religious may have obligations beyond the local Church, such as the formation of candidates and the care of the elderly in other countries.

For their part, religious, especially members of exempt institutes, generally think in terms of the expression of their charism in the universal Church. As laudable as this way of thinking is, it may

[15] JOHN PAUL II, Ap. Exhort. *Vita Consecrata*, 48.

[16] *Ibid.*, 50.

contribute to their inadequate insertion into the local Church. The praxis of their autonomy or exemption becomes problematic when it is characterized by excessive independence from the pastoral plan (where one exists) or the abandoning of valuable apostolates without any prior consultation of the bishop.

Only from a theological outlook – more than juridical – will we be able to understand autonomy or exemption, on the one hand, and dependence, on the other, of religious as well as their greater openness to the universal Church as well as their need and obligation to collaborate in the pastoral plan of the diocese.

Neither autonomy nor exemption can justify a lack of solidarity or absolute independence. Nor can cooperation with the hierarchy reduce religious to inert instruments in the hands of the bishop. Hence both parties – bishops as well as religious, have to encourage knowledge of the doctrine regarding the episcopacy and religious life, the theology of the local Church as well as their mutual relations.[17]

Means for enhancing the relationship between bishops and religious

What does this mean, in practical terms?

- First, there is a need for mutual respect and effective communication between the diocesan bishop and the major superiors of religious who serve in the diocese. A bishop should treat serious matters with the major superior instead of limiting his communication to the local superior, pastor, school director, etc.
- The diocesan bishop will want to create with major superiors different occasions for regular communication as well as promote extraordinary celebrations, such as the annual commemoration of consecrated life (February 2nd). Reciprocal visits have also proven

[17] Sacred Congregation for Religious and for Secular Institutes - Sacred Congregation for Bishops, Directives for the mutual relations between bishops and religious in the Church, *Mutuae Relationes*, 29.

to be helpful in fostering communion between the diocesan bishop and religious.

• The bishop ought to appreciate persons and structures that will enhance his pastoral care for religious, such as the nomination of a diocesan vicar or delegate for consecrated life.

The CICLSAL can provide a valuable service at the time of the *ad limina* visits by encouraging the bishops to create a forum for regular dialogue with the religious in their respective Churches. The Congregation can exploit its frequent contact with general superiors to urge religious to establish and maintain respectful and open communication with the ordinaries of the dioceses where their members serve.

The story of Simon Bruté College, Indianapolis

I submit for your consideration an example of a decision by a religious order to alienate a significant temporal good that has resulted in great benefit for the local Church as well as for the religious involved. In 1932, a monastery of Discalced Carmelite nuns was erected in the city of Indianapolis. For more than fifty years, the monastery flourished, maintaining a community of twenty nuns, while founding two daughter monasteries.

In the last decades, vocations diminished and by 2008, the community had been reduced to nine elderly nuns. The prioress approached my predecessor, Archbishop Daniel Buechlein, OSB, to discuss the possibility of selling the monastery. The nuns had decided to move to a vacant building on the property of the motherhouse of Congregation of the Sisters of the Third Order of St. Francis, located in a small city approximately 150 kilometers southeast of Indianapolis. The Franciscan Sisters welcomed the monastic community and offered them the use of their infirmary, when needed.

At the same time, Archbishop Buechlein was looking for a residence to accommodate a growing number of diocesan seminarians, who were studying at a Catholic university that was sponsored by the Franciscan Sisters. The original monastery of the Carmelites was located within walking distance of the university and seemed to be an ideal site for the seminary. The Carmelite nuns arranged for several professional estimates of the value of the property and later agreed to sell it to the Archdiocese of Indianapolis.

The archdiocese recently augmented the former monastery and the seminary now accommodates 46 seminarians from Indianapolis and the surrounding dioceses. The Carmelite nuns are very satisfied with their new home and, because they received a just price for their former monastery, the nuns have sufficient funds to provide for their monastic life and care for the sick. Finally, the Franciscan sisters have welcomed to their faculty of philosophy a growing number of students.

The mutual benefit to the religious and the diocese is clear. It should also be noted that the decision engendered much admiration and goodwill among the faithful, who witnessed and approved the fruitful collaboration. This solution was possible because the different religious institutes involved and the diocesan bishop had already established respectful and transparent relations, which made this concrete collaboration possible. I am grateful to be the heir of this example of communion among the different vocations that enrich our local Church.

Conclusion: "mutual relations" among disciples

According to the Gospel of Matthew, shortly before his passion Jesus speaks with his apostles about the way they should relate with each other. He counsels against adopting a model of "mutual relations" that was prevalent in their society: "You know that the rulers of the Gentiles lord it over them, and the great ones make their authority over them felt. But it shall not be so among you" (*Mt* 20:25-26).

Without a system of mutual relations that is based on the principle of communion, there is the real possibility that other forms of relationship will enter the Church: that of a commercial corporation, a parliament of opposing interests or the law of the jungle, where only the strongest survive.

The strength of the Church is found in communion, which is the real source for projecting the mutual relations among the disciples of Jesus Christ. The Magisterium and canonical disposition can favor a harmonious and fruitful collaboration among bishops and major superiors. But not all the problems presented by life are resolved by the application of norms. The search for the common good of the Church, love and a genuine desire, together with a lively sense of communion and an appreciation for creative dialogue will always provide the best help.[18]

✠ JOSEPH W. TOBIN, CSsR
Archbishop of Indianapolis (USA)

[18] Cf. T. Bahíllo Ruiz, Las relaciones entre obispos y religiosos en la Iglesia: realidad y perspectivas a los XXX años de la *Mutuae Relationes*, en *Estudios Eclesiásticos*, vol. 83 (2008), núm. 327, p. 565.

ECCLESIASTICAL GOODS AND THEIR PURPOSES IN THE CODE OF CANON LAW

YUJI SUGAWARA, SJ

Introduction

Book V of the Code of Canon Law, titled *The Temporal Goods of the Church* (cann. 1254-1310), clearly indicates that the Catholic Church has the innate right to possess and to use goods to pursue its ecclesial purposes through the many juridic persons who are under the supreme authority of the Roman pontiff. As is indicated in the book's first canon, the right of the Church to goods is linked to the fact that it has its own proper purposes to be pursued (can. 1254 § 1), for which temporal goods are also necessary. Similarly, when can. 1260 expresses the innate right of the Church to require from the faithful those things which it needs, the norm states that it exercises this power only as much as is necessary for the purposes proper to it.

The expression "proper purposes" can be substituted sometimes by the analogous term "mission." The patrimonial right of the Church is derived from the mission that the church carries out in the world, that is, the salvific mission received from the Lord himself. The licit nature of the Church's ownership of temporal goods is directly linked to the achievement of its purposes and if the goods do not serve those purposes, such ownership is not justified. As the Second Vatican Council made evident, the Church makes use of "temporal things insofar as her own mission requires it," indeed, she will "give up the exercise of certain rights which have been legitimately acquired, if it becomes clear that their use will cast doubt on the sincerity of her witness or that new ways of life demand new methods."[1]

Can. 1254 § 2 highlights the purposes of the goods owned by the Church, particularly those purposes *proper* to it. They are principally: to order divine worship, to care for the decent support of the clergy and other ministers, and to exercise works of the sacred apostolate and of charity, especially toward the needy.[2] The purpose specified in § 2, charity, especially towards the needy, historically and still today, has held the top position among those purposes. The preferential option for the poor is one of the burning issues that occupies an important place in the conciliar and post-conciliar Magisterium[3] both for the entire Church and consecrated men and women. The Code not only speaks of the right of the Church to require the necessary goods from the faithful but also clearly of the goals for which these goods are destined.

The Code of Canon Law indicates different principles that guide a correct administration of goods. From the practical point of view, it would not be possible for each institution in the Church to maintain its diverse entities or carry out its apostolic activities if it did not have any economic capacity. At the same time, it is impossible to bring credibility to the message of the Church in the modern world without the correct and just administration of goods and any mistakes in this area, in fact, can cause (rather, in reality, they have caused) serious hardship in the particular churches and in institutes of consecrated life.

[1] SECOND VATICAN ECUMENICAL COUNCIL, Past. Const. *Gaudium et spes*, 76.

[2] In the current Code, Book II, can. 222 § 1 speaks explicitly of the obligation "to assist with the needs of the Church" and lists, as examples, the same aspects: "for divine worship, for the works of the apostolate and of charity, and for the decent support of ministers." The canon speaks not only of clerics but also of other ministers, including consecrated persons and lay people who offer their service to the Church.

[3] For example, SECOND VATICAN ECUMENICAL COUNCIL, Decr. *Apostolicam actuositatem*, 8; Past. Const. *Gaudium et spes*, 42.

1. The goods of the institutes of consecrated life

In the Church, goods are only considered "ecclesiastical" when they belong to public juridic persons (can. 1257 § 1) which are ordered "for a purpose which is in keeping with the mission of the Church" (can. 114 § 1) in order to "fulfill in the name of the Church, [...] the proper function entrusted to them in view of the public good" (can. 116 § 1). According to can. 634 § 1, not only religious institutes, but also their provinces and houses, are defined as public juridic persons *ipso iure*, which is why the temporal goods owned by all these entities are considered "ecclesiastical goods" and are governed by the canons regarding the temporal goods of the Church, unless other provision is expressly made otherwise (can. 635 § 1).

Although the temporal goods of institutes are established as "ecclesiastical," can. 1256 affirms that they belong to the institutes themselves as a juridic person which has acquired them legitimately, and not to another higher authority in the Church, for example, the particular church in the case of institutes of diocesan right. These goods are administered and alienated according to their own abilities and under their own management and responsibility with the freedom to judge the quality and quantity of goods that are necessary for their purposes, as a manifestation of the internal governance of the institutes that enjoy a just autonomy of life (can. 586 § 1). As the Second Vatican Council teaches, consecrated life is inseparably united to the mystery of the Church and it belongs to its life and holiness.[4] The conciliar decree recognizes that institutes have the right to possess whatever goods are required for their temporal life and works they seek to accomplish.[5] Following the reasoning of the Council, institutes have the right to possess and administer temporal goods, given that they participate

[4] SECOND VATICAN ECUMENICAL COUNCIL, Dogm. Const. *Lumen gentium*, 44; cf. can. 574 § 1.

[5] SECOND VATICAN ECUMENICAL COUNCIL, Decr. *Perfectae caritatis*, 13.

in the mission of the Church. The goods of the institutes and their use, therefore, should be understood within the purposes and needs of the Church, which is limited to possessing and using all the means necessary and to making use of "temporal things insofar as her own mission requires it".[6]

Respecting then the strong guidance of Vatican II, every institute must pursue its proper purpose by faithfully grounding itself on the aims and intentions of its founders.[7] The just autonomy of governance, recognized in can. 586 § 1, includes the administration of temporal goods as part of governance. Needing or not needing temporal goods for pursuing its purposes is to be evaluated clearly and, although much will also depend on the views of the various superiors and officials in concrete decisions, there can be no other criteria for the institutes of consecrated life other than the founding charism of each institute. This approach requires that each institute establish norms for the administration of goods, including the collective practice of evangelical poverty, which reflect its own founding charism. Can. 635 § 2 affirms that the poverty of the institute must be "fostered, protected, and expressed" through the norms concerning the use and administration of goods. The norms of each institute, therefore, must express not only the limits to the use and administration of goods, but also the right to poverty according to the ideals of the founders. The key criterion for establishing the norms for the administration of goods in proper law should be the institute understanding that its proper purpose is evangelical poverty; the efficiency of a strict administration of goods or the efficacy of the apostolate is not its primary goal.

The document *Starting Afresh from Christ* indicates that the constitutions of each institute are "always open to new and more demanding interpretations" and that this dynamic sense of spirituality offers the opportunity to develop a deeper spirituality that is

[6] Second Vatican Ecumenical Council, Past. Const. *Gaudium et spes*, 76.

[7] Second Vatican Ecumenical Council, Decr. *Perfectae caritatis*, 2.

more ecclesial and communitarian and generous in apostolic choices.[8] As the understanding of the charism deepens, ever new possibilities of carrying it out will be discovered.[9]

2. Difficulties experienced

From the beginning, the Church received many temporal goods from the faithful so that it could respond to the many needs it encounters both within the Church and in the world. What matters is the intention for which the goods were offered to the Church and the reason why the Church possesses them, that is, its supernatural purpose: the salvation of souls (can. 1752). The difficulty in the field of administration comes from the existence of a canonical norm which is based on factors that are strictly ecclesial, that is, the spiritual and pastoral needs in the Church require a particular style of life and apostolate. While the canonical norms must focus, as we saw above, on safeguarding the ultimate purposes of the goods offered, administrators actually are obliged to deal with technical norms before the different parties involved in the management of goods.

Even within consecrated life, a key issue concerns the relationship between the ideal of evangelical poverty it professes and the difficulty of renouncing material goods needed to advance its life and works. The institutes can possess and administer goods because they participate in the purposes of the Church. But when the quantity of goods begin to increase in the institute, often the question seriously arises of how it may be possible to maintain and protect those goods both to support its members and support its mission effectively. The spiritual question can easily turn itself into a technical issue and balance is lost.

[8] Cf. Congregation for Institutes of Consecrated Life and Societies of Apostolic Life, *Starting Afresh from Christ*, 20.

[9] Cf. *Ibid.*, 31.

The Code of Canon Law does not offer a quantitative definition for the administration and alienation of goods, rather, it is limited to regulating the praxis with a criterion based on ultimate purpose. When it comes to resolving problems, one might wish there were a list of concrete measures that demand special attention as well as all the necessary procedures, for example, acts of extraordinary administration. But the modern economy would not permit an approach of determining things with such detail because of the complexity of the activities involved today compared with the past. It would not be possible to list at the level of universal law either, all the categories of extraordinary acts when such rapid changes that were previously unimaginable are underway concerning the nature and means of economic activity.

In the end, while financial management is not the only thing in the organization of the Church, it is something that requires special attention because different areas and different levels in the Church suffer from a lack of experts. In the world of economics today, the Church needs experts in the management of goods and pastors who understand the urgency of this issue. The Church, in fact, is no longer an exception when it comes to financial affairs in the world and it can no longer ask for leniency and tolerance before civil legislation. Rather, transparency in the administration of material goods is an important part of ensuring the credibility of the Gospel message to a world that suffers various injustices and new forms of poverty.

3. The response from the Code

With the objective of preserving the ecclesiastical patrimony by bearing in mind its proper purposes, the Code imposes certain formalities when following the required procedures and using consultative bodies to find the best ways and to avoid errors and abuses in the acts of administration and alienation. In every situation, the Code requires the presence of a leader who can pave the way for the goods entrusted to it to be used to achieve its proper purposes at every level and category, which means it foresees there be a superior overseeing the persons and an administrator of the goods.

Certainly, it must be recognized that there are not many norms in the Book on the temporal goods of the Church and the norms are general since they are promulgated for the entire Church. Church law limits itself to regulating just some of the more important aspects and to setting a number of principles; for the rest it refers to or "canonizes" civil law regarding financial affairs. Furthermore, in the Code of 1983, almost all of the canons in Book V have corresponding canons in the Code of 1917, which means that we have a 100-year-old and stable tradition in the Church on the subject in question and, at the same time, we are abiding by principles that have been valid for at least 100 years (certainly even more) for responding to the needs of today's economic world.

Therefore, we need two elements that perhaps require innovation in the legal structure and in the mentality of the persons involved: first, to use well what little exists in canon law concerning the administration of goods, and second, to form capable members within the institute who can learn to collaborate with lay faithful who are competent in the social teachings of the Church and civil law. Obviously, a norm does not produce the spiritual reality. Nonetheless, without a juridic structure, the spirit of the institute and its sound traditions run the risk of disappearing.

a) *Canons to protect purposes*

Different canons in Book V make reference to the protection of goods. Can. 1281, which addresses the extraordinary acts of administration, states that in order to place acts which exceed the limits and manner of ordinary administration (§ 1), the administrators must first obtain written permission from the ordinary,[10] and

[10] There are acts that are placed in a different category from the point of view of the purpose and at a different level of the measure and they are considered extraordinary administration; these acts require a particular procedure according

such acts must furthermore be defined in the statutes (§ 2). In such a way, when the act responds to the purposes and the service that the juridic person should provide based on its statutes, the administration is held to be ordinary. Given that religious institutes have proper law to determine the acts that exceed ordinary administration, according to can. 638 § 1, it is up to them to establish specifically that it be the competent superior to give the requested permission.[11]

Every juridic person, like a religious institute or a religious house with its own works, has a stable patrimony or capital. Some goods are considered indispensable by their very nature, in the sense that without such goods, the juridic person would not have the means necessary to accomplish its purposes, for example, a school building or a library at a university. Can. 1291 talks about "stable patrimony" regarding the act of alienation and it shows the need for such goods to be clearly assigned. These goods are part of the *stable patrimony* in order to either maintain them or not alienate them, according to the nature and purposes of the juridic person; they require a particular procedure for their alienation.

The Code does not prohibit alienation, but it establishes how to alienate the goods that once served as a religious witness; it requires a decision about to whom the property is to be transferred or to demonstrate the reason why the institute is letting go of the administration of the ecclesiastical goods. Furthermore, can. 1292 asks the episcopal conference in each country or region to determine the amounts beyond which would require the per-

to canon law. In a careful reading of the canons that use the expression "*finem (fines) et modum*," Cardinal De Paolis observes that administration can be extraordinary both in reference to purposes or to measure. According to the author, when the act responds to the purposes and the service that the institute must give, based on its proper law, the administration is considered ordinary. Cf. V. De Paolis, *I beni temporali della Chiesa*, Bologna 1996, 146-148.

[11] Furthermore, can. 1284 § 2, 6°, states that one of the main tasks of administrators is to set aside money left over after expenses to be used towards the purposes of the Church or the institute.

mission of a competent authority for alienation. The maximum amount is determined by the Holy See for the alienation of goods owned by religious institutes. According to can. 638 § 3, however, it is up to the institute's internal authority to determine the minimum amount, beyond which permission from the internal authority of the institute is required. The alienation of ecclesiastical goods, in fact, requires a just cause and the Code lists, besides urgent necessity or evident advantage, "piety, charity or some other grave pastoral reason" and certain norms are offered that intend to guarantee and to protect the purposes of the acts of alienation of ecclesiastical goods (cann. 1293-1294).[12]

Respecting the wills of those who donate goods to the Church or of benefactors or founders is particularly important in canon law, as can been for example, in can. 1300 on pious wills.[13] Their intentions must be respected with the utmost care and precision, because by offering goods to the Church, the faithful are seeking to fulfill their responsibilities, to honor God, to practice fraternal charity and to support the ministers who work in the Church (can. 1254 § 2). This obligation is, in fact, a norm that has always been respected in the history of the Church. Equally, in cases of "offerings given by the faithful for a certain purpose" (can. 1267 § 3) and of "goods which have been donated or left to it for pious causes" (cf. can. 325 § 2), the will of the founder or donor who bequeaths his or her goods, for example for works of piety, charity and the apostolate, must be respected.

[12] The constitutions, or the fundamental code, of every institute must give instructions of a general nature and of principle regarding administration and alienation, leaving the mutable elements to the norms contained in other codes of the institute (can. 587 § 1 and § 4).

[13] The canon uses the very strong expression "*diligentissimeimpleantur*" (they must be scrupulously fulfilled), which asks that, with the acceptance of goods, the donor's religious motives be respected with the utmost diligence.

b) *Required consultative bodies*

As regards consultative bodies, can. 1280, which is a new canon compared with the Code of 1917, requires that every juridic person have its own finance council or at least counselors who assist the superior in the fulfillment of his or her task.[14] Since ecclesiastical superiors are not often elected or appointed based on their ability to administer temporal goods, the council, which is set up or added to, offers considerable or virtually indispensable help in the world today, where the management of goods demands particular skill. According to the canons, this council must be established in every juridic person; in the case of a diocese, the group, which must be presided over by the bishop himself or delegate, consists of at least three Catholic faithful, who are experts in finance and civil law and are outstanding in integrity (can. 492). While the finance council will have the task of paying special attention to the technical and financial aspects of the act that the superior must carry out, caring for the pastoral aspects is up to the college of consultors, which is a post-Conciliar creation (can. 502). According to the norms of Book V, the bishop must have the prior opinion of these bodies concerning acts of great importance or he must have their consent if it regards acts of extraordinary administration (can. 1277) with the specific consequences listed in can. 127 that are required for the acts to be valid.

In the case of religious institutes, Book V states that the consent of the competent superior's council is required (cf. can. 638 § 3). All the same, nothing prevents the superior, in his or her governance, from having another body for financial affairs determined by proper law. Can. 636 § 1 prescribes that in every institute and province governed by a major superior, there must be a finance

[14] The canon says "*quaevis persona iuridica*," therefore, the norm concerns any juridic person, whether public or private. For the act to be valid, their eventual opinion or consensus is required after they have been notified, according to the norm of can. 127 § 1. In the case of the appointment of two counselors, they are taken as individuals, for whom can. 127 § 2 is applied.

officer distinct from the major superior and constituted according to the norm of proper law, who manages the administration of goods under the direction of the respective superior. While the finance officer will have the task of drawing special attention to the technical and legal aspects of the act that the superior must carry out, it is up to the council (can. 627) to assist the superior in certain particular aspects: the discernment of pastoral choices and how to pursue the proper purposes and the relationship with the local Church. For the sound governance of the temporal patrimony of the institute, it is first of all necessary that the superior be adequately and sufficiently informed about the real economic situation of each single entity, both about its resources and needs so that they can do what is necessary for the good of the juridic person.

Special attention is needed concerning the fact that extraordinary acts of administration exist in addition to acts of ordinary administration, regulated by Book V in the current Code under the title of administration of goods (Title II; cann. 1273-1289). Another category of acts exist that Church norms specifically regulate under the title of acts of alienation (Title III; cann. 1291-1298) and they are distinct from those regarding administration.[15] This distinction of economic factors is also found in the field of the goods of religious institutes in can. 638 §§ 1-3. Furthermore, in the administration of economic activities, there exist different regulations in civil laws and legal agreements.

Superiors and their councils, administrators and finance officers in the institutes must know the distinction between these different kinds of acts, as well as the related procedural requirements in canon and civil laws for the sound governance of the institutes. But how is all of this seriously achievable without the help and involvement of experts, particularly lay experts? And how can

[15] For example, in Book V, can. 1277 provides for the diocese to determine the extraordinary acts of administration and can. 1281 for other juridic persons, while can. 1292 deals with acts of alienation.

laypeople verify whether their administration was right without knowing the spirit and fundamental character of the institute? An expert in canon law should understand the application of civil legislation; the finance officers should not ignore the norms of canon law. The assistance or utilization of lay experts is not enough, rather what is needed is real collaboration between consecrated and lay persons based on the correct understanding of the institute's mission. It is necessary to get the people concerned involved in the particular charism of the institute for greater collaboration and service.

Conclusion

As we have said so far, the Code seeks a balance in the delicate questions concerning the centrality of proper purposes in acquisition, administration and alienation. In fact, not all superiors are equipped with the right skills to adequately administer goods and many administrators of goods are occupied instead with the complicated and detailed procedures of acquisition, reserves, property improvements and maintaining the patrimonial situation of each entity. The Code of Canon Law's respect for the purposes of the goods owned by ecclesiastical entities is constant. Faced with the very complicated reality of the economic world, which is experiencing rapid change, the norms of Book V seem useless and powerless. But the Code seeks to demonstrate the principle of the legal protection of the Church's goods with those few canons with their general nature, and always to underline that the main principle is the purpose of the Church, that is, service to humanity.

We must admit that these purposes are not always clear in concrete situations with regards to the technical and legal aspects of temporal goods. In such a situation, it is necessary there be the clear conviction that goods are means and not ends, and that the top priority is not the goods themselves, but the juridic person, through whom the goods can be dedicated in order to pursue their ecclesiastical purposes. It is important to ask oneself if the goods in one's possession are truly serving the proper and spiritual purpose for which the institute was founded and exists – service to the person and works of charity and the apostolate to glorify God – so that a correct way of acquiring, maintaining, administering and alienating goods may lead both the entire Church and the institutes to demonstrate evangelical coherence, and that the norms regarding temporal goods serve to achieve this objective.

YUJI SUGAWARA, SJ
Professor of Canon Law
Dean of the Faculty of Canon Law
of the Pontifical Gregorian University – Rome

CHARITY, JUSTICE AND LEGALITY

AN INSTITUTES ASSETS AND THE ORDERING OF THE STATE

MIROSLAV KONŠTANC ADAM, OP

1. Introduction

The contribution I wish to make offers an analysis of the relationship between charity, justice and legality and the management of the assets of religious institutes based on the abovementioned values in relation to state order – an issue that is quite complex.

2. The relationship between justice and charity

The famous Dominican Father Reginaldo M. Pizzorni was a professor of the philosophy of law his whole life at Rome's Pontifical University of St. Thomas Aquinas and the Pontifical Lateran and Urbanianum Universities. He wrote in his book, *Justice and Charity*, in 1995: "The question of the relationship between justice and charity is very old. It is a question that deeply marks the development of western thought all the way from the beginning, and that is posed as a foundational question whenever, over the course of history, philosophical speculation takes on the greatest problems of the foundations of human coexistence – of the basis of social relations and, therefore, more specifically, of the nature of law and of its function in the human family [...]. We must admit that today we live in a world that has always been governed less by reason and love. The modern-day mentality favors justice and has a patronizing attitude toward charity. We live in an age in which charity is in crisis and is rejected in the name of a presumed social justice, and, in such a way, one runs the risk of losing both one and the other. In this manner, our world perishes from its egoism, from the unbridled frenzy for profit: it dies for having betrayed justice and above all charity, the gift of self. But is justice then possible if within and beyond justice itself there is no charity?"[1]

Since the 1800s an objection has been raised against the Church's charitable activity, formulated by the famous French man of letters Montesquieu: "The alms given to a naked man in the street do not fulfill the obligations of the state, which owes to every citizen a certain subsistence, a proper nourishment, convenient clothing, and a kind of life not harmful to health [...]."[2]

This means the poor would not need works of charity, but rather justice. It would be necessary to create a just order in which everyone receives his or her share of the world's goods and, therefore, does not need works of charity anymore. Therefore, from the worldly point of view, " 'the supreme secular value, as an alternative to charity, is justice. If there were more justice, there would be no need for charity.' That is the assertion of Norberto Bobbio, one of the greatest Italian scholars of law in the second half of the 1900s. In reality, justice is not, as Bobbio and many like him maintain, an *alternative* to charity. It represents rather the first (and the poorest) of the conditions of possibility."[3] "Therefore, for Christianity, justice and charity are intimately connected to each other, whilst remaining clearly distinct from each other: united but distinct. This teaching recurs repeatedly in the discourses and documents of the recent supreme pontiffs and had widespread recognition in the doctrine of the Second Vatican Council."[4] The final answer to social questions will be charity, which, how-

[1] R.M. PIZZORNI, *Giustizia e carità*, Bologna 1995, 5.

[2] "*Quelques aumônes que l'on fait à un homme nu dans les rues, ne remplissent point les obligations de l'état, qui doit à tous les citoyens une subsistance assurée, la nourriture, un vêtement convenable, et un genre de vie qui ne soit point contraire à la santé*" (MONTESQUIEU, *De l'esprit des loix*, tome troisième, XXIII, 29, à Amsterdam et à Leipzig 1763, 43-44), cit. in F. D'AGOSTINO, *Diritto e giustizia. Per una introduzione allo studio del diritto*, Turin 2000, 87-88.

[3] F. D'AGOSTINO, *Diritto e giustizia*, cit., 38-39.

[4] R.M. PIZZORNI, *Giustizia e carità*, cit., 7.

ever, must not substitute justice, but presuppose it, as Pius XI noted in his encyclical *Divini Redemptoris*: "Charity will never be true charity unless it takes justice into constant account."[5]

Father Pizzorni explains it: "There cannot be true charity this way without justice: *charity presupposes justice*, because the first charity, the first proof of love toward the other is precisely to apply justice to him, to carry out first and foremost and completely our duty of firm justice, and to integrally respect rights and to give that which is due; otherwise it would be hypocrisy, a mask of injustice. We cannot give in the form of alms that which is due a worker by right. Before speaking of charity it is necessary to satisfy justice: to give each his or her due; if one wants, one can aim for giving *more than his or her due*, that is, what is *ours* and, if it is necessary, even *ourselves.* True charity is beyond yet *not beneath* justice; it begins where justice ends. Before giving one's own and oneself as *gift*, we need to have given what is *due*, that is, what is due the other, one will not be able to pass off what is due as gift, on the contrary, we will have to believe, perhaps, that everything is due."[6]

On the other hand, "there cannot be true justice either without charity: *justice presupposes charity*, inasmuch as justice is, in its own way, a form of love oriented as it is toward serving mankind, and it is love that drives an ever more adequate and deeper knowledge of the rights of the other. Not without foundation, therefore, was it said that 'the charity of today is the justice of tomorrow, just as the justice of today was the charity of yesterday.'"[7] We can then assert with Pius XII that it is always love that orders human relationships and informs social relations because "if charity be not joined with strict and rigid justice in a kind of brotherly bond, the eye of

[5] Pius XI, Encycl. Lett. *Divini Redemptoris*, March 19, 1937, n. 49, in *Enchiridion delle Encicliche*, 5, bilingual ed., Bologna 1995, n. 1246.

[6] R.M. Pizzorni, *Umanesimo sociale cristiano. La Chiesa come permeazione cristiana nel mondo. Ad uso privato*, Rome 1973-1974, 381.

[7] Cf. V.G. Séailles, *La philosophie du travail*, Paris 1923, 117.

the mind is very easily clouded and thereby hindered, so that it does not discern the rights of another; the ears become deaf, so that they do not hear the voice of that equity which has the power, by explanation to the wise man willing to listen, to make clear in reasonable and orderly fashion whatever may be the matter of dispute, even the bitterest and the rudest of differences."[8] True charity must be the complement and perfection of that justice and equity John XXIII outlined, inviting Christians, with solemn commitment, to the "reintegration of relationships in the life of human society in truth, in justice and in love."[9] Also Francesco D'Agostino, a contemporary philosopher of law, explains: "Nor can justice pretend to render charity superfluous, nor can charity pretend to replace justice. Without charity, justice is Phariseeism, but without justice, charity is a mere and empty form."[10]

We must remember that Christ revealed to us that God – origin of every creature – is love (cf. *1Jn* 4:8). This way Christianity goes even further and launches a new message: *the message of love, of charity*; and the Church, including in its name, was defined in the first centuries as love (*agápe*). Therefore, if positive law in itself and in the understanding of the ancients tends toward justice, virtue, peace and, higher still, friendship, then love in the Christian understanding is associated with law: love must integrate law. Therefore law needs charity for the perfect attainment of its own juridical goals. Christian-Thomistic doctrine of law thus establishes a harmonious communion or circularity between divine law, natural

[8] "*Qua propter, si rigidae destrictaeque iustitiae caritas fraterno foedere non coniungitur, facilius mentis oculi quadam praepediuntur caligine, ne aliena iura cernant; auresque obsurdescunt, ne vocem illius aequitatis audiant, quae, si volenti sapientique studio edisseratur, asperrimas etiam ac salebrosas causas, quae in controversiam cadunt, ordine rationeque enodare atque explanare potest*" (PIUS XII, *Easter Homily for Peace*, April 9, 1939, in *Discorsi e radiomessaggi di Sua Santità Pio XII*, I, Milan 1941, 39).

[9] Cf. JOHN XXIII, Encycl. Lett. *Mater et Magistra*, May 15, 1961, IV, 1, in *Enchiridion delle Encicliche*, 7, ed. bilingual, Bologna 1994, n. 434.

[10] F. D'AGOSTINO, *Diritto e giustizia*, cit., 89.

law and positive law, between justice and charity, because, as St. Thomas Aquinas wisely affirms, "love is the first principle of all that we do."[11]

The Second Vatican Council also recalled that everything must be done with justice accompanied by charity: "*Iustitia duce, caritate comite*" (*GS* 69), works of justice must be achieved under the inspiration of charity: "*Ad opus iustitiae, inspirante caritate, perficiendum*" (*GS* 72). For this reason, according to the Conciliar Constitution *Gaudium et spes*, the fundamental law of charity is the basic law of human perfection and, therefore, also of the world's transformation. In fact, in Jesus, true man showed himself to be a man who generously dedicates himself and expends himself for his brother, revealing to us real true man and, with that, the basic law of human progress (cf. *GS* 38).[12]

This doctrine of law does not, therefore, say to mankind: either law or love, either justice or charity; but law and love, justice and charity. In his "*Speech on development*," given in Bogatá on August 23, 1968, Pope Paul VI said: "The promotion of justice and the safeguarding of human dignity be your charity," and remembered that "the justice is the minimum measure of charity." [13] John Paul II, too, in his encyclical *Dives in misericordia* in 1980, recalled "that justice alone is not enough, that it can even lead to the negation and destruction of itself, if that deeper power, which is love, is not allowed to shape human life in its various dimensions." [14]

Pope Benedict XVI looked at the question in his encyclical *Deus caritas est* in 2005, explaining that we can "determine more pre-

[11] "*Quodlibet agens ex amore agit quodcumque agit*" (ST. THOMAS AQUINAS, *Summa Theologiæ*, I-II, q. 29, a. 6).

[12] Cf. R.M. PIZZORNI, *Umanesimo sociale cristiano*, cit., 383-385.

[13] "*La promoción de la justicia y la tutela de la dignidad humana sean vuestra caridad*" (PAUL VI, *The "Day of development,"* Bogotá, August 23, 1968, in *Insegnamenti di Paolo VI*, 1968, Vatican City 1969, vol. VI, 394).

[14] JOHN PAUL II, Encycl. Lett. *Dives in misericordia*, November 30, 1980, n. 12, in *Enchiridion delle Encicliche*, 8, bilingual ed., Bologna 1998, n. 175.

cisely, in the life of the Church, the relationship between commitment to the just ordering of the state and society on the one hand, and organized charitable activity on the other. We have seen that the formation of just structures is not directly the duty of the Church [...]. The direct duty to work for a just ordering of society, on the other hand, is proper to the lay faithful. As citizens of the state, they are called to take part in public life in a personal capacity. [...] Even if the specific expressions of ecclesial charity can never be confused with the activity of the state, it still remains true that charity must animate the entire lives of the lay faithful and therefore also their political activity, lived as 'social charity.'"[15] The first year of Pope Francis' pontificate could be expressed as a commitment to put into practice "a word already made flesh and constantly striving to take flesh anew" and, therefore, "to perform works of justice and charity, which make that word fruitful."[16]

"In the situation of today, and in close relationship to the commitment of the new evangelization, there is a need to 'think big' about the witness of charity as well, articulating it in its many, correlated dimensions. In reality, authentic charity innately possesses the demand for justice: therefore translating into an impassioned defense of the rights of everyone. But it is not limited to this because it is called to bring justice to life, inserting a sign of gift and of interpersonal relationships in the various relationships protected by law. A bureaucratic attitude, anonymity and legalism are dangers that threaten our society; often it is forgotten that those who turn to all the many social services are real people. Furthermore, charity knows how to individuate and answer the ever-new needs that emerge in a rapidly changing society. With its preventative and prophetic works, charity commits itself – both by raising awareness and by taking advantage of the political and institutional instru-

[15] BENEDICT XVI, Encycl. Lett. *Deus caritas est*, December 25, 2005, n. 29, in *Enchiridion Vaticanum* 23, Bologna 2008, n. 1585.

[16] FRANCIS, Ap. Exhort. *Evangelii gaudium*, November 24, 2013, n. 233.

ments destined for this – so that needs, when they are authentic and when resources and the situation permit, are recognized as rights and are protected by the social organization." [17]

3. Some definitions

Justice is the respect of dignity and the rights of others; respecting in the other what is his, giving to each his own: *unicuique suum.*[18] The fabric of justice, in fact, is the "*exteriores actiones et res.*" [19] This way we have relationships of social justice founded on the essential needs of the human person, which is reason why social justice demands that all the means necessary to live and to live in a manner worthy of *man* are provided for.

Charity-friendship, as a natural virtue, is goodwill and love, that sees in the other an "*alter ego*," for whom one desires all the good that one would want for oneself. This, however, tends to focus on the unique and inimitable nature of the close personal relationship... In this way we have relationships of social charity that lead to wanting – to whatever extent possible – the integral good of all the persons who make up the social community – the good that is due, and also that which is not strictly due. Charity, therefore, wants that all members of the community come to the aid of their brothers and sisters in need, as much as they can, so that they become *more human*, so that they can realize fully in themselves that dignity and those gifts which they each carry. It is *philanthropy* – love of *amicus humani generis.*

[17] THE ITALIAN BISHOPS' CONFERENCE - JUSTICE AND PEACE COMMISSION, *Evangelizzazione e testimonianza della carità. Orientamenti pastorali dell'Episcopato italiano per gli anni Novanta*, n. 38, in SEGRETERIA GENERALE CEI, *Notiziario della CEI*, n. 12, December 8, 1990, 348-349.

[18] The very old and extraordinary definition of justice, also recorded in the *Digest*, comes from Ulpian (III century AD), according to whom *justice* consists in *giving to each his own* (*justitia est constans et perpetua voluntas jus suum cuique tribuendi*). Cf. F. D'AGOSTINO, *Giustizia. Elementi per una teoria*, Cinisello Balsamo 2006, 12.

[19] ST. THOMAS AQUINAS, *Summa Theologiæ*, I-II, q. 58, a. 8.

But *Christian love* (*agápe*), as supernatural virtue, wants something more... Love, as opposed to friendship, tends towards the universalization of personal relationships, to the point that every one, every individual possible, becomes my "neighbor" to love as myself.[20]

Since the virtue of justice is ordered toward the common good, it prepares for and supports the exercise of brotherly charity, after having been the vehicle for the realization of the basic requirements of the selfsame charity; for that reason the recognition of the rights of others is the first step required by charity.[21]

The last term remaining to clarify is *legality*. "Insofar as every member is justified to deem a law as *unjust*, it remains a fact that, as a matter of principle, everyone must recognize the existing presumption that supports the law's *obligatory* nature, especially if the law has been issued by a legislature deemed by society to be democratically legitimate. From this perspective *legality* appears as a fundamental value in every order. Nevertheless, even in cases in which the unjust nature of a law may appear to be beyond dispute, the value of the principle of legality is not diminished if disobedience or, worse still, the resistance to the unjust law has the paradoxical and objectively predictable effect of an increase in the social injustice overall, rather than its defeat or mitigation. Regardless, the right of every member of the community to *criticize unjust laws* still holds as they unite in their duty of working, within the limits of each person's possible efforts, so that such laws may be abrogated or modified." [22]

[20] Cf. R. PIZZORNI, *Giustizia e carità*, cit., 11-12.

[21] Cf. R. CAMBARERI, *Il cristiano in politica. La domanda di giustizia nel mondo contemporaneo*, Bologna 1995, 76-77.

[22] F. D'AGOSTINO, *Giustizia*, cit., 49-50.

4. The relationship between justice, charity and legality

To observe just laws is a matter of justice. The warning of the Second Vatican Council is greatly relevant: "Let everyone consider it his sacred obligation to esteem and observe social necessities as belonging to the primary duties of modern man" (*GS* 30). Christians know that "there is no authority except from God" (*Rm* 13:1) and that, therefore, every just order and every true law must see the disciples of Christ ready to obey for the building up of the common good. For this reason, obedience to civil laws appears reasonable: the good of the single individual or the intermediate groups on the one hand, and the good of society on the other, are closely linked. In a word, the common good is the heart and the justification of the principle of legality.[23] "Legality, understood as respect for and the observance of the laws, is a particular form of justice. For this reason, from the deep roots of justice and legality spring morality and they take the form of love – and for the faithful they take the form of charity or evangelical love – toward each person and toward the community."[24] Precisely thanks to the gift of charity, the faithful are asked to be a critical conscience and concrete witness of the true sense of legality within today's society.

5. Code of the Church's charitable activity

Works of charity derive their meaning from "love-agápe," from the love that God had for us in Jesus Christ and who fully revealed himself in the Paschal mystery. From this perspective works of charity do not simply have a philanthropic meaning, but are an essential part of the Church's proclamation of the Gospel. Works of charity are closely linked to evangelization, which the conciliar

[23] Cf. L. LORENZETTI, *Educare alla legalità: "Obbedire alle leggi giuste,"* in www.chiesadimilano.it/polopoly_fs/1.43717.1310480954!/menu/standard/file/foglio_145bis.pdf

[24] G. VOLTA, *Sintesi del documento della Commissione Giustizia e Pace della CEI "Educare alla legalità"*, April 4, 1991, 8, in www.chiesadimilano.it/polopoly_fs/1.43717.1310480954!/menu/standard/file/foglio_145bis.pdf

decree *Apostolicam actuositatem* speaks about (n. 8). A code of the Church's charitable activities has been drawn from the text of this decree and is proposed in the following points:

1. To see God's image in the other, who was created in God's image, and the image of Christ the Lord, to whom is truly given that which one gives to those in need;
2. To have regard for, with great sensitivity, the freedom and dignity of the person who receives help;
3. To not stain the purity of intention with seeking one's own personal benefit or with the desire for domination;
4. To satisfy first and foremost the demands of justice so that what one offers as a gift of charitable activity may not be that which is already due in the name of justice;
5. To eliminate not just the effects, but also the causes of all ills;
6. To predispose institutions and charitable activities to have as their fundamental rule wanting to lead the people they assist, bit by bit, to be free from depending on third-parties and to become self-sufficient.[25]

In this regard, one of the best canonists today, Cardinal Velasio De Paolis, proposes some further reflections:

1. Every work of the apostolate draws origin and strength from charity;[26]
2. Some works by their very nature are aimed at becoming vivid expressions of the same charity. This certainly involves both corporal and spiritual works of mercy, and works of charity. Among the purposes of ecclesiastical goods, the Second Vatican Council lists "for the exercise of the works of the holy apostolate or works of charity, especially on behalf of the needy" (*PO* 17);

[25] Cf. L. Bogliolo (editor), *Il decreto sull'apostolato dei laici: genesi storico-dottrinale*, Latin text and translation in Italian: presentation and commentary, Turin-Leumann 1966, 209.

[26] Saint Thomas says that charity is the mother and the root of all the virtues (cf. St. Thomas Aquinas, *Summa Theologiæ*, I-II, q. 62, a. 4).

3. One must recall the whole Church's history: it has been defined as a "channel of charity" and its goods have been called the "patrimony of the poor." The sick, children, widows, the handicapped, the different categories of poor of every era, etc. are the privileged classes for the attention and pastoral concern of the Church. The construction of hospitals, orphanages, leprosy homes etc., is part of the Church's history. The saints particularly stand out in works of charity. The history of the Church is the history of charity. "Charity is the heart of the Church." [27]

6. Laws that regulate ecclesiastical goods

Ecclesiastical goods, precisely because they belong to the Church and are meant to serve its purposes, are under the governance of the Church and sustained by its laws. Can. 1254 § 1 recalls that the right to goods as well as their administration does not come to the Church from civil power but from the founder. Therefore, the control and administration of them are regulated by canon law (cf. cann. 1255-1256) under the supreme authority of the Roman pontiff (cf. can. 1256). The point of reference for the administration of goods is the law of the Church: the universal, general regulations of Book V of the *Code of Canon Law*, the special law for religious (cf. cann. 634-640), and the norm of proper law (cf. cann. 635 § 2 and 687).[28]

Can. 1257 § 1 spells out what ecclesiastical goods are: "All temporal goods which belong to the universal Church, the Apostolic

[27] Cf. V. De Paolis, *I beni temporali della Chiesa*, Bologna 1995, 262-263 and 265-266.

[28] Handling this should be integrated with civil legislation as well, which the Code refers to (cf. can. 1290) and, in Italy, with the law of the Concordat, especially when referring to the recognition of the public juridic personality, to acts of purchase and exemption from taxes. To this is added the study of the revised Concordat (February 18, 1984) and the *Norme circa gli enti e i beni ecclesiastici in Italia* (*Norms concerning the entities and ecclesiastical goods in Italy*) (November 15, 1984). Cf. E. Gambari, *I religiosi nel Codice. Commento ai singoli canoni*, Milan 1986, 196, note 106.

See, or other public juridic persons in the Church are ecclesiastical goods..." In fact, religious institutes, as well as the entities which they are divided into, that is, provinces and religious houses that are erected, are entitled to the same canonical legal order of the nature of public juridic persons. Precisely for this reason can. 634 § 1 tells us that, by simply applying cann. 1255 and 1256, "institutes, provinces, and houses are capable of acquiring, possessing, administering, and alienating temporal goods unless this capacity is excluded or restricted in the constitutions." This is why administrators of ecclesiastic goods need to know well the legislation and the spirit of both the Church and one's own religious institute in order to mirror them in their own behavior.

One cannot forget, however, that the Church lives in the present day and has a continuous relationship with contemporary political society: between them there is continual reciprocal osmosis. Civil societies can offer the Church much, especially from the technical and cultural point of view, just as the Church can give them much, presenting them the Gospel message and the values it holds. Throughout history such osmosis was particularly strong in the field of law. We cannot forget that the Church developed in a culture where Roman law was in force and reigned. If such law offered valid foundations to the organization and structure of the Church, the law also experienced great beneficial influences from the Gospel message. This influence was particularly strong in the field of property law. We find the principle of referring to the civil law of nations in the Code of 1917, particularly in can. 1529. The reasons are many, but we cannot get into all of them. It suffices to say that the majority of modern states do not recognize canon law as an autonomous source of law. If the Church wanted to push this point at all costs, there would be frequent disputes.

It is obvious then that law is very diverse according to different nations: if the Church were to pretend to regulate the entire sector of temporal goods with its own universal regulation, a minimum of uniformity would be difficult if not impossible. It would end up that the entire regulation of temporal goods would demand such a mountain of laws that they would weigh ecclesial life down enormously to the point of making it nearly impossible. For that reason, the Church, in its prudence, chose a wise road in line with the rest of tradition: it issued a very limited set of norms that touches on the essential principles and matters dealing with ecclesiastical goods.

Book V is the shortest book in the Code. In all other respects, it received – "canonized" – civil legislation. By means of canonization, the Church on the one hand retains the principle of its exclusive competence over that which concerns its own life and, on the other, it adapts to local situations. Laws formally incorporated are ecclesiastic laws, meaning that the civil laws obligate the faithful within the Church by prescript of the same ecclesiastical authority: they are real and actual ecclesiastical laws. Materially, however, in terms of content, they are the laws of the nation in which the Church lives. Can. 22 gives us the general principle on the canonization of civil laws: "Civil laws to which the law of the Church yields are to be observed in canon law with the same effects, insofar as they are not contrary to divine law and unless canon law provides otherwise." Therefore, contracts of any nature will need to observe the norms of civil law, according to can. 1290.

The norms that refer to civil law, however, must be distinguished from canonization, either for reasons of prudence or precisely because it is pursuant to civil legislation. Here are a few examples: can. 668 § 4 urges that the renunciation of goods be done in a form that is also valid, as far as possible, to civil law, so as not to result in any difficulties before civil law and to avail oneself of the advantages that come from its civil effects. The same can be said of can. 1274 § 5, which wants the institutes being talked about in the canon to have standing in civil law as well. Another measure of prudence is seen in the norm of can. 1284 § 2, 2°, which wants to ensure that the ownership of ecclesiastical goods is safeguarded in ways which are also valid in civil law, and canon § 2, 3°, which calls for special care to be taken so that not observing civil law does not result in damaging the Church. Concerning alienation of goods, can. 1293 § 2 imposes that "other precautions prescribed by legitimate authority are also to be observed to avoid harm to the Church." Can. 1299 § 2 urges that "In dispositions *mortis causa* for the good of the Church, the formalities of civil law are to be observed if possible." But it specifies that if they were omitted, "the heirs must be admonished regarding the obligation, to which they are bound, of fulfilling the intention of the testator." Can. 1296 poses the hypothesis of the alienation of ecclesiastical goods that is invalid according to canon law, but valid according to civil law. Instead, the norm of can. 1286, which refers to civil laws regarding workers and pay, is simply a reference to an obligation that in and of itself is put into force by civil law.[29]

7. "*Sana cooperatio*"[30]

State systems are not all equal; they are very different, especially in Europe.[31] With regard to works of education and charity carried out by the Catholic Church, in particular by religious institutes, the

[29] V. DE PAOLIS, *La vita consacrata nella Chiesa*, Revised and expanded edition, edited by V. Mosca, Venice 2010, 409-412.

[30] "Vatican II persistently repeats hopes for a *sound cooperation* between the Church and the political community, saying they will be more effective the more they are in accordance with the foundation and purpose the Council assigns them. A collaboration that is justified since both, while 'under different titles, are devoted to the personal and social vocation of the same human persons' (*GS* 76). The conciliar constitution observes that man is 'not limited only to the temporal order; while living in the context of human history, he preserves intact his eternal vocation,' and for her part, the Church, 'by preaching the truths of the Gospel, and bringing to bear on all fields of human endeavor the light of her doctrine and of a Christian witness, she respects and fosters the political freedom and responsibility of citizens' (*GS* 76)" (G. DALLA TORRE, *La città sul monte. Contributo ad una teoria canonistica sulle relazioni fra Chiesa e Comunità politica*, Rome 1996, 111-112). On the arrangement of religious institutes and the jurisdiction of the Italian state see C. CARDIA, *Ordinamenti religiosi e ordinamenti dello Stato. Profili giurisdizionali*, Bologna 2003, 148-158.

[31] Cf. W. LOSKAND, *Církevní majetek ve Spolkové republice Německo*, in *Revue církevního práva* 1 (1995) 101-112; J. LISTL, *Vztah mezi státem a církvemi v Německu*, in *Revue církevního práva* 2 (1996) 1-10; H. KALB, *Rakouské konfesní právo v současné politické diskusi*, in *Revue církevního práva* 2 (1996) 19-28; R. SOBAŃSKI, *Teoretické základy a praktické uskutečňování vztahu stáu a církve v*

hostile situation of past liberal, anticlerical and socialist governments has changed notably. Different secular governments, especially in former socialist countries that had been governed by communists for 40 years and for more than 70 years in the former Soviet Union, believed they were resolving the question of social justice once and for all. Without a doubt, much was done in the social sphere. It is true that the fundamental rule of the state must be the pursuit of justice and that the aim of a just social order is to guarantee each person, in respect of the principle of subsidiarity, his or her share of the common good. With the change of political systems and the reestablishment of democracy and religious freedom, it must be observed, however, that poverty, both spiritual and material, has not disappeared, and there is a need for charitable works, which before had been not permitted, and were even prohibited.

In these countries, the state is used to being completely responsible for the social sphere, and it continues to fulfill this obligation of justice. At the same time, it has permitted the Church, which is operating throughout each nation's territory, to introduce and carry out works of education and charity – works which are carried out, for the most part in fact, by different religious institutes, both men's and women's. Benedict XVI confirms this in his encyclical *Deus caritas est*, published in 2005: "Love – *caritas* – will always prove necessary, even in the most just society. There is no ordering of the state so just that it can eliminate the need for a service of love. Whoever wants to eliminate love is preparing to eliminate man as such. There will always be suffering which cries out for consolation and help. There will always be loneliness. There will

některých evropských zemích, in *Revue církevního práva* 2 (1996) 83-94; J. LISTL, *Základy současných vztáhu mezi státem a církví v moderních západních demokraciích*, in *Revue církevního práva* 2 (1996) 95-103; N. MICHEL, *Církev a stát ve výcarsku*, in *Revue církevního práva* 2 (1996) 105-122; H.C. VERYSER, *Financování činnosti církvi ve Spojených státech amerických*, in *Revue církevního práva* 2 (1996) 169-178; H. MARRÉ, *Systémy financování církví v zemích Evropské unie a v USA*, in *Revue církevního práva* 4 (1998) 65-79.

always be situations of material need where help in the form of concrete love of neighbor is indispensable. The state which would provide everything, absorbing everything into itself, would ultimately become a mere bureaucracy incapable of guaranteeing the very thing which the suffering person – every person – needs: namely, loving personal concern. We do not need a state which regulates and controls everything, but a state which, in accordance with the principle of subsidiarity, generously acknowledges and supports initiatives arising from the different social forces and combines spontaneity with closeness to those in need. The Church is one of those living forces [...]. In the end, the claim that just social structures would make works of charity superfluous masks a materialist conception of man: the mistaken notion that man can live 'by bread alone' (*Mt* 4:4; cf. *Dt* 8:3) – a conviction that demeans man and ultimately disregards all that is specifically human."[32]

It is interesting to note that in many of these countries (Czech Republic,[33] Slovakia,[34] Hungary, Romania, Lithuania,[35] Latvia[36]) the state not only permits works of education and charity, it also makes an effort to offer the necessary means, such as buildings, equipment, supplies and financial assistance starting at 50% or more, and in some cases, more than 80%. In the meantime, it asks the

[32] BENEDICT XVI, Encycl. Lett. *Deus caritas est*, n. 28, in *Enchiridion Vaticanum* 23, n. 1584.

[33] Cf. J. PALLA, *Daňově zvýhodněné dary církvím*, in *Revue církevního práva* 1 (1995) 35-36; J.R. TRETERA, *Stát a církve v České republice*, Kostelní Vydří 2002, 92-107, 131-132 and 145.

[34] Cf. M. NEMEC, *Právne postavenie a činnosť cirkví v Slovenskej republike*, in *Revue církevního práva* 2 (1996) 151-168; J. MARČIN, *Sytuacja ekonomiczna Kościoła Rzymskokatolickiego na Słowacji w świetle prawa kanonicznego i prawnego porządku Republiki Słowacji*, Košice 2013, 160-169 and 176-186.

[35] Cf. G. PENEMOTE, *Fundamento antropológico do princípio de "sana cooperatio" – Justificação das relações jurídicas actuais entre a Igreja e a Comunidade Política*, Thesis ad Doct. in Utroque Iure apud Pont. Univ. Lateranensis, Rome 2004, 181-183.

[36] Cf. G. PENEMOTE, *Fundamento antropológico*, cit., 180-181.

Church to offer personnel, like priests, brothers, sisters and experienced and skilled lay Catholics, who are paid, and, as a matter of fact, hired by the state so as to carry out the noted activities on the condition of observing state laws. The governments in these countries permit it and do it by invoking the name of justice and saying that it would be unjust to ask that citizens who pay taxes pay yet again for services offered by the Church's educational, social and charitable institutions; in fact this would be discrimination when compared to citizens who turn only to state institutions.

In closing, there are not enough people who are available to perform some very urgent and necessary services. For this reason, secular governments ask the Church for help with personnel and they are ready to finance projects run just by religious, for example, the National Anti-drug Center in Bratislava, Slovakia, entrusted to the Salesian Fathers, and also the work entrusted to different male and female religious congregations who offer education to gypsies in different parts of Slovakia. All of this is guaranteed with the stipulation of a kind of concordat, "Basic Accord between the Holy See and the Slovak Republic," from November 24, 2000.[37]

To illustrate the above-cited facts, the text of articles 16 and 17 of the "Basic Accord between the Holy See and the Slovak Republic" says:

> "Art. 16, 1. The Catholic Church has the right to develop activity of a pastoral and spiritual nature, and religious training and upbringing in all formative state institutions, educational and medical institutions, state institutions providing social services, including those used for obligatory institutional education, and for the care and social reinstatement of drug dependent persons, in accordance with conditions agreed between the Catholic Church and the respective institution. The Republic of Slovakia will ensure that conditions are fit for the exercising of this right. Persons who are under the care of these

[37] Cf. KONFERENCIA BISKUPOV SLOVENSKA, *Základná zmluva medzi Svätou stolicou a Slovenskou republikou s komentárom*, Bratislava 2001, 18-27.

institutions have the right to participate in Mass on Sundays and on holy days of obligation and are granted the liberty to fulfill all religious acts.

2. The above parties will collaborate in realizing communal projects in areas of medical care, of training and upbringing, and in those offering assistance to the elderly and to the sick. These projects will apply to schools, educational and medical institutions, institutions offering social services, therapy and the rehabilitation of drug dependants. The Holy See guarantees that the Catholic Church will promote these projects particularly with the staff of the institutions; the Republic of Slovakia will make provisions in proportional measure, but particularly materially and financially."[38]

"Art. 17, 1. The Catholic Church has the right to develop activity of a formative, training, experimental-scientific, missionary, charitable, medical and social nature. This right also includes the setting up, ownership and the management of institutions of this kind in accordance with the conditions laid down by the legal system of the Republic of Slovakia.

2. As far as reimbursements for medical services are concerned, provided by the agency of obligatory insurance, the institutions referred to in paragraph 1 have the same rights and duties as state institutions of the same type.

3. The Holy See guarantees that the Catholic Church will participate in the financial insurance of these institutions. The financial contribution for these religious institutions from the state budget of the Republic of Slovakia will be determined in a special agreement in accordance with Article 20 of the present concordat."[39]

8. Conclusion

It is fundamental that religious institutes apply, in the management of their temporal goods, the values of charity, justice and legality, and that patrimonial policies are effective on the civil level, too, being implemented in conformity with civil legislation of the

[38] Konferencia Biskupov Slovenska, *Základná zmluva...*, cit., 24.

[39] Konferencia Biskupov Slovenska, *Základná zmluva...*, cit., 25.

nation in which they are located. In this case, the unique situation arises of two distinct authorities – the religious and the civil – that serve the same people in the same territory. Hence, this offers a further reason for collaboration between the two authorities – the religious and the civil, each one possessing clearly differentiated aims but with the intention of regulating matters of common interest.

MIROSLAV KONŠTANC ADAM, OP
Professor of Canon Law
Rector of the Pontifical University "Angelicum" – Rome

SECOND SESSION

Moderator

SISTER NICLA SPEZZATI, ASC

Under-secretary of the CICLSAL

THE COMPLEXITY IN THE MANAGEMENT OF INSTITUTIONAL GOODS: THE RELATIONSHIP BETWEEN THE GOVERNING AUTHORITY AND THE SERVICE OF TREASURERS

ÁLVARO RODRÍGUEZ ECHEVERRÍA, FSC

Introduction

As the title indicates, I will explain with what follows the relationship that ought to exist between the general governing authority and the service of the treasurer of a congregation or institute. In the first place, I think that we are able to shed light on this relationship with the Gospel. In order to do that, it is good to contemplate the way a community of Jesus is to act. Later, we will situate this relationship in the globalized world in which we live. I think it is important to shed light on the actual complex economic reality with the Word of God. The economy is an essential dimension of life and, as such, Jesus recognizes it in the New Testament, in particular in the Gospel of St. Matthew – a former tax collector:

- "The Kingdom of Heaven is like a treasure buried in a field... or a pearl of great price" (*Mt* 13:44-46).
- "Which of you wishing to construct a tower does not first sit down and calculate the cost to see if there is enough for its completion?" Jesus asks (*Lk* 14:28).
- Other parables speak about the master who comes and the need to know how to employ people's talents so that they bear fruit (*Mt* 25:14-30; *Rev* 22:12); the contract and salary due to the tenants (*Mt* 20:1-16); and the king who decided to settle accounts with his servants (*Mt* 18:23-35).

• Jesus describes the characteristics of the good administrator and he praises him: "Who, then, is the faithful and prudent servant, whom the master has put in charge of his household to distribute to them their food at the proper time?" (*Mt* 24:45). These words define well, in my opinion, how our general treasurers ought to be.

• St. Paul, in turn, warns the one who aspires to be bishop and "does not know how to manage his own household" (*1 Tim* 3:5).

• Of course, we also see that Jesus puts the value of money in perspective when he says to his disciples: "Do not take gold or silver or copper for your belts; no sack for the journey, or a second tunic, or sandals, or walking stick." But we must not forget that he adds immediately after: "The laborer deserves his keep" (*Mt* 10:9-10).

Matthew had experience in economic matters, but despite this and the citations here on the subject, he was not the treasurer of the apostolic community. We know that it was Judas, certainly a way to show us what treasurers ought not to do and to help us live out this responsibility, not with fear and trembling, but rather with transparency and honesty.

I believe that where we are (willingly or unwillingly) is clear – in a globalized world, and our point of reference ought to be the Gospel. At the assembly in May 2002, the Union of Superiors General reflected thoroughly on the economy and the mission in consecrated life in the world today. During that assembly, it was ascertained that the economic world today is in a process of globalization owing to the integration, interdependence and globalization of the market and available resources. For some people, it is "a false dawn" that favors individualism, isolation and social fragmentation. Others believe it possible to humanize economic globalization by fostering an economic ethics that is careful to protect the environment and the rights of the excluded. Faced with this we can ask ourselves if humanizing the globalized economy and placing the economy at the service of the person, beginning with our institutes and our central governments, may not be a concrete way to live out our charism in today's world and be one of the best ways to serve the Church and her mission of salvation, as, indeed, Pope Francis has asked of us repeatedly.

Fortunately, we are able to count on institutional norms to aid us in developing our role of superior general or general treasurer. In this regard, I recall the following canons:

- Can. 635 § 1: "Since the temporal goods of religious institutes are ecclesiastical goods, they are governed by the prescripts of Book V, The Temporal Goods of the Church."
- Can. 635 § 2: "Nevertheless, each institute is to establish suitable norms concerning the use and administration of goods, by which the poverty proper to it is to be fostered, protected and expressed."
- Can. 636 § 1: "In each institute, and likewise in each province which is governed by a major superior, there is to be a finance officer, distinct from the major superior and constituted according to the norm of proper law, who is to manage the administration of goods under the direction of the respective superior. Insofar as possible, a finance officer distinct from the local superior is to be designated even in local communities."
- Can. 636 § 2: "At the time and in the manner established by proper law, finance officers and other administrators are to render an account of their administration to the competent authority."

1. Vision

The great challenge that we have before us, which is accentuated by the economic and financial crisis, is to demonstrate in thinking and behavior that the traditional principles of social ethics – namely, transparency, honesty and responsibility – cannot ignored or attenuated.[1]

[1] Cf. BENEDICT XVI, Encycl. Lett. *Caritas in veritate*, 36.

Vision: keeping in mind the Gospel values, how do we want to be seen by others – by civil authorities, society, the Church, etc.? In my opinion, we all want others to see us – leaders and administrators – as people who are able to carry out our roles ethically and with transparency, honesty and a sense of responsibility. Some time ago, the *Wall Street Journal* presented an in-depth study on the finances of the Catholic Church in the United States. The authors of the study ensure, on one hand, that the money of the Church is administrated honestly and, on the other hand, that decisions are based more on compassion towards those making the requests than on objective and technical criteria that are in line with good administration. One runs the risk of acting according to reasons motivated by trust, driven by kindness towards others, in the desire to respect the conscience of others, etc, and not so much in order to act according to previously established objectives.

The press and the television have vilified – or at least, have tried to vilify – the image of administrators of institutions of a Christian character. More than ever, we have to act with truth and transparency before society. It is time to hold on to and/or recover our image and credibility. We will succeed if we conduct our management with the spirit of the Gospel and, at the same time, with competence and professionalism.

2. Complementarity in service

Let me refer to an experience our institute had. The central government of the institute is at the service of the brothers and the mission they carry out in the provinces or administrative divisions. The provinces have their due administrative autonomy within the limits established by Canon Law and from our juridical norms that are collected in the Administrative Directory, the latest version of which was published by the superior general and his council in 1998.

It is prudent and opportune also to maintain the principle of subsidiarity in the administrative context. Concretely, the superior general does not administer and manage the goods of the institute, but he guarantees that this administration is carried out in a manner that complies with Canon Law and the proper law of the institute. The financial and administrative autonomy of the province is an essential good because it makes it possible to preserve a level of finance culture and local economic responsibility, but it must be regulated by a general administrative directory that indicates the limits that must be observed.

It is a matter of shared responsibility, by both the superior general and the general treasurer, and each one of them holds a moral responsibility as well in the performance of their respective roles. We can say, clearly and simply, that the *administration* corresponds to the general treasurer and the *leadership* to the superior, alone or with his council. Naturally the treasurer must have the vision of the institute's charism while performing his administrative duties because we are not talking about a business enterprise, but about an evangelical mission, and this is what must guide administrative decisions – that they always support the mission of the institute. It is necessary, then, that a charismatic-ecclesiological collaboration be established between the two and that it be lived with fidelity and ethical rigor. The general treasurer, however, can never be reduced to being simply a delegate representing the superior.

In this shared mission, the treasurer stands in a relationship of responsible and mature dependence upon the superior, to whom he or she must be accountable regarding administration. But this mission is not reduced to that of a simple bookkeeper. In fact, he or she has to ensure the management of goods in all aspects regarding their conservation, correct use and investment. As I have said already, the treasurer enjoys a certain amount of freedom and personal initiative as indicated by the proper law of each institute, and in our case by the Administrative Directory. He or she also counts on the precious assistance of an economic council, which in our case is an international council. For the superior, he maintains the administration's direction by guiding it along the course marked out by the charism and the fundamental choices made in the destination and use of the goods, while always respecting the ecclesial identity of the goods themselves.

In our institute the tradition is that the superior general carries out, together with the general council, his responsibilities with regard to financial administration, which is to say, that all the members of the general council are involved in the process in order to ensure that the administration respects the laws within and external to the institute. This kind of management is not only shared, but it is also followed, valued and assumed by the whole general council, together with the superior. As a consequence, the general treasurer administers the goods of the institute under the authority of the superior general and the general council.

This complementarity in the administrative service of the institute is reflected explicitly in our Administrative Directory, especially in relation to the general council's functions. It is logical that the general treasurer is answerable to the superior general and the general council, who is held accountable for his or her work. The rapport between the general treasurer and the superior as well as with his council should not make us forget that governance in a religious institute is not collective, but personal, and that, consequently, in economic matters and economic decisions, the final responsibility rests with the superior general.

3. Functions of the general treasurer

Before pointing out the functions of the general treasurer, it is helpful to recall that can. 636, cited above, requires that the treasurer of an institute or a province be distinct from the superior general or provincial. This wise obligation allows the superior to feel more free in his mission of leadership and in the guidance of the institute, avoiding the always negative concentration of responsibilities and, consequently, of power in one and the same person.

The functions of the general treasurer include the following aspects: management, oversight, assistance and advice, training and information. I will limit myself just to some examples, because it is not possible in the time provided to offer a complete vision as is spelled out in our Administrative Directory.

1. Management
   a) Administers the goods of the central government.
   b) Prepares the annual budget of the central government and presents it to the brother superior and to his council for study, discussion and approval.
   c) Manages the different funds of the center of the institute, the investments..., etc.

2. Oversight
   a) Oversees the implementation of the budget during the year with the assistance of the International Economic Council.
   b) Periodically oversees the results obtained by the "operators" entrusted with managing our investments.
   c) Examines the financial reports that each province sends at the end of the financial year.

3. Aid/Advice
   a) Acts as the principal adviser of the brother superior general in all economic and financial matters.
   b) Studies the requests submitted by the provinces concerning the authorization of expenditures on construction, the purchase of land, the sale of land or buildings, and gives an opinion before the general council's vote.
   c) Can be sent by the brother superior or his council on a mission to study or to advise the provinces when they are in difficulty; with the agreement of the brother superior, the treasurer may delegate another person to carry out this mission.

4. Formation
   a) The treasurer is particularly involved with the training of the future treasurers (bursars) of the provinces.
   b) Depending on how much it is needed, he/she organizes training sessions in accounting for the young provinces and seeks to help them establish standardized methods of working and bookkeeping.
   c) Organizes regional meetings of provincial treasurers and, when appropriate, meetings for the provincial treasurers of the whole Institute.
   d) The rapid changes underway in the world of finance require the general treasurer have ongoing, permanent formation.
5. Information
   a) Regularly informs the brother superior general and his council about the financial situation of the central government.
   b) Prepares a financial report for the general chapter that covers the whole period since the last chapter.
   c) Sends information to the provincial brothers and their treasurers annually concerning the financial situation of the central government and audit reports.

4. Institutional relations

The treasurer's relations of dependence are institutional, that is to say, they are ruled both by Canon Law and by proper law, and in particular, by the Administrative Directory of the Institute. The figure of the administrator as "a proxy" who passively carries out decisions made by others is no longer accepted by society or even by the law: the administrator must be fiduciary. In his or her capacity as a trusted administrator, the general treasurer is then, by law, accountable to the general council and the law regarding the management of the institution's goods in a professional, ethical, and legal manner.

The treasurer must take on the responsibility of accurate accounting, that is: with figures that truly reflect all of the institution's assets and liabilities; where all financial transactions are registered correctly; accounting practices that are in compliance with the country's regulations or standards. When it comes to giving an account to the general council, the general treasurer will have time-frames and ways suggested by the superior general that come at least every trimester in order to offer assurances that transparency in the institute's administration is the norm. Transparency refers to the treasurer or administrator's duty to present and have examined by the authority and the council the information relevant to management, the use of resources that the institution has put in their hands, and the criteria followed in making decisions.

5. Importance of the general council

The general council, which is the institutional body legitimately elected by the general chapter, must be aware of the ultimate responsibility that it has in regard to the goods of the institute. Events today invite people to recognize the responsibility – even legal responsibility – that comes from not acting and from not fulfilling institutional obligations.

This responsibility must be pro-active, which is to say:

- The general council needs to nominate an economic or finance council that will accompany the general treasurer in the management of the institute's goods.
- Beyond the functions that internal law assigns to the finance council, the general council can request other functions or services of the said council.
- Furthermore, it is up to the general council to establish the expense limits for the general treasurer.
- Importantly, the general council must study and, if the case demands it, approve the financial reports presented by the general treasurer.

• It must ratify the manual that outlines the roles of the staff working in administration.

• One of its tasks is to establish the criteria for institutional administration.

• In accordance with internal regulations, the general council must sanction acts of extraordinary administration.

• One obligation of the general council is to approve the institute's annual ordinary budget after accurate study.

• The appointment of external auditors is up to the general council.

6. Ordinary administration

The institute's ordinary administration is regulated by the ordinary annual budget, which is prepared by the general treasurer, in collaboration with the economic council, before it is definitely approved by the general council. The budget must help promote the objectives of the institute's government, namely, by manifesting the priorities for the current fiscal year. The extraordinary and multi-year budgets and their liquidation are essential documents for assessing their implementation by the general treasurer and the economic council.

The superior general will make sure that transparency is the norm throughout the whole process of ordinary administration. Transparency demands that there be no secret transactions or secret accounts. Transparency in management presumes having a well-organized archive that preserves accounting documents for the length of time established by law. Transparency requires placing the information at the disposal of the competent authority and the general council:

• We are not owners of the goods that we administer or of the information that protects those goods.

• Having a monopoly on information about administrative matters produces serious problems for the institute.

7. Extraordinary administration

For purchases, maintenance operations, construction, etc. that exceed the maximum monetary limit fixed beforehand by the general council, and that do not make up part of the regular annual budget of the institute, transparency demands that there be open competitive bidding (invitation to tender).

The general treasurer, with the approval of the economic council, presents the general council with the extraordinary budget, which corresponds to the operations of extraordinary administration. In order to proceed, the written approval of the general council is necessary.

The general council will be vigilant in order to avoid possible conflicts of interest in the administration of the institute. If management aims to be ethical and transparent, transactions that have been subtly influenced by personal gifts are not acceptable, and personal favors must never influence administrative decisions either.

8. The management of patrimony

The institute's economic council, together with the general treasurer, supervises the investment of its patrimony. The superior general is vigilant to make sure that investments are socially responsible and Catholic ethical principles are applied.

Since the institute is a religious congregation, it is unacceptable its portfolio include ventures that are high-risk or lack internal transparency, such as speculative funds – "hedge funds," non-publicly traded shares, venture capital activities, structured products...

9. The audit – external review

For reasons of transparency and to inform the institute that the administration is complying with its administrative norms and respecting civil laws and the ethical principles of social responsibility, the superior general guarantees there be an annual management audit. It is up to the general council to appoint the auditors. In fact, transparency and legality in the administration of the institute demand that the administrative audit should be performed by an independent entity.

Just so you know, an audit is not a sign of mistrust towards the administrators, but rather, it confirms, in an objective and impartial way, that they are performing their job well, and it is an impartial guarantee for the whole institute. In fact, the transparency and legality of their management does not depend solely on their criteria or on their conscience, but rather counts on a specialist and impartial opinion that protects them both within the organization and, especially, before the law.

Without a doubt, the external audit involves a cost. As a matter of appearance, transparency, and justice due to administrators, it is necessary to realize it should be money well spent; it helps create a good image and good dividends because it guarantees that management is following the law by fulfilling its obligations related to labor, taxes and salaries.

If there are any discrepancies in the process of preparing the official report, the institution is protected because the external audit shows that it was not the institute's intention to hide anything, and that it followed the recommendations of external experts.

10. International solidarity

Practical questions pertaining to the administration of financial assistance for projects of solidarity have always concerned us in our institute. Initiatives and campaigns of solidarity have always taken place in the form of projects or sectors, which do have the economic resources, giving to other areas of the institute that experience serious economic difficulties.

Until a few years ago, the supervision of this solidarity exchange was entrusted to the office of the general treasurer. But since the chapter of 1986, the solidarity exchange service was removed from the role of the general treasurer. As of that date, a secretariat was created, which is globally responsible for the solidarity exchange or the interdependence among sectors.

Conclusion

Together with the general council, we published a circular in 2009 titled, *Towards Self-Sufficiency*, in order to promote awareness about a change underway caused by the decrease in the number of religious in provinces with more economic opportunities, and growth in provinces with greater economic difficulties. This situation made it impossible to continue a policy that was satisfied simply with giving outside aid and not worried about looking for resources locally.

I believe the invitation we have received to live out a prophetic realism can be applied to the subject we have been discussing. "Without realism, life becomes anxious and stressful. Without realism, utopias and visions lose their transformative capacity and become spectacular but not dynamic. [...] Practicing this principle, we need to find the right balance between two different forces that ask for different policies. Shall we have absolute trust in Providence or pursue fundraising and savings? Shall we follow our charism or institutional norms? Shall we focus on inspiration or production? The principle of 'getting real' asks from us, on the one hand, not to look for projects that exceed our capacities. On the other hand, it asks us to exploit all our capacities and pursue all the possibilities we have. To be consistent with our role as 'realistic prophets' we need to start by looking to those seemingly impossible projects with our eyes set upon simple and modest steps. These steps eventually will lead us to the more complex and ambitious goals we desire."[2]

Álvaro Rodríguez Echeverría, fsc
Superior General, Brothers of the Christian Schools

[2] Circular 460, *Towards self-sufficiency*, September 2009, General Council.

THE MANAGEMENT OF GOODS CONCERNING THE *SODALES* AND THE MISSION

SANTIAGO Mª GONZÁLEZ SILVA, CMF

Perhaps we can begin by saying that the economy is something much too serious because it is left solely up to the treasurers. In fact, the first approach to the situation that we are going to look at shows a configuration of power that is ill-suited to the Gospel inspiration of consecrated life.

> "Then Jesus summoned them and said to them: 'You know that those who are recognized as rulers over the Gentiles lord it over them, and their great ones make their authority over them felt. But it shall not be so among you. Rather, whoever wishes to be great among you will be your servant; whoever wishes to be first among you will be the slave of all. For the Son of Man did not come to be served, but to serve and to give his own life as a ransom for many'" (*Mk* 10:42-45).

St. Basil the Great sees in these words an essential dynamic of communal life,[1] that was right at the heart of his experience. When Benedict developed his Rule, it arose, deliberately, in the wake "of our Holy Father Basil."[2] If we want a deep understanding of the correspondence and respect that ought to determine the

[1] Basil of Caesarea, *Regole brevi*, Introduction, translation and editing by L. CREMASCHI, Bose 1993, n. 115, 306.

[2] *Sancti Benedicti Regula*, Introduction, text, apparatuses, translation and editing by G. PENCO, Florence 1970, cc. 71-73. From hence, *RB*. Indispensable for in-depth knowledge of the matter is A. DE VOGÜÉ, *La Regola di San Benedetto, commento dottrinale e spirituale* ("*The Rule of Saint Benedict: A Doctrinal and Spiritual Commentary*"), Praglia 1998.

management of goods with the members of an institute, here we find the decisive reference. Whatever the organizational layout, it is necessary to evaluate it based on a spiritual reciprocity that links participation to an identical consecrating grace. Because we want to talk about this life, our reasoning will draw happily from history and, within it, from those who give witness, namely, the saints.

From joyous sharing

We have already named the first: Benedict. Three reasons stand behind this choice. He was a founder, the father of monasticism in the western Church and a prudent legislator. The originating force of his charism is expressed in broad wisdom. The first point is suggested by the name chosen: cellarer – the one who takes care of the supplies in the cellar. Though based on hard reality, the norm seeks some steadfast qualities: "Wise, mature, sober." This last quality consists in keeping away from possible excesses: "Not a great eater, not haughty, not excitable, not offensive, not slow, not wasteful."[3] There is a degenerative logic that needs to be fought because it ends in the abandonment and neglect of the task. We can read in this a summarized version of experience, which is very useful for analysis.

However, we are not looking at pop psychology. Expressed as an adversative, here is the required principle – that the person be "a God-fearing man."[4] "It is interesting that Benedict desired that the responsible treasurer be God-fearing, convinced that the engagement with worldly things presupposed a spiritual profundity."[5] Authentic profundity because it would be able to communicate itself: "A father to the whole community. Let him have charge of everything."[6] This solicitude can overflow until it gener-

[3] *RB* 31.1.

[4] *RB* 31.2.

[5] A. Grün, *Benedetto da Norcia*, Brescia 2006, 94. From now on: A. Grün.

[6] *RB* 31.2-3.

ates a pre-eminence. Instead, he ought to remain at his post: "He shall do nothing without the Abbot's orders, but keep to his instructions."[7]

This lesson still holds true today. Perhaps even more so because the economy is recognized in society as a *de facto* power. When interacting with other confreres, the treasurer might interfere with the sense of authority. Certainly, norms guiding consecrated life are incredibly varied. Yet there is a permanent practice of placing this position at the level of an office, instead of an authority. The treasurer is an official, but not a superior. The treasurer has a subordinate role. Rather than make decisions, it is their job to carry them out. When these purposes are inverted, the life of the community and the individuals is gravely altered in its nature. Authority, understood first of all as spiritual,[8] deteriorates into a mere administrative exercise. The whole setting becomes conditioned by scheming and personal interests.

The risk of abuse of power looms: "Let him not vex the brethren. If any brother happens to make some unreasonable demand of him, instead of vexing the brother with a contemptuous refusal he should humbly give the reason for denying the improper request."[9] It is not necessary to provoke the brothers or to deliberately humiliate the sisters. Even when confronted with undesirable requests, the treasurer must speak humbly without using cutting phrases that are insensitive in exchanges with the sisters. The fear of God is shown above all in the respect shown to individuals. Benedict is aware of the peril that power comes with money and he points out to his confreres their dependence on money. This power comes through, unfortunately, in a thousand different ways, such as by making someone plead repeatedly for something or showing indifference to someone's expressed needs. Instead, the fear of

[7] *RB* 31.4-5.

[8] Congregation for Institutes of Consecrated Life and Societies of Apostolic Life, *Faciem tuam*, 13a.

[9] *RB* 31.6-7.

God leads to the fear of men. Everyone merits respect, even the person who is difficult and has exorbitant needs. The treasurer cannot be self-righteous, cannot judge or reprimand someone who expresses a desire. Treasurers ought to take all people seriously while being aware of their limits as well as the amount of financial resources they have available.[10]

Benedict issues a transcendental warning: "Let him guard over his own soul."[11] This reflective attitude is, above all, liberating. Preoccupied with a thousand things and details, treasurers ought to return to the origin of their call. Unhindered, one can hear himself or herself. Personal aspirations expand beyond recurring patterns of calculation. If treasurers become bitter and harsh, then aggressivity and dissatisfaction will spread inside them. On the contrary, if they care for their soul, their task remains spiritual and does not become the mere work of administration.[12] It is necessary, however, to take the proper amount of time – seeking it out during those periods with less pressure from deadlines. One needs to get there before the situation precipitates. We learn from the meek Francis de Sales: "When I wanted to review my soul at this, my return, it made me feel great compassion, because I found it so weakened and defeated that it seemed dead. It, I can well believe, had had almost no time to breathe. I will be near to it for all the next winter and will seek to treat it well."[13] From this personal perspective, he draws near his neighbor. "Let him take the greatest care of the sick, of children, of guests, and of the poor, knowing without doubt that he will have to render an account for all these on the Day of Judgment."[14] The cellarer has the task of

[10] Cf. A. GRÜN, 94-95.

[11] *RB* 31.8.

[12] Cf. A. GRÜN, 96.

[13] FRANCIS DE SALES, Letter to the Baroness of Chantal, the end of October 1606, in *Tutte le lettere*, ed. L. ROLFO, Rome 1967, I, 816. For correction, *Œuvres de Saint François de Sales*, Annecy 1904, XIII, 222 et seq.

[14] *RB* 31.9.

re-awakening life. This instruction is also the most important strategy in the economic governance of a monastery.[15]

Material things are then discussed: "Let him regard all the utensils of the monastery and its whole property as if they were the sacred vessels of the altar. Let him not think that he may neglect anything."[16] Even that which belongs to the world is sacred. The fear of God means taking the realities of this world seriously. Some communities are depleted of resources because they escape into a world of illusion that does not consider concrete reality.[17] A realistic spirituality is the best guarantee of balance and justice: "He should be neither a miser nor a prodigal and squanderer of the monastery's substance, but should do all things with measure and in accordance with the Abbot's instructions."[18] We all know some kind of administration where it skimps on necessities, most of all for the least and the last, and then consultants are paid not only handsomely, but even amidst the smell of corruption.

What Benedict demands more forcefully is humility: "Above all things, let him have humility; and if he has nothing else to give let him give a good word in answer."[19] A true doctor in this field, he spells out his 12 Degrees of Humility during one marvelous seventh chapter of his code, recommending all of it with a phrase culminating in charity. The same connection, in the person of Christ, seals the chapter on humility, as an aid to carry out the divine will.[20] Even the observations of psychologists confirm it – humility protects us from those projections heaped onto us from the outside. It leads us to ourselves, to our own truth, and allows us to be at peace.[21]

[15] Cf. A. GRÜN, 95.

[16] *RB* 31.10-11.

[17] Cf. A. GRÜN, 94.

[18] *RB* 31.12.

[19] *RB* 31.13.

[20] A. DE VOGÜÉ, *La comunità, ordinamento e spiritualità*, Praglia 1991, 182-183.

[21] Cf. A. GRÜN, 97.

This whole premise keeps the treasurer from abusive measures: “Let him have under his care all that the Abbot has assigned to him, but not presume to deal with what he has forbidden him.”[22] Because interference is often accompanied with defects in carrying out the duties pertaining to the office. Benedict points out the treasurer ought to distribute the “appointed allowance of food without any arrogance or delay, that they may not be scandalized, mindful of the Word of God as to what he deserves ‘who shall scandalize one of the little ones.’”[23] The seriousness of this call draws attention to the arrogance and carelessness of the servant, and are held up as intolerable behaviors. Benedict warns that every brother is to be treated amicably, and not to do it as if from on high.[24]

Because of the number of confreres, the need for extensive management is foreseen: “Let helpers be given him, that by their assistance he may fulfill with a quiet mind the office committed to him.”[25] In fact, were this work conceived of in exclusive and personal terms, it would very easily lead to delusion. The person carrying the burden will not see his own efforts recognized and will suffer the limitations of his collaborators. Equanimity is the presupposition for fruitful and peaceful management.[26] Benedict proposes this final aim – equanimity at all times and in all interactions, so “that no one may be troubled or vexed in the house of God.”[27] Sadness drags a person down and creates an atmosphere of heaviness and depression, which is the greatest obstacle that can be placed in one’s life[28] and particularly in communal life.

[22] *RB* 31.15.
[23] *RB* 31.16.
[24] Cf. A. Grün, 95-96.
[25] *RB* 31.17.
[26] Cf. A. Grün, 96-97.
[27] *RB* 31.19.
[28] Cf. A. Grün, 96.

In fact, the treasurer often forgets the authentic root of consecrated poverty. It is not based on ascetic deprivation, but is born rather from a brotherly-sisterly sharing in the joy of the Gospel. If our point of view sees only the suffering of detachment, it remains ensnared by pettiness and stinginess, which are characteristic of many religious administrations. Thus, one ends up with the parsimony of an obsessively domestic economy, incapable of overcoming the peasant horizon in which it was born, while institutes of today are active on global horizons. Many suffocating and repressive practices are rooted here, which weaken enthusiasm and youthfulness as they only worry about preserving "decrepit carcasses." The small number of useful people are exploited under false pretences to maintain the anachronistic comforts of a privileged circle. Canonical visits ought to concentrate on identifying these abuses to remove them, roots and all. There is nothing of the Gospel here, but only a contrary spirit identified by its sign of arrogance. But we have seen the consequences, which are clearly before everyone's eyes: "Whenever a worldly mentality predominates, the result is rivalry, jealousy, factions."[29] This is something very much opposed to the community.

Evangelical poverty, on the other hand, breathes new life: "For redeemed by Christ and made a new creature in the Holy Spirit, man is able to love the things themselves created by God, and ought to do so. He can receive them from God and respect and reverence them as flowing constantly from the hand of God. Grateful to his Benefactor for these creatures, using and enjoying them in detachment and liberty of spirit, man is led forward into a true possession of them, as having nothing, yet possessing all things (*2 Cor* 6:10). 'All are yours, and you are Christ's, and Christ is God's' (*1 Cor* 3:22-23)."[30]

[29] FRANCIS, *Homily, consistory for the creation of new Cardinals*, February 22, 2014.

[30] SECOND VATICAN ECUMENICAL COUNCIL, Past. Const. *Gaudium et spes*, 37.

All the way to reaching the least

We now have a trinomial (Gospel, poverty, liberty) that guides us inexorably to St. Francis.

In his first Rule, the theme of poverty immediately appears bound vocationally to the mission. A candidate encounters the brothers as itinerants. We read two recommendations: benevolence and poverty. If someone "comes to our brothers, let him be kindly received by them"; "let the brothers take great care not to meddle with his temporal affairs, but let them present him as soon as possible to their minister." Let him "receive him kindly, and encourage him, and diligently explain to him the tenor of our life." An approach still marked by fraternity and frankness. Then one will see: "If he be willing and able, with safety of conscience and without impediment, let him sell all his goods and endeavor to distribute them to the poor." The choice is done in complete spiritual freedom and without interference: "Let the brothers and the ministers of the brothers be careful not to interfere in any way in his affairs." The reason for this repeated insistence is explained: "And let them not receive any money, either themselves or through any person acting as intermediary." The prohibition is reaffirmed when the sole exception is admitted: "If however they should be in want, the brothers may accept other necessaries for the body, money excepted, by reason of their necessity, like other poor."[31]

Chapter II in the approved Rule reaffirms abstention: the brothers and their ministers guard themselves from being concerned about temporal things, for they should freely do so as God inspires them. "If they ask advice, the ministers may refer them to some God-fearing brothers through whose counsel their possessions may be distributed to the poor."[32] The only variation consists in

[31] E. CAROLI (ed.), *Fonti Francescane*, Padova 2004, 5-6, p. 62. From hence, *FF*.

[32] *FF* 78, 90.

favoring outside assistance in discernment in order to keep themselves far from all self-interest.

Francis, in the unapproved Rule, does not even contemplate a brother being installed as treasurer. He relates every decision to the ministers. They see their responsibilities delineated right from the start: ministers and servants of the other brothers must "often visit and spiritually admonish and console them. And let all my other blessed brothers diligently obey them." A spiritual task, as one can see, that is centered on encouragement and perseverance. With unequivocal emphasis, it comes directly from the Gospel: "And let the ministers and servants remember that the Lord says: I have not 'come to be ministered unto, but to minister' " (*Mt* 20:28).[33]

Participation in economic life is recognized in a way that always maintains the proper style: "Let the brothers in whatever places they may be among others to serve or to work, not be chamberlains, nor cellarers, nor overseers in the houses of those whom they serve, and let them not accept any employment which might cause scandal, or be injurious to their soul, but let them be inferior and subject to all who are in the same house."[34] Minority is the guarantee of fidelity in the friar. The approved Rule integrates notable elements. A significant phrase comes at the beginning: "Those brothers whom the Lord favors with the gift of working." There is a fundamental appraisal of the reality of work. After this, there is the added invitation to work faithfully and devotedly so that idleness is chased away. He does not want the brother to extinguish "the spirit of holy prayer and devotion, which all other temporal things should serve." Only at this point can one then accept: "As payment for their labor let them receive that which is necessary for themselves and their brothers, but not money. Let them receive it humbly as befits those who serve God and seek after the holiest

[33] *FF* 13-14, 65. There is not an equivalent chapter in the approved Rule.

[34] *FF* 24, 67-68.

poverty."[35] The precise exclusion of all monetary compensation puts a limit on pragmatic arrangements, which are strongly perceived as being devoid of divine inspiration.

The threat looms. Francis, with his excellent merchant experience, intuited it with extraordinary lucidity. In the earlier Rule, he proclaims and further justifies the ban that the friars not receive money. It starts off directly: "The Lord commands in the Gospel: 'Take heed, beware of all malice and avarice and guard yourselves from the solicitudes of this world, and the cares of this life'" (*Lk* 12:15; 21:34). The juxtaposition of the texts reinforces the dilemma. It is a choice between two antithetical aims, between the Lord and economic cupidity. He reasons from this: "Therefore let none of the brothers, wherever he may be or whithersoever he may go, carry or receive money or coin in any manner." He goes beyond rational logic. He identifies money with economic domination, at a time when this was only just the beginning. He does not accept it "indeed for any reason, except on account of the manifest necessity of the sick brothers. For we ought not to have more use and esteem of money and coin than of stones." He is drastic in rejecting the value of trade. He shuns entering into that chain of production. He keeps saying that there is an alternative option: "Let us therefore take care lest after having left all things (cf. *Mt* 19:27) we lose the kingdom of heaven for such a trifle. And if perchance it should happen that any brother should collect or have money or coin, except only because of the aforesaid necessity of the sick, let all the brothers hold him for a false brother, a thief, a robber, and one having a purse, unless he should become truly penitent." He repeatedly uses the imperfect subjunctive to express how absurd, to the point of impossible, he believes such a supposition to be. The prohibition does not allow them to receive money even by way of others. "And let the brothers in nowise receive money for alms or cause it to be received, seek it or cause it to be sought." It specifies, in favor of the excluded, the exception already noted:

[35] *FF* 88, 93.

"The brothers may however for the manifest necessity of the lepers ask alms for them." He closes, still reiterating: "But let them be very wary of money." He puts them on guard, at the end, against the eventuality of being carried away by this evil power: "But let all the brothers likewise take great heed not to search the world for any filthy lucre."[36]

In the approved Rule, the thought is the same. Here we have a much more concise version, reinforced further by the fact that it preceded the chapter on how the friars may work. He personally exhorts them in an imperative tone: "I strictly forbid the brothers to receive money in any form either directly or through an intermediary." He adds the needs of the sick and the clothing of the brothers, as necessity may seem to demand: "Nevertheless, the ministers and custodians can work through spiritual friends to care for the sick and clothe the brothers," according to the circumstances. That responsibility is restricted to ministers and custodians, and they ought to carry it out through other people. He holds onto this point to reestablish: "This must be done, however, in such a way that they do not receive money."[37]

Many administrators will lament – happily – that this lofty spiritual reflection lacks applicability. They are, however, deceived. This is sound and more relevant than ever. It would be interesting to know more about the disasters that resulted from the financial crises of religious men and women. There is undoubtedly much more to it than what we are able to read about in the newspapers. Certainly it is not because they embarked greedily into speculation, but because they put their trust in capital, in money, rather than in God. Before the collapse of the economy, it was common to hear from treasurers: "Without overlooking Providence, we have now guaranteed the greatest returns on our assets." It was not necessary to bother with heaven anymore. They had taken care of it.

[36] *FF* 28, 69-70.

[37] *FF* 87, 92.

The temptations of the Church in its mission are seen in the temptations overcome by Christ: "[The devil] took him up and showed him all the kingdoms of the world in a single instant. The devil said to him, 'I shall give to you all this power and their glory; for it has been handed over to me, and I may give it to whomever I wish. All this will be yours, if you worship me.' Jesus said to him in reply, 'It is written: You shall worship the Lord, your God, and him alone shall you serve' " (*Lk* 4:5-8). Unfortunately, many times the community succumbs. It really seems more than reasonable to accumulate every resource and all power in order to serve the kingdom. Still, the saints following the Gospel did not think this way. Francis Xavier sailed to the missions of Asia. António de Ataíde, Count of Castanheira, considered it improper that a papal legate should wash his own laundry and go into the kitchen to make something to eat. Francis reflected on how to start evangelizing. He responds: "Your Highness, gaining public esteem and authority with the means that you say, brought the Church to the state in which one finds it, together with its prelates. The way to go forward in order to be credible is to do the laundry yourself and to season the pot without need of another and, further, to seek to work in the service of the souls of one's neighbors." [38] In the year as his death, when he embarked for his last voyage, he left this recommendation to the person who would replace him as vice provincial: "And mind well that the honor of the society is not in having importance and honor in the world, but only in being at peace with God." [39]

[38] *Monumenta Xaveriana*, II, 387. Cited in J.M. RECONDO, *San Francisco Javier*, Madrid 1988, 294.

[39] FRANCIS XAVIER, Letter to Father Gaspare Barzeo, April 6-14, 1552, in A. CARBONI (edited by), *Dalle terre dove sorge il sole. Lettere e documenti dall'Oriente 1535-1552*, Rome 2002, 452.

In open communion

We know that the Spirit blows far and, starting from last year, strong as well. It is time for the new evangelization. Pope Francis, in his apostolic exhortation, *Evangelii gaudium*, says: "This is why I want a Church which is poor and for the poor. They have much to teach us. Not only do they share in the *sensus fidei*, but in their difficulties they know the suffering Christ. We need to let ourselves be evangelized by them. The new evangelization is an invitation to acknowledge the saving power at work in their lives and to put them at the center of the Church's pilgrim way." [40] This formulation of the preferential option for the poor is definitive. The Church "is able to be the Church only if it is the Church for the others." [41] As a reflection of identity, the communal employment of goods and the spirit with which they are managed in the mission beg to be changed.

The first place to look is at our brothers and sisters. Treasurers will do well to remember that they are administrators, not proprietors. A quick and immediate clue can be found in how they use possessive pronouns. If the first person singular predominates, there is a problem, perhaps even just at an early stage.[42] In any case, the point to be examined, above all, is certainly the work. It ought to be carried out in the communion of goods and in a perspective that goes beyond simple economic returns. So many religious men and women are overwhelmed with burdens propping up impossible structures and with work schedules that go far beyond normal healthy conditions. There is a whole wide and vast set of problems which demands urgent intervention because it is becoming tolerated as being normal.

[40] FRANCIS, Ap. Exhort. *Evangelii gaudium*, 198.

[41] G. MÜLLER, *Povera per i poveri. La missione della Chiesa*, Vatican City 2014, 21.

[42] F. TORRES, La administración de los bienes en tiempos de crisis, in *Vida Religiosa* 111 (2011) 83.

One effective remedy would be transparency and co-responsibility in management at every level. The Magisterium of Pope Paul VI taught us: "Two aspirations persistently make themselves felt in these new contexts, and they grow stronger to the extent that he becomes better informed and better educated: the aspiration to equality and the aspiration to participation, two forms of man's dignity and freedom."[43] But this is not applied even to the members of the general chapters, where the economic memorandum is often shrouded by a lack of clarity and verification is hindered by procedural measures.

Subsidiarity should be implemented particularly in the economic arena. Because of the legal requirements of taxation, things have been heading increasingly towards a centralization of the economy. This activates a dangerous mechanism here, founded "on the enormous power that money has taken on today, a power seemingly superior to any other."[44] It is fed by a tendency that encourages decisions to be made by experts in isolation, many of whom do not belong to the institute. Gradually, it comes to be managed from the outside, to the point of necessitating the inclusion in the constitution precise requirements for authorization by the general government in order to avoid sudden sweeping maneuvers that are foolish and ruinous.

The ideal figure is found in the administrator who has a vocational identity, who never thinks of claiming for himself or herself a right of veto, who never blocks everything new without even evaluating it, repeating: "It is not possible." By contrast, they enthusiastically put themselves at the service of the proper charism, instead of acting like the accountant of the status quo. They are authentic procurators, as a particular tradition has called them. They manage to make possible the ministry that is needed at the time and place in which the Gospel is proclaimed. It is time to remember that the apostolate, if it wants to be evangelical, must remain poor – at least,

[43] PAUL VI, Ap. Lett. *Octogesima adveniens*, 22.

[44] FRANCIS, Preface, in G. MÜLLER, *Povera per i poveri*, cit., 5.

with that poverty of heart that can recognize that the work of the Gospel is always greater than the means employed.[45]

As Pope Francis explains: "We might think that this 'way' of poverty was Jesus' way, whereas we who come after him can save the world with the right kind of human resources. This is not the case. In every time and place God continues to save mankind and the world *through the poverty of Christ*, who makes himself poor in the sacraments, in his word and in his Church, which is a people of the poor. God's wealth passes not through our wealth, but invariably and exclusively through our personal and communal poverty, enlivened by the Spirit of Christ." [46]

Even small communities think of themselves in reference to others. The preferential option for the poor is "central to all entities." [47] We cannot close ourselves up inside a shell. Sharing goes beyond domestic boundaries: "When the goods which one has available are used not only for one's own needs, they multiply by being spread around, and often bear an unexpected fruit." [48] We vitally learn that "alone, we are not able to give ourselves all that we need. The honest recognition of this truth invites us to remain humble and to practice solidarity with courage as a virtue essential to life itself." [49] Universal generosity in the mission strengthens an authentic communion among the members of the same community.

SANTIAGO Mª GONZÁLEZ SILVA, CMF

Professor of theology of apostolic life and social doctrine of the Church
Dean of the Institute of the Theology
of the Consecrated Life "Claretianum"
Pontifical Lateran University – Rome

[45] Cf. R. VOILLAUME, *Lettres aux Fraternités*, Paris 1960, I, 364.

[46] FRANCIS, *Lenten Message 2014*, 6.

[47] G. GUTIÉRREZ, L'opzione preferenziale per i poveri ad Aparecida, in G. MÜLLER, *Povera per i poveri*, cit., 220.

[48] FRANCIS, Preface, in G. MÜLLER, *Povera per i poveri*, cit., 8.

[49] *Ibid.*, 9.

THE MISSIONARY PROJECT AND ECONOMIC CHOICES

Yvonne Reungoat, FMA

Introduction

I am happy to greet the prefect of the Congregation for Institutes of Consecrated Life and Societies of Apostolic Life, His Eminence Cardinal João Braz de Aviz, the other superiors of this dicastery, and all the participants in this symposium, and to reflect on a subject that is important for the prophetic witness of consecrated life today. Consecrated life has the duty to offer a significant evangelical witness in a world in which the top 85 richest people in the world hold the resources of half of the world's population – about 3.5 billion people, according to statistics published on the occasion of the Davos Forum.

In his message addressed to Professor Klaus Schwab, Executive Chairman of the *World Economic Forum*, on January 17, 2014, Pope Francis emphasized: "Ours is a time of notable changes and significant progress in different areas which have important consequences for the life of humanity. [...] Nonetheless, the successes which have been achieved, even if they have reduced poverty for a great number of people, often have led to a widespread social exclusion. Indeed, the majority of the men and women of our time still continue to experience daily insecurity, often with dramatic consequences. [...] I ask you to ensure that humanity is served by wealth and not ruled by it."

Religious congregations and societies of apostolic life have received a founding charism from the Holy Spirit in order to be a prophetic sign in the historic moment in which they came into being, and that includes having enormous potential for the future. Every charism holds within itself a powerful force which asks only to be unleashed in order to be a force of social transformation in the setting in which it is lived and shared, grounded in a coherent evangelical life. Above all, every charism contains a great missionary impulse. Consecrated life in itself is mission in Jesus' image, "whom the Father has consecrated and sent into the world" (*Jn* 10:36). This powerful apostolic spirit impels many consecrated men and women today to risk their lives in every part of the world, above all where the needs are greatest, in order to bring the Good News of the Gospel and to be a sign of God's love in the midst of his people. Every charism is the source of inexhaustible creativity because the principle actor is the Holy Spirit, who is creative love!

All the founders have listened to the Spirit of love in the cry of the poor, have heard their uproar and have found new ways to try to make their lives more human. For this purpose, they founded different apostolic works according to their particular charism. Each time, the starting point has been the creative force in their heart – compassion before the urgent needs of a significant part of the human race. From there arose many missionary projects that came to fruition through prayer and a deeply spiritual life, an expression of the "passion for Christ and the passion for humanity." The fire that burns in the hearts of the founders has been shared by people and communities that have embraced the same call from God. Almost everywhere, the beginnings were poor with regard to the people and the economic means, but rich in faith and unlimited trust in the Lord, in apostolic audacity and in the forceful conviction that love is stronger than life. Today, the rapidity and profundity of cultural and social shifts require continuous discernment in order to bring about the necessary adaptations with a view to responding adequately to the real needs of the beneficiaries.

We have often experienced that from a small, apparently insignificant seed, a great tree is born that gradually extends throughout the whole world. That is the case with our institute and for the entire Salesian Family. If our cofoundress, St. Maria Domenica Mazzarello, who was following in the footsteps of St. John Bosco, had not risked, just five years after the founding of the institute, sending a group of very young sisters, who had no experience and no economic means, to America, we would not be present in five continents today. This radical audacity in the faith is also important today, because what is important is spreading the kingdom of God throughout the whole world! I am convinced that we are called to share with the poorest, not our surplus, but that which is necessary, both in economic means and human resources.

Keeping this foundation in mind, we were asked to relate the missionary project to economic decisions. I will attempt to share some fundamentals that can help us reflect. In fact, in the running and the governance of our institutes, we constantly find ourselves having to face decisions that need to be taken in this regard.

The missionary project and the economic dimension

The reason for which a new missionary project is launched, a new presence is established or a new work begun, is above all in order to respond to a need, to a request that is believed to be important after adequate discernment by the general or provincial council and, inasmuch as it is possible, with the involvement of the whole congregation. Like Mary at Cana, we realize that humanity "has no more wine." A new work or project is never launched for economic reasons. In the same way, when shutting down a work, the determining factor is not economically motivated, even if that is important to keep in mind. But in the process of discernment in regard to starting a missionary project, keeping the economic dimension in mind along with the other factors is necessary.

A prior assessment of sustainability, including economic, permits opening up a horizon of hope for the project's beneficiaries. This is especially important when it is a mission that serves the poorest so as not to disappoint their hopes and expectations after having built up their hope for a better future. Not having the economic means at the project's design phase ought to be an impetus to track down the necessary resources – people and funds – to guarantee the life of the project rather than be an obstacle to moving forward. A missionary project's objective is a process of integral development that promotes nurturing human dignity and transforming the social context according to the God's plan for humanity. It is, then, always important to develop a well-rounded vision that takes into consideration all aspects of human life where one wishes to manifest concretely God's love and render it visible and comprehensible. In the life of our institutes it is often difficult to link all these aspects together and, in particular, to put the economic dimension in its proper place in relation to the other dimensions. We are called to a change of mentality so as not to leave the concern for this dimension to just one person, for example, to the treasurer. The whole council and the whole community are interested in participating in a process of a holistic vision of the mission.

The Church's recent social Magisterium invites us to overcome the apparent dichotomy between mission and economy: "The great challenge before us [...] is to demonstrate, in thinking and behavior, [...] that in commercial relationships the principle of gratuitousness and the logic of gift as an expression of fraternity can and must find their place within normal economic activity." [1] Economic choices are aimed at realizing a missionary project that promotes a culture that sees development as moving from conditions that are less human to conditions that are more human. The human being is always measured according to the Gospel.[2] But which principles ought to guide a sound economic plan for opening a mission? I will list some.

The missionary project and trust in divine providence

Throughout the history of religious congregations, the founders and foundresses have been enlivened by a great apostolic impulse, allowing themselves to be moved by and to live with compassion

[1] BENEDICT XVI, Encycl. Lett. *Caritas in veritate*, 36.

[2] Cf. INSTITUTE OF THE DAUGHTERS OF MARY HELP OF CHRISTIANS, *Cooperazione allo sviluppo. Orientamenti per l'Istituto delle Figlie di Maria Ausiliatrice*, Bologna 2007, 17-18.

with regard to people's suffering, as Jesus did. They ventured out without a great amount of economic resources and with a small number of people. We have, in our history, great experience of the Father's providence. Indeed, we immerse ourselves in the mystery of the self-emptying of Jesus, who, being abundant, became poor in order to enrich us with his poverty. With him we make ourselves available without reserve for the mission entrusted us by the Father and we abandon ourselves with a filial attitude to his providence.[3]

Living in a social context that makes us confront a business-focused mindset toward management, it is important to deepen the idea of divine providence, which was so dear to our founders. Experience proves that when we develop projects for the poorest, divine providence never fails. This, at least, is from my own personal experience and our institute's. One needs to have the courage to take risks and to be certain that the Lord never abandons his people, especially the poorest – his favorite people. This courage stems from a passion that no hardship can extinguish.

Our founders were convinced that divine providence could never abandon them. They did not have the concept of a God of entitlement, but of a Father who turns those whom He calls to collaborate with him in building up his kingdom into protagonists. Don Bosco affirmed, "Divine providence has inexhaustible treasures. We all do what little we can, and God will supply what is lacking. While we then place unlimited confidence in the goodness of the Lord, we do not shun our own cooperation."[4] For Don Bosco, the "*da mihi animas caetera tolle*" was a fire that blazed in his heart and made him ready for any sacrifice in order to find the money needed to further his work for the poor children of Turin. His passion touched the hearts of benefactors, who were unable to turn down his requests.

[3] Institute of the Daughters of Mary Help of Christians, *Costituzioni*, art. 18.

[4] E. Ceria, *Memorie Biografiche di don Giovanni Bosco*, Turin 1933, XIV, 672.

The wisdom and pragmatism of our founders urge us to know we can trust in divine providence, not with a passive attitude, but driven by a great creative audacity. In this regard, we have sought to strengthen a mindset of coordination in the institute. In order to teach a culture of solidarity and to form new generations in this outlook, it is important to nourish in them hope and creative audacity, with the view of constructing a more just world with more solidarity and to promote the creation of networks for uniting forces towards the realization of a common project. Along these lines, we have promoted the creation of development offices in the religious provinces that have as their objective the coordination of projects and mediating between different entities. These offices also play an important role in training in development and planning by teaching techniques for examining the situation and developing the projects themselves. They also have a significant impact on overcoming a mentality of entitlement in favor of a solidarity that is ingrained in the organization's structures and networked. The development offices are a way of being pro-active in the search for the ways of divine providence, who always shows up for the appointment! At the same time, they let people experience how creating synergy around a common goal is an irresistible and contagious life-changing force. This process intrinsically evangelizes and humanizes. The quality of relationships in the exchange network plays an essential part as it is a privileged channel through which God passes.

The communion of goods for the benefit of the mission

Religious institutes have chosen to live in imitation of the early Christians, pooling everything together, as a sign of the vow of poverty. The communion of goods represents a considerable force: it permits the achievement of great things with the few resources of many people who put all that they have together. It allows for sharing resources with those who have fewer possibilities in order to reduce the number of those in need and to curtail rising inequalities, which have now become an intolerable scandal. The communion of goods is also, however, a fragile good, as demonstrated by what happens in the account of Ananias and Sapphira in the Acts of the Apostles. In order to make the communion of goods effective, it is necessary to embark on a journey of conversion to the love that leads to making choices freely and willingly along these lines.

This involves not only a formal following of the rules of each institute's constitution, which may encourage courageous choices, but also a committed embodiment by each person and by the community of greater solidarity with the poor. When talking about the importance of putting things together to have in common, Don Bosco's words resound out almost prophetically: "There are some practical and very effective things [...] and among these I note: *the unity of spirit and the unity of administration.*"[5] These words were written during the time Don Bosco was working to get approval of the constitutions, and they reveal one of his most ardent desires. "Everything stays in common: the more you give to the house, the more divine providence sends."

The communion of goods, in addition to strengthening fraternity, opens the door to solidarity and makes more funds available for the mission of serving the poorest. Please allow me to cite an article from our constitutions. Every one of us can make reference to his or her institute's rule of life: "In view of imitating the early Christians, each one of us willingly places at the disposal of the community, more than material goods and the fruits of one's labor, but also one's time, gifts and personal skills. This sharing and fraternal communion extend from the local community to the that of the province via the provincial, and to the global community via the general superior, in such a way that everything may be put at

[5] A. AMADEI, *Memorie Biografiche di don Giovanni Bosco*, Turin 1939, X, 1098.

the service of the apostolic purpose of the institute, according to the needs of different situations."[6]

The international reality of the institute always challenges or us: one family is present in the world's richest countries and the poorest countries, and we are called to carry out the same educational mission and to give witness by means of our experience of sharing that it is possible to build a world that has more solidarity, that is more just and more human. Different experiences of global solidarity in times of emergency are a concrete sign of belonging to this great family that lives the joys, the sufferings, the hopes and the concerns of all its members near and far. The choice to inspire the creation of micro-enterprises and enhance micro-credit has changed the lives of many families in some parts of the world, empowering them to improve their living conditions to the advantage of the whole local community. In some places, civil authorities have been inspired by these models. But I want to emphasize that the majority of these initiatives have arisen as a result of prayer, inspired by the Holy Spirit. In this case it involves not only finding the necessary funds for a missionary project, but living out the experience itself as a missionary experience!

Planning skills and economic choices

A missionary project requires a planning approach because the decision made at the present moment contains the seeds of a future yet to come. It seems to me to be very important to develop, in our councils at the different levels, this planning mentality. In this one finds the signs of hope in a world where it is often difficult to plan for the future, especially for the younger generation, on account of the economic crisis in which we are living, but also because of the problems connected to peace being threatened in different parts of

[6] Institute of the Daughters of Mary Help of Christians, *Costituzioni*, art. 25.

the world. Building a project means believing in the future and creating the objective conditions for instilling hope.

For the realization of any kind of missionary project, it is important to focus on a quality formation of people. The primary resource needed to carry the project forward is found in the people. Structures can fail, as happened at Haiti where the earthquake caused schools, hospitals and churches to collapse, but those who were in charge of these works continued the mission with everyone's cooperation, adapting to the circumstances in order to not leave people abandoned: children, young people etc. A solid, charismatic and professional formation is the basic element that must be considered a priority. This indispensable economic investment will find its fruitfulness in the future, provided that everyone accept sacrificing the urgency of the moment for the quality of the future. This choice requires a vision of planning and a long-term outlook that is shared be everyone, not only within the council, but also in the congregation's global community, so that they can take on courageous choices together in support of the mission. Before starting a new work it is necessary to take the time to form the people who will carry it through. Often we get caught up in the urgency. Nevertheless, we are aware that what does not get done at the start is difficult to achieve afterwards.

From an economic point of view, the budget forecast and plan are tools that are at the service of communion and of planning in the mission. These help in the planning of our works and our mission if they are used as instruments for communion and realistic planning, and not used just for their technical aspects. They are like a compass that shows the way and makes us understand whether we are being faithful to the project or deviating from the goal we have set for ourselves. They help us not waste resources with activities that would be leading us astray and would keep us from reaching our objectives. For an apostolic project to come about, it is always important that the project and the economic conditions be considered together and that these aspects be discussed in every discernment. Keeping the apostolic spirit alive lets people face all the realistic information concerning the different aspects of management. Even if our work has some features in common with businesses, I think it is important we do not simply enter into the kind of management dynamics typical of businesses; even though such management is kept in mind, it is important we develop a prophetic dimension of management that can be a sign for others in society. Even the language that we use is not neutral.

Planning ahead, when it is lived in the communion of goods and with in-network coordination, is the key to sustainability. This is not just economic sustainability, but also relational and spiritual, and it lets us inspire others – youth and adults, in their search for an alternative style of life. Planning ahead requires a new culture, for example, a culture in which the economy is considered to be just one element among all the others (formation, pastoral...) and to capable of contributing to the overall goals. It is not about being in opposition, but in alliance. For this to happen, different people need to work together and reflect together with transparency and common purpose. We must never forget that the missionary projects we dedicate ourselves to are not ours, they are the Church's, and the mission is first and foremost a gift of God. The mission is always lived in the midst of his active and mysterious presence. The Lord asks us to collaborate in the realization of his plan, but he chooses to go along the paths that we open up together with him.

As educators by vocation, we are aware that we teach by how we live and if we want to teach new generations a culture of solidarity, it is necessary that we are the first to begin a process of conversion. All consecrated men and women are called to contribute to the development of a culture of solidarity in order to build a world according to God's plan. For that reason, our economic choices have to be an expression of a new way of life. When we make the choice to be with the poorest, as a sign of the Church's preferential option for them, we must be forever creative in order to remain faithful to our charism. Today is a favorable moment for this prophecy!

With the Church in missionary outreach

Planning requires betting on the future by starting with a present that is animated by the fire of the Spirit. To use Pope Francis' expression, it requires we be a *Church in missionary outreach*, a Church that is not removed from the world, but is close to the joys, the sorrows and the hopes of mankind, and is rich in faith in her Lord. We need to be a poor Church with the poor, and thus, capable of sharing, of being impassioned, of building energy and a mindset that plans ahead. And above all, we need to be a Church capable of living its founding purpose: to proclaim the kingdom of God, especially to the poor. A Church which *goes forth* takes the initiative, it leaves all comforts behind, it participates and plans for reaching the peripheries that need the Gospel;[7] it shortens distances, it becomes engaged in human life, touching the suffering flesh of Christ in the people.[8]

Pope Francis calls for a pastoral and missionary conversion in which the poor are the protagonists. They have much to teach us. We are called to discover Christ in them, to lend our voice, but also to be their friends, to listen to the mysterious wisdom which God wishes to share with us through them.[9] The martyred Archbishop Oscar Arnulfo Romero stressed, *The world of the poor is our true place*. If we desert them, we distance ourselves from Christ. We want to stay in this place, recognizing that every person is immensely sacred and, therefore, worthy of our affection and our dedication.[10] We want to embrace the simplicity of the Gospel and a life according to the Beatitudes, confident that our lives will also become more joyful, open and available, capable of inspiring fresh energies for the mission, of opening up horizons of hope and of renewing vocational vitality. Important life choices can

[7] Cf. FRANCIS, Ap. Exhort. *Evangelii gaudium*, 20.

[8] *Ibid.*, 24.

[9] *Ibid.*, 198.

[10] *Ibid.*, 274.

come to fruition in the joy of poverty and this life can be spread to others. The Church in missionary outreach is above all the Church that dwelt in the Cenacle where it received the Holy Spirit and was filled with the audacity to proclaim the kingdom beyond all boundaries.

Conclusion

The word "economics" derives from the Greek word *oikos-nomos*, which literally means "household management," and where "house" can mean the walls of our domestic home, and also everyone's home: our planet. Good economics, then, is linked to caring for the planet and all of its inhabitants. Religious institutes are called to be prophetic in living within the economy, too, so as to be able to say with their life and works: *"No" to an unjust economy. "No" to an economy that excludes, "Yes" to an economy that promotes life, true human promotion, that promotes a more just society and the building up of the kingdom of God.*

I hope that this symposium may be an occasion for us to begin again with fresh enthusiasm and with some decisions aimed at guaranteeing members of our congregations, the many lay collaborators and the millions of people we touch an effective coherence between quality of life, health, sobriety, education, training, infrastructure and employment opportunities that are dignified and justly compensated. May these decisions help us give witness to the gratuity in the gift of our life, animated by a strong apostolic passion, sustained by sound and sensible economic management. We are happy to be able to contribute to the building of a new civilization of love and communion that chooses to be present at the frontiers still not reached by the Church.

YVONNE REUNGOAT, FMA
Superior General, Daughters of Mary Help of Christians

THIRD SESSION

Moderator

BROTHER JEAN PAUL MULLER, SDB

General Econome
of the Salesian Society of Saint John Bosco

GREETING FROM CARDINAL GIUSEPPE VERSALDI

President of the Prefecture for the Economic Affairs of the Holy See

I would like to thank the Congregation for Institutes of Consecrated Life and Societies of Apostolic Life, represented by the Prefect Cardinal João Braz de Aviz, not only for the invitation to preside over this session of the symposium, whose theme is "The management of the ecclesiastical goods of institutes of consecrated life and societies of apostolic life," but especially for having wanted this symposium, which in and of itself is a service to the mission in the Church.

Together with my warmest greetings to everyone, from the illustrious speakers to the participants, I want to contribute with a reflection that does not fall under this theme, but wishes to express my personal witness. I believe I was invited because of my role as president of the Prefecture for the Economic Affairs of the Holy See (which, as has been noted, is destined to be transformed within the economic-administrative reform initiated by the "Motu proprio" *Fidelis dispensator et prudens* of February 24, 2014). It has been precisely in my latest responsibility, begun in 2011, that I have experienced firsthand (first as priest and then as bishop) the problems tied to the management and administration of the temporal goods of the Church.

Here I understood the complexity and also the importance of the relationship between temporal goods and spiritual goals of the mission of the Church. On the one hand, in fact, whoever administers must do it with the spirit of a good father of a family, who seeks not only to protect the patrimony, but also to help it grow so that it can support the works necessary for the spiritual mission. On the other hand, however, in doing this, we come up against a worldly reality in which the rules are not always exactly compatible with the values that guide the Church's mission. A problem thus emerges that makes the job of administrators in the church difficult as they are caught up by the need to make gains in the economic and financial world that is objectively dominated by the market and by the law of profit and, and on the flip side, they run the risk of being a counter-witness of a Church that is not very poor and is compromised by the world of business.

This problem, which affects every state of life in the Church, becomes even more evident when one enters the world of consecrated life where the testimony of detachment from earthly goods is directly assumed with the vow of poverty. That vow, together with the vows of obedience and chastity, characterize religious life as prophetic and as anticipation of the eschatological reality according to these words of the Second Vatican Council: "The religious state, whose purpose is to free its members from earthly cares, more fully manifests to all believers the presence of heavenly goods already possessed here below. Furthermore, it not only witnesses to the fact of a new and eternal life acquired by the redemption of Christ, but it foretells the future resurrection and the glory of the heavenly kingdom" (*Lumen gentium*, 44).

Special attention must be paid to this specific charism of consecrated life when it comes to the management of the institute's goods so that the institute does not contradict its own witness or lack the means necessary to service and carry out its work (especially when the purpose is directly apostolic). Clearly contrary to this would be the idea that the purpose of charity towards the poor could lead to overlooking proper procedures for acquiring and taking in temporal goods, because a good end never justifies any means. (Unfortunately I was able to verify this directly in some cases, as sometimes the poverty of individual religious men and women is preserved, while justifying the accumulation of wealth of the religious institute).

But I would like to underline here the particular value that a religious institute's correct management of temporal goods can have as an instrument for evangelization and the transformation of the worldly dimension, as it is inevitably necessary to operate in the economic and financial fields. Here, the social doctrine of the Church, which is always brought up to date with the papal Magisterium, is the point of reference for every finance offer or professional who wants to be consistent with his or her faith. In regards to this final point, I refer to the teaching of Benedict XVI, especially in *Caritas in veritate*, as well as the Magisterium of Pope Francis, which is particularly insistent on the need to address the structural causes of poverty, eliminate inequity and overcome the blind and invisible forces of the market with policies aimed at shaping an economy seen as "the art of achieving a fitting management of our common home" (*Evangelii gaudium*, 206). So when religious administrators follow these criteria to the best of their abilities, they not only give coherent witness by renouncing maximum earnings in favor of an economy that is more just and based on solidarity, but they also, in their own small way, contribute to changing from within the very rules of the world. They show that it is possible to maintain the legitimacy of profit and keep as a priority the goal of the common good and solidarity that aims to eliminate unjust inequalities. That this inherent witness in the world of economy and finance would come from religious men and women strengthens the conviction that faith in God docs not ignore the reality of this world, but, on the contrary, it is a further guarantee of bringing about the kingdom of God from the temporal and earthly world. This is what Benedict XVI was driving at in his encyclical letter *Deus caritas est*, when he upheld the role of religion in the public sphere: "The Christian religion and other religions can offer their contribution to development only if God has a place in the public realm, specifically in regard to its cultural, social, economic, and particularly its political dimensions" (56). The same concept is taken up again by Pope Francis in his apostolic exhortation *Evangelii gaudium*: "I am firmly convinced that openness to the transcendent can bring about a new political and economic mindset which would help to break down the wall of separation between the economy and the common good of society" (205).

It is obvious that every religious administrator must know these principles not only in theory, as updated by the Church's social doctrine, but they must also apply them with the means they have. They need to harmonize, as has been said, the need to make the goods entrusted to them bear fruit (because just tucking them away to return them whole and without fruit would not be evangelical!) with their witness of consecrated life. The witness of one's charism must be even more shining and credible for religious men and women than for Christians living in the world.

I wish that all administrators, particularly you who have gathered here, may experience a growing conviction of how precious your ministry is. I hope it may be rescued from a certain mentality (I don't know if this belonged in the past or if it is still present) that thinks that those who deal with material goods necessarily end up getting their hands dirty or that the steward's role is beneath others and must be endured. Rather, it is a means that is necessary for the spiritual mission and it is, in and of itself, a source of positive witness in a field that has become so sensitive for the world (as the scandals by a few in the field of economics-finance have demonstrated). As the Second Vatican Council recalled, there are not two Churches with one that is invisible and spiritual and another that is visible and earthly, but there is one Church, instituted by Christ as "the community of faith, hope and charity, as an entity with visible delineation through which He communicated truth and grace to all." This "society structured with hierarchical organs and the Mystical Body of Christ, are not to be considered as two realities, nor are the visible assembly and the spiritual community, nor the earthly Church and the Church enriched with heavenly things; rather they form one complex reality which coalesces from a divine and a human element" (*Lumen gentium*, 8).

Therefore, you administrators are not children of a lesser god, who work for an earthly Church separate from the spiritual one; but, just like your fellow brothers and sisters who dedicate themselves to education or spiritual formation, you carry out a precious and demanding ministry that is equally necessary so long as the Church is a pilgrim on this earth. I think that only this kind of high regard for your work can be the needed incentive to not let yourselves become trapped by a resignation to bring in profitable outcomes by whatever means possible. That comes with the risk of either following the worldly mentality or letting harm come to those resources that, through the great work and generosity of the faithful, have been given to the Church and religious institutes as a sign of faith and esteem for a spiritual mission that the world needs now more than ever. We also need to evangelize the way we look at and manage temporal goods in religious life. I think and hope that this symposium may be an important step in this direction.

PAPER

ECONOMIC BEHAVIOR IN A CHANGING SOCIETY

STEFANO ZAMAGNI

1. Premise

As is well known, individualism is the philosophical stance which says the individual is the one who gives value to things and interpersonal relationships. And it is always the individual alone who decides what is good and what is bad, what is lawful and illicit. Said another way, anything the individual attributes value to is good. Objective values do not exist according to axiological individualism, but only subjective values. In the essay *Individually, Together*, Zygmunt Bauman clarifies that "casting members as individuals [and not as persons] is the trademark of modern society."[1] This individualization, continues Bauman, is in the transformation of human identity from a "given" into a "task," and giving the actors the responsibility for carrying out that task and for the consequences of their actions.[2] Bauman's thesis, therefore, is that "individualization brings to the ever growing number of men and women unprecedented freedom of experimenting, but it also brings an unprecedented task of coping with the consequences." So, the ever widening gap between the "right of self-assertion" on the one hand and the "capacity to control the social settings" in which such self-assertion should take place, "seems to be the

[1] Z. BAUMAN, *Individually, Together* (Italian edition: *Individualmente Insieme*, Parma 2009, 29).

[2] *Ibid.*, 31.

main contradiction of the 'second modernity.'"[3] Just think about the condition of women working outside the home and the problem of millions of people without work, especially young people.

On the other hand, libertarianism, which is very much the trend today, is a thesis put forth by many philosophers who say, in order to establish freedom and individual responsibility, it is necessary to turn to the idea of self-causation. For example, Galen Strawson argues, like many others, in his paper, *Free Agents* (Italian edition: 2012), that the only truly free agent is an agent that is self-caused, self-made, and in his words, *causa sui*, like God. (A strong and convincing critique of this thesis is by Adina L. Roskies in *Don't Panic: Self-Authorship without Obscure Metaphysics*, in *Philosophical Perspectives*, 2012).

The radicalization of individualism in libertarian terms, and therefore antisocial terms, has led to the conclusion that each individual has "the right" to extend himself or herself as far as his or her own power permits. The dominant idea in cultural circles today is freedom is seen as the termination of all ties. Since having ties limits freedom, ties are what needs to be undone. Because the concept of a bond is mistakenly equated with the concept of constraint, the conditioning of freedom – limits – are confused with the conditions of freedom – having ties.

Michel Foucault considered this aspect with rare perspicuity. When he addressed the problem of gaining access to the truth, he wondered if it were true that today we live in a time in which the market has become a "place of truth." That is, where people's entire lives are subsumed by economic efficiency and where it is still up to the market to ensure that government, in order to be a model of "good governance," should operate according to that place of veridiction: "The market must tell the truth; it must tell the truth in relation to government practice" and "Henceforth, and merely secondary it is [the market's] role of veridiction that

[3] *Ibid.*, 39.

will command, dictate, and prescribe the jurisdictional mechanisms, or absence of such mechanisms on which [the market] must be articulated."[4]

2. Towards the civil market

2.1. Today's great cultural and political challenge is to go beyond the traditional model of a free-market economy without, however, giving up the benefits that this model has so far ensured. It is not true, as some would like to believe, that if one wants to preserve and extend the social order founded on the market, one must necessarily accept (or endure) the market's traditional capitalist form. There is a widespread conviction across large swaths of public opinion at this time that says the model of so-called "turbo-financial capitalism" has already run out of steam. This precious opportunity to rethink the way we make sense of the market is before us right now.

Indeed, in the near future, the market will increasingly be asked not only to produce wealth and ensure a sustainable growth of income, but also to focus on integral human development. That is to say, the kind of development in which the material, the social-relational and the spiritual dimensions can progress in harmony. While the capitalist market has ensured an impressive advancement in the material world – that of growth – it has worsened significantly the social-relational and spiritual situation. And that is the cause of the truly alarming increase in the so-called social costs of growth. On the altar of efficiency – erected for the new myth of modernity – non-negotiable values have been sacrificed, such as democracy, distributive justice and positive liberty. Today, the myth of efficiency has found its full expression in the theory of financial markets: the so-called "market efficiency hypothesis." (Care must be taken not to confuse the following: the capitalist

[4] M. FOUCAULT, *The Birth of Biopolitics* (Italian edition: *Nascita della biopolitica*, Milan 2003, 40).

market is indeed compatible with commutative justice and with negative liberty, but not with distributive justice or with positive liberty. On the other hand, it is well-known that the capitalist market can go – and, in fact, has gone – "hand in hand" with brutal dictatorships, but not for long, as I will explain in a moment).

This sacrifice, which the economic and social history of the post-industrial revolution has talked about in a timely and exhaustive manner, found its theoretical justification, and therefore, cultural legitimacy, in the principle of NOMA (non-overlapping magisteria). This says that ethical principles have as much impact on economics as they have on the laws of physics and chemistry. That is to say, the field of economics must be kept scrupulously separate from the fields of politics and ethics because the infiltration of those values and principles into the market could put at risk reaching the market's ultimate goal: efficiency and, therefore, growth. This is how the capitalist market succeeded in gaining acceptance for the principle that must be used to measure those who work in the areas of politics and ethics: a political arrangement is acceptable if it serves to increase efficiency; an ethical norm is embraced and applied if it promotes growth. Now carefully reflect on the meaning of the following passage from the famous volume, *The Principles of Scientific Management* by F.W. Taylor: "Now one of the very first requirements for a man who is fit to handle pig iron as a regular occupation is that he shall be so stupid and so phlegmatic that he more nearly resembles in his mental make-up the ox than any other type. [...] Therefore the workman who is best suited to handling pig iron is unable to understand the real science of doing this class of work."[5] Taylor, who wrote a century after the analogous thinker, the Englishman Charles Babbage, used this idea as the basis for the design of the well-known model of the assembly line – a model that certainly can leave no room either for individual initiative or for a worker's intellectual development.

[5] F.W. Taylor, *The Principles of Scientific Management*, New York 1911, 28.

Why can't the market and democracy be separated for too long? We know that one of the chief merits of the creation of the market is to provide an efficient solution to the problem of how to mobilize and manage knowledge that is dispersed among a multitude of individuals. Friedrich von Hayek had already clarified, in a famous essay from 1937, that in order to channel efficiently the knowledge possessed by the different members of society, a decentralized mechanism of coordination is necessary, which is, in fact, the price system. But in order for this to operate in the way that is required, it presupposes – as Carlo Tognato observed – that people participating in the workings of the market understand and share the "language" of the market. It's worth an analogy. Pedestrians and motorists stop in front of a red light because they share the same understanding of the meaning of a red light. If, for some people, the light meant endorsing a particular political stance and, for others, it signaled danger, it is evident that no coordination would be possible and it's easy to imagine the consequences. The example suggests that the market needs not one, but two kinds of knowledge in order to fulfill its main task. The first kind is individual knowledge that is stored in each individual and – as Friedrich von Hayek had well understood – can be conveyed by the normal mechanisms of the market. The second type of knowledge, however, is institutional, and that has to do with the common language that enables a large variety of individuals to share the meaning of the different patterns of speech that are used and to have mutual understanding every time they meet.

It is a fact that, in any society, many different kinds of language coexist, and the language of the market is just one of these. If this were the only one, there would be no problems – the usual market-based instruments would be enough to mobilize local individual knowledge efficiently. But it's not like this, for the simple reason that contemporary societies are multicultural settings in which the individual type of knowledge must travel across language borders and that is what poses formidable difficulties. Mainstream economics was able to avoid that difficulty by implicitly assuming that the problem of the institutional type of knowledge did not exist at all because all the members of society share the same value system and accept the same principles of social organization. But when this is not the case, as reality forces us to recognize, and one has a "multilingual" society to govern, it becomes necessary to have another institution that is different from the market and that can bring forth a language of relationship capable of helping members belonging to different language communities be able to dialogue. Well, this institution is called democracy. This helps explain why the problem of managing knowledge in our society today, which is ultimately the problem of development, assumes that the two institutions – democracy and the market – are able to work together, side by side, mutually influencing each other. Instead, the separation between market and democracy has been unfolding over the course of the past 150 years, riding the wave of the exaltation of a certain cultural hyper-efficiency and exaggeratedly possessive individualism. And this separation of market and democracy has made people – even informed scholars – believe that it were possible to expand the market's reach without worrying about dealing with strengthening democracy.

Two major consequences flowed from this. First, the pernicious idea that the market would be a morally neutral area that would have no need for submitting to ethical judgment because it already had a solid core of its own moral principles that were sufficient for its social legitimacy. On the contrary, because the market is unable to be self-founded, it had to presuppose that a "language of relationship" had already been established in order to come into existence. This consideration alone would be enough to defeat all pretense of self-referentiality. Second, if democracy is left to slowly decay, it may happen that the market is prevented from channeling and efficiently managing knowledge. Therefore, it may happen that society ceases to progress without letting the "failures" of the market be to blame, but rather lets the blame fall on some shortcoming of democracy. The best and most glaring empirical confirmation of this proposition is the ongoing economic and financial crisis that broke out in the US in 2007. It is, in fact, a crisis of an entropic nature, not a dialectic one as it was in 1929.

That's why it is necessary to rejoin the market and democracy in order to avoid the twofold danger of possessive individualism and centralized statism. There is individualism when every member of society wants to be the one and only; there is centralism when one entity wants to be everything. In the first case, diversity is so exalted that it kills the unity of the human community; in the other case, in order to maintain uniformity, diversity is sacrificed. An analogous argument – but not identical – ought to be made with regard to bridging the divide between the market and ethics. What do we find as being behind this split? The thesis liberal individualism does not pursue or seek to impose is a specific concept of the good. Rather, it limits itself to providing a neutral structure of fundamental rights and freedoms which enables individuals to freely pursue their own ends and to respect the freedom of choice of everyone else. What follows is that individual rights cannot be sacrificed forthe benefit of the common good and the principles of justice that specify those rights cannot be based on some notion of solidarity. This means that commutative justice can be acceptable, but no concessions can be made to distributive justice.

2.2. But there are values – which are recognized by Whately, Wicksteed and many others all the way up to Milton Friedman, the founder of the influential Chicago school of thought, that the market must bargain for; but these values are, so to speak, way upriver, that is, they refer to the conditions required for the market to come into existence and work well. One thinks of such values as honesty, loyalty and trust. But it is recognized that these are necessary values, because without freedom of enterprise or without freedom to enter into exchange relationships, the market could not even exist. Similarly, if economic agents do not respect the commitments they have made as well as the legal regulations that are in force, and especially if a strong network of relationships built on trust has not been established between them, the market – as we already know – certainly could not operate efficiently. But according to this reductionist approach to economics, everything must already be in existence before the market begins to function, exactly as Thomas Hobbes had surmised in his famous *De Cive* of 1642 when he wrote that men enter into the public sphere already formed, just like mushrooms suddenly springing up after a heavy rain. In any case, it is not up to the market to take any steps; the task is rather up to civil organizations or state organizations or both.

Clearly, with this argument, those who support this view of market society are not even fazed by doubts that any outcomes stemming from the economic process could ever end up eroding that core of values upon which it itself stands, and without which no market economy would ever last through the morning. For example, if market outcomes do not meet even the most minimal criterion of distributive justice, could one possibly believe that the patrimony of values, such as honesty and trust, would remain unchanged over time? Without the bonds of trust, contracts do not get signed, at least not without prohibitive transaction costs, as we know. Why should economic agents trust each other and keep the commitments contractually made if they know the results of the economic game are manifestly unjust? Also, what about the interests or the fate of those who, for one reason or another, cannot take part in the economic game or they are kicked out because they are judged to be inefficient and, therefore, not competitive? Can one honestly believe that remedies from a compassionate state or private philanthropy can be sufficiently relied upon? Absolutely not, because these kinds of remedies increase, rather than reduce, the gap between a paradigm concerned with judgements of efficiency and the paradigm of ethical judgments. And this is for a twofold reason.

In the first place, it is because they bolster the conviction that the market is a mechanism that allocates and can function *in vacuo*, regardless of the type of society in which it is immersed. Namely, it is an ethically neutral mechanism, whose results, if some ethical standard deems them unacceptable, can always be corrected *ex post* by the state. In the second place, it is because that line of reasoning lends legitimacy to the false idea that says the world of the market coincides with the world that defends just individual interests, and the world of the state coincides with the world that defends collective interests. From this we get the well-known, dichotomous model of social order in which the state is identified with the space for the public interest (or solidarity) and the market with the space for private life (i.e. the pursuit of individualistic goals). It is the "public" that is identified only with the state, which ought to occupy itself with solidarity through redistribution; it is the "private" (that is to say, the market) that must concern itself only with efficiency, i.e. the maximum amount of production one's assets will allow.

Today, we now know that to ensure the sustainability of a thriving market economy there needs to be a continual injection of values from outside the market itself, just as the Böckenförde paradox suggests. The paradox says that the liberal secularized state lives by prerequisites which it cannot guarantee itself. The essence of the paradox is that the liberal state can exist only if the freedom it promises its citizens is regulated by the moral substance of the individual and by social structures pursuing the common good. Instead, if the liberal state attempts to impose regulation, it gives up its very own liberal nature and ends up resorting back to that same totalitarianism from which it declares to be free. *Mutatis mutandis*, the same argument holds true for the market. Although the market economy postulates equality among those who take part, it generates, however, *ex-post* inequality in the outcomes. And when equality in being diverges too far from equality in having, that is the very reason why the market is called into question. More generally, the market economy lives by and is fueled by prerequisites that it itself is not capable of creating and that, in any case, can be preserved over time as long as the logic of efficiency

– which in itself remains essential – does not displace the other values which penetrate all the channels of community integration.

The democratization of the market then is the first task that must be taken up by all those who want to strengthen this institution. In a recent book,[6] the authors Daron Acemoglu and James Robinson distinguish between "extractive" and "inclusive" economic institutions. The first kind favors the transformation of the added value created by production into parasitic income and drives the allocation of resources toward financial speculation. The second kind, on the contrary, are institutions that are good at facilitating the inclusion of all resources into the market, especially labor, in a way that respects basic human rights and ensures reducing social inequality.

Branko Milanovic confirmed for us that social inequalities have increased everywhere over the last three decades, much more than the aggregate income has increased. Above all, he has informed us that these inequalities have become by now endemic in the market system.[7] And yet, inequality is not a given and it isn't even a historical constant. It is not something destined because it has to do with the rules of the economic game, that is, with the institutional structure that a community of people joined together in a nation decided to give it. It is not a historical constant because there are countries where inequalities are significantly greater than elsewhere. It serves very little to call for more growth in the hopes of reducing inequalities, if, at the same time, one does not change the rules of the game of the market. A point which Alexis de Tocqueville had already made clear in 1835 in his famous treatise, "Democracy in America," in which he wrote that equality is encountered only at the two furthest extremes of civilization.

[6] D. ACEMOGLU - J. ROBINSON, *Why Nations Fail: The Origins of Power, Prosperity, and Poverty* (Italian edition: *Perché le nazioni falliscono. Alle origini di potenza, prosperità e povertà*, Milan 2013.)

[7] Cf. B. MILANOVIC, *The Haves and the Have-Nots: A Brief and Idiosyncratic History of Global Inequality* (Italian edition: *Chi ha e chi non ha. Storie di disuguaglianze*, Bologna 2012).

2.3. It begs the question: Is it realistic to strive for a civil market economy in today's current historical conditions? A "yes" answer can be sought in the fulfillment of a specific condition: that it establish itself *within* the market (and not outside of it, that is, *a latere*) until it reaches a critical threshold – an economic space occupied by subjects whose economic behavior is based on the principle of reciprocity. Unfortunately, and this is the indicator of serious cultural underdevelopment, the principle of reciprocity continues to be confused with the exchange of equals. And yet, the difference between the two is great. In fact, in the relation of exchange, the determination of the exchange relationship (i.e. the equilibrium price) precedes the transfer of the object to be exchanged – only after the buyer and seller have agreed on the price of the object of the transaction can the exchange take place. While when it is a relation of reciprocity, the transfer precedes, both logically and in time, the compensation, about which the subject who initiates the relationship cannot claim a right, but only an expectation. In addition, the connections of reciprocity tend to change the outcome of the economic game itself. That's because either the practice of reciprocity goes to consolidate pro-social behaviors in subjects that find themselves interacting in situations like "the prisoner's dilemma," or the culture of reciprocity tends to modify endogenously the subjects' preference structure. It's worth giving a simple example. If I find myself needing the help of others in a situation in which I cannot credibly bind myself to some commitment in the future, a rational agent – in the sense of someone operating according to an individualistic rationale – certainly will not help me even though he is able to help me, because he knows that I, too, am a purely self-interested person. Therefore, he will suppose that I will have no interest whatsoever in reciprocating the favor. This is not the case, however, if my potential helper knows that I am the kind of person who practices reciprocity.

That is why, unlike what happens with the exchange of equals, reciprocity cannot be explained only in terms of self-interest: the motivations and arrangements in respect to the other are essential ingredients in the concept of reciprocity. This is why the prevailing economic literature, based as it is on the utilitarian subject, is unable to account for the notion of reciprocity because it systematically interprets it as a special case in the exchange of equals, in which the subjects practice enlightened self-interest. The fact remains, once relationality – *primum movens* of reciprocating action – is expelled from any discussion about economics, it is obvious that there is nothing more to do than think of it as a form of altruism or moral emotion.

This reductionist choice is due to the culture of modernity, a choice according to which a contract and incentive, along with an appropriate system of laws, would be enough for the market. In so doing, it gives up trying to understand that reciprocity and its logic of overabundance always opposes the logic of equivalence of contract. The essential characteristic of reciprocity is that the exchanges it generates are inseparable from human relations – the object of any transaction cannot be separated from those who put them into being, and so they cease being anonymous and impersonal. This is why, with reciprocity, it is possible to give without losing and take without depriving. And so, the value of the civil market is in the three principles it considers as being co-essential in the foundation of a solid social order: the exchange of equals; redistribution; and reciprocity.

To avoid any misunderstanding, I wish to clarify that I do not mean to argue that human behavior is driven only by intrinsic motivations (these are the motivations of a person who acts not because some economic advantage can be gotten from it, but because he or she "believes" in its symbolic value). I wish to simply say that such motivations *help* explain human behavior and, in particular, are an integral part of the definition of rationality. All the more reason I do not wish to assert that it is at all possible to govern a market economy on the sole principle of reciprocity as seen as being in opposition to the principle of the exchange of equals. Rather, I maintain that a market organization that knows how to stimulate pro-social behaviors of at least some of its members, instead of demeaning them, will tend to operate not only more efficiently by substantially reducing the level of operational transaction costs, it will also tend to operate in a way that is more "felicitous," that is, satisfying for everyone.

In fact, the human being is not fundamentally or purely individualistic, as axiological individualism would have it. Nor is the human being purely a "socializer" as a structural-organismic approach would have it. But people instead will tend to develop those inclinations that are given the most incentive in the social setting in which they operate. The thesis that says pro-sociality and reciprocity are "exceptions" that must be explained in the light of the "natural and historical supremacy" of self-interest, appears then as extreme as the opposite one. Not only that, but this thesis has been debunked today on the grounds of empirical evidence associated with new evolutionary theories that demonstrate how cooperation and competition are perpetually intertwined. The first, in fact, plays a role in evolution that is just as important as mutation and selection.[8]

The fact is that, in their extraordinary behavioral complexity, human beings can be guided by a great variety of motivational configurations; efficiency and public happiness in a market society will depend then on its ability to leverage the individual's *best* motivations, thus letting economic agents be free to seek – both at the same time – the maximum well-being for one's self and others through a "reasonable" mediation between the two. The thing that keeps the indispensable networks of trust and mutual assistance standing, which, in turn make the market sustainable, is this continuous ability to mediate, which naturally presumes there also be "enlightened self-interest," but doesn't find its answer in it. It could be of interest to remember that even in the tradition of jurisprudential thought in the United States until after the Second World War, the existence of capitalist enterprise was justified

[8] Cf. J. Haidt, *The Righteous Mind. Why Good People are Divided by Politics and Religion*, London 2012.

exactly and only within the logic of service. The eminent legal expert E. Merrick Dodd wrote regarding this issue: "Business is permitted and encouraged by the law primarily because it is of service to the community rather than because it is a source of profit to its owners." [9]

2.4. One could ask: how widespread is the practice of reciprocity in reality? Contrary to what it may seem, even casual observation suggests this phenomenon is quite widespread in our more advanced societies. Not only is it at work in various forms and degrees in the family, in small informal groups and in voluntary associations, but networks of transactions based on reciprocity are present in all those kinds of business that include: cooperatives, in which reciprocity assumes the particular form of mutuality; social enterprises; organizations of production that have given life to fair trade; ethical finance; socially responsible investments; cash mobs; microcredit, etc. Given the economic results achieved so far by these entities and the concrete ways by which they operate, the empirical evidence out there now is ample and accurate. There's no need to take up more space here on the subject, so I'll refer people to read Leonardo Becchetti (2013). I will limit myself just to say that, as many studies on Italian economic development have highlighted, the so-called model of the "New Competition" presupposes, because of its practicality, both the agents' disposition to cooperate and a complex network of transactions – the structure of which is very similar to what characterizes relationships of reciprocity. It is precisely in this that lies the secret of the success of our industrial districts. However, they are stories that, while they continue to receive increasing attention from scholars and foreign professionals, still stir up regret over the difficulties in applying them elsewhere, especially in Southern Italy.

[9] E.M. DODD, For Whom are Corporate Managers Trustees?, in *Harvard Law Review* 45 (1932) 1147.

It is a widely documented fact that the model of New Competition has become more cohesive and has flourished in those regions that have seen the emergence and solidification of strong networks of reciprocity over the course of time. An important confirmation of what has just been said comes to us from recent trends in North America where it is no longer unusual to find capitalist-like enterprises that, in lieu of building up a corporate charitable foundation dedicated to the traditional practice of philanthropy, have begun starting new businesses that are non-profit but operate completely according to business logic. They produce and manage goods and services in sectors such as: social services; public or community assets (the commons); cultural assets, and more. To list just a few examples, there is: Pacific Community Ventures; The Emancipation Network; B-corporations (benefit corporations); and low-profit limited liability companies – first established in 2008 and now rapidly expanding. Benefit corporations do not operate to maximize stockholder dividends, but to achieve specific goals of public interest (having a positive impact on society and the environment, public housing, education, setting up employment for those who are disadvantaged etc.) So far in the last three years, seven states in the United States have approved laws allowing for and authorizing the creation of this type of business.

There is still another type of business that is particularly effective when one wants to create something for the collective interest and needs significant financial resources. They are called *participatory nonprofit enterprises*, which are authorized to issue shares (not just bonds). They guarantee the underwriter extensive tax benefits under the one condition that when the shares are sold, the proceeds are to be newly invested in other businesses of the same type. If investors wish to retain the proceeds, they will have to pay back the tax cuts they had benefited from. A similar trend is underway in Europe after *community interest companies* emerged in Great Britain in 2005 and after the European Commission of the European Union, in a November 2011 resolution, explicitly encouraged the 27 countries of the union to pursue "social businesses" defined as: "Companies that have a positive social impact and address social objectives as their corporate aim rather than only maximizing profit for its members." The declared objective is promoting the emergence of responsible, not speculative, capital markets.[10]

That framework helps explain the rapid spread, in Italy as well, of such web-based phenomena like *social lending* (also called peer-to-peer lending in which an online platform helps loan supply meet investor demand) and *crowdfunding* (potential donors select projects they believe should receive their funds). Even though crowdfunding right now is still limited, it has high development potential. The point that deserves attention is that crowdfunding is an example of a cooperative type of process among people who are eager to make their resources (monetary or otherwise) available to others in order to give life to new businesses or even to create new markets for goods and services. With crowdfunding and social lending, one ultimately aims for creating a real and true shareholding of the people, promoted over the web, which is capable of providing "business coaching" services, too. Therefore, it aims to give wings to the establishment of new types of enterprises, other than the traditional capitalist business.

As I showed in my book, *Impresa Responsabile e Mercato Civile*, (which translates as "Socially Responsible Businesses and the Civil Market"),[11] beyond the details that distinguish one enterprise from another, one basic goal unites these different forms of organization: to strive for achieving a genuine democratization of the market through a plurality of different types of enterprises that can operate within it. That's why it does not make sense, nor does it help, to frame the problem as choosing between the principle of reciprocity and the principle of the exchange of equals. It does not make sense because we lack an indisputable set of criteria upon which to base

[10] *http://ec.europa.eu/internal-market/social-business/index-en.htm*

[11] Il Mulino, Bologna 2013.

this choice. To avoid any misunderstandings, this criteria certainly cannot be about Pareto efficiency, since, by its nature, this notion of efficiency could not be applied to a system of economic relations based on the principle of reciprocity. On the other hand, it does not benefit anyone, rather it is harmful, because an advanced economy requires that both principles be able to find concrete fulfillment. It is naive to think of successfully basing all types of transactions on the culture of the exchange of equals. If this culture were to become hegemonic, then individual responsibilitywould coincide with what was contractually agreed upon. Each side would always and only do what falls within his or her "jurisdiction" with grotesquely imaginable consequences. If the culture of the exchange of equals does not become a hybrid with the culture of reciprocity, the system's ability to progress will suffer. Hence, the urgent need to make it understood that the aim of economic policy is not simply to offer incentives that encourage self-interested agents to invest in line with objectives set by policy-makers. But it also becomes about creating the conditions for the growth of a pro-social base and for its intelligent use in the pursuit of the common good.

Basically, the position that must be defended is that pluralism is not just necessary in politics – which is obvious – but also in economics. The market economy that has room for more principles of economic organization – the exchange of equals, reciprocity, redistribution – and does not let the institutional setting privilege one principle over another, is a pluralistic, and therefore, democratic market economy. In an authentically liberal society, it is the actual competition (not just the virtual) between different subjects offering various types of goods (from private goods to public goods, from merit goods to common goods) that determines who has to produce what and how much. It is, ultimately, the proper meaning of a business' civic responsibility, a notion that is quite recent (known as corporate social responsibility) and that makes up the last link in that chain begun after World War II in the United States.

3. The perspective of the common good

Now I wish to talk about a second problematic area. It concerns the need to get the perspective of the common good – a true and real part of Catholic ethics in the field of social-economics – back into the contemporary cultural debate. As John Paul II clarified on several occasions, the Social Doctrine of the Church is not to be considered just the latest ethical theory in a whole line of theories already found in literature. Rather, it is to be seen as the "common grammar" of all of them because it is based on a specific point of view: taking care of the human good. In fact, while different ethical theories place their foundation either in the search for rules (as happens in positivistic legal naturalism, according to which ethics are derived from legal norms) or in action (Rawlsian neo-contractualism or John Harsanyi's neo-utilitarianism come to mind), the Social Doctrine of the Church takes its Archimedean point as "being with." The sense of the ethics of the common good, which is needed in order to understand human behavior, requires putting oneself in the shoes of the person who acts (see *Veritatis Splendor*, 78), not (as legal naturalism does) in a third-person perspective, that is to say, the perspective of the impartial spectator (as Adam Smith had suggested). In fact, because the moral good is a practical reality, the person who knows it best is the one who does not theorize about it, but who practices it. This is the person who knows how to pick it out and choose it with confidence every time it's under discussion.

In the Bull of Indiction of the Great Jubilee of the Year 2000, *Incarnationis Mysterium*, we read that one of the aims of the Jubilee was helping to create *"an economic model which serves everyone"* (12, italics added for emphasis). This passage must be emphasized. It had never happened throughout the long history of jubilee years that a task of this nature be intentionally chosen by a pope to be a purpose of a jubilee versus it being a more or less unintended consequence of something else. Even more explicitly, his message for January 1, 2000, entitled "Peace on Earth to Those Whom God

Loves," reads: "In this context we also need to examine the growing concern felt by many economists and financial professionals when, in considering new issues involving poverty, peace, ecology and the future of the younger generation, they reflect on the role of the market, on the pervasive influence of monetary and financial interests, on the widening gap between the economy and society. [...] Perhaps the time has come for a new and deeper reflection on the *nature* of the economy and its *purposes*. [...] Here I would like to invite economists and financial professionals, as well as political leaders, to recognize the urgency of the need to ensure that economic practices and related political policies have as their aim the good of every person and of the whole person" (15 and 16). What is new and, in some ways, surprising, is the actual invitation to address the problem we are discussing at the level of its theoretical foundations, or, rather, its cultural presuppositions. Facing the capitalist squalor of the tendency to reduce human relationships to an exchange of equivalent products, the spirit of contemporary man rises up and begs for a different story.

The keyword that expresses this need better than all the others is the word "fraternity." The word was once used for the flag of the French Revolution, but was then abandoned by the post-revolutionary order for well-known reasons, and then eventually removed from the political-economical lexicon. It was the Franciscan school of thought that gave this term the meaning it has retained over the course of time, which is to complement and supersede the principle of solidarity. In fact, while solidarity is the principle of a social organization that allows people who are unequal to become equal, fraternity is the principle of a social organization that allows people who are equal to be different. Fraternity allows people who are equal in their dignity and fundamental rights to express their plan of life or their charism in different ways. The seasons of time we have left behind during the 19th and especially the 20th centuries have been marked by great battles, both cultural and political, in the nameof solidarity, and this has been a good thing. Let us consider the history of the trade-union movement and the struggle for attaining civil rights. The point is that a good society cannot be satisfied just with the sphere of solidarity, because if a society were only united and not fraternal, it would be a society in which everyone would try to distance themselves from each other. The fact is that, while a fraternal society is also a united society, it is not always true the other way around.

People have forgotten the fact that a human community is not sustainable when the sense of fraternity dies out and everything is reduced to, on the one hand, improving transactions based on the exchange of equals, and on the other hand, increasing transactions carried out by government public assistance. It gives us the reason why, no matter how great the intellectual abilities of those experts in the field, a credible solution still has not been found for the big trade off between efficiency and equity. A society is not capable of having a future if its principle of fraternity fades away. That is, society is unable to make any progress if the only thing that exists is "giving to receive" or "giving out of duty." This is why neither the liberal-individualistic worldview, in which everything (or just about everything) is "exchange," nor the state-centric vision for society, in which everything (or almost) is about "duty," is a reliable guide to get us off the shoals our societies appear mired in today.

If there is a setting in which the recovery of the concept of fraternity shows all its potential for development, the setting is a transition from a "welfare state" to a "welfare society." In order to understand its importance, it's worthwhile remembering the three great U.S. industrialists – John D. Rockefeller, Henry Ford and Andrew Carnegie, together with others who were not as well known – who signed an agreement in the early 1900s that gave rise to what, from then on, was called "welfare capitalism," that is, a capitalism of welfare, of wellbeing. Fundamentally, the agreement anticipates that companies must take responsibility for the wellbeing of their own employees and their families, based on the principle of restitution. This way, the company gives a part of the profits it has earned from its activities back to the local community.

This principle has been engraved in American culture – one must give back *post factum* a part of what has been obtained thanks also to the contribution of the community's productive activities. Welfare-capitalism met with immediate success in the United States, but right from the start it showed its Achilles' heel: it lacks a universal aspect. In fact, if a citizen is lucky enough to work for a company which has agreed to this pact, he or she will know he or she can utilize the benefits provided. But that will not be the case, if he or she works elsewhere.

This is the reason why, twenty years later in 1939 in England, the great and well-known economist, John Maynard Keynes, wrote the article, "Democracy and welfare." In it he defends the thesis that if you want to talk about welfare, it has to be universal, not particularistic. That is, you cannot just cover certain categories or groups of individuals. Based on this insight, Lord William Beveridge, the British economist, succeeded in drawing up in 1942 in the midst of war, the famous "Beveridge Report," which would give rise to: the National Health Service; free assistance to the disabled and care-dependent elderly; and free, basic education up to a certain age for everyone. That is how the well-known welfare state got its start in England, where it is the state and not the company that is in charge of its citizens' welfare. In this regard, this quote by Lord Beveridge is still famous in which he says the state must protect the citizen from the "cradle to the grave." No one certainly can deny that this model was a real achievement of civilization. It spread first throughout England, and then to the rest of Europe. In the United States, the opposite happened – the welfare state never took root. There has been welfare capitalism, a model which U.S. citizens were, are and always will be particularly fond of.

After several decades, however, the welfare state model started to show two Achilles' heels. The first was financial sustainability. If welfare services want to be of any quality, they have increasing costs over time and the only revenue source the state has available to cover those costs is a general tax. Now, if this were the only source for covering all spending, a tax burden ratio far greater than

50% would have to be imposed. But this would reduce the GDP alarmingly. It is then clear that if the resources needed to finance the welfare state were to come exclusively from general taxation, the tax burden would only increase. But this fact, from a political point of view, would jeopardize the democratic structure of the country.

The second reason behind the crisis of the welfare state is the bureaucratization of the system. I use the word "bureaucratization" in a technical sense to mean the standardization of the ways of meeting needs. The problem is that people's needs cannot be standardized. A trivial example can explain the imbalance between people's needs, which are different, and how they are covered by social services, which are distributed evenly. Two people with the same disease and with the same diagnosis will have different reactions to the same drug. What may be good for one will certainly not be good for the other, since different human bodies respond differently to the same type of care. This is why social services are always shrouded by a dark cloud of discontent. The low opinion citizens have of public services in Italy is closely linked to the lack of tacit quality, even though the mandated quality is high.

That's why, for the past 15 years here, they have started talking about going from a model of the welfare state to a welfare society. According to this model, all of society, and not just the state, must take responsibility for the welfare of its citizens. Parallel to this idea, the principle of *circular subsidiarity* has begun to pop up. If society as a whole is to take care of all its citizens universally, then it's clear that the three sides of the magic triangle must strategically interact. The three sides that make up the whole of society are: public entities (state, provincial, regional, government-related bodies, etc.); business or rather, the business community; and groups and associations in civil society (volunteers, social-advocacy associations, social cooperatives, non-governmental organizations, foundations). So, the whole idea of "circular subsidiarity" lies here – the three sides must be able to find ways to systematically interact both when planning what action is needed in the field and for ensuring its management.

The advantage of implementing the welfare society and the subsequent principle of "circular subsidiarity" is having the possibility of overcoming the two *aporias* of the welfare state we talked about earlier. First of all, this model would make it possible to find the needed resources from the business world. When people say "there aren't enough resources," they are referring to public resources, not private, which, on the contrary, are easily on hand. The point is that so far no one has thought of tapping into these resources from the business world and channel them towards providing welfare services. Secondly, the presence of the public sector becomes fundamental within this mechanism since it must be vigilant and guarantee universal coverage. The danger of excluding certain groups of society from using these services must always be kept in mind. The world of civil society, which we continue to call the "non-profit" world or the "third sector" (a better name for it, however, would be "civil society organizations"), occupies a special place in the triangle as the sector that possesses detailed awareness. Who knows better than an association of volunteers if there is someone who has a special need in a certain part of the city? This information can come only from those who work on the ground, close to people. In addition, these people are in a good position to make sure that the way things are run are done so in a way that can improve people's quality of experience.

That is why circular subsidiarity will prevail as the model for the near future. There's only one alternative to such a model and that's a return to welfare capitalism – the liberal model of welfare, which relies on companies, according to their preparedness, to face the social responsibility of satisfying the needs of the people. However, if people insist on keeping the old model of the welfare state alive, it will lead in time to welfare capitalism, and this would be a real paradox. Recently, British Prime Minister David Cameron effectively reduced the public health care service of an entire nation – England, the very country in which that service had been born.

In order to avoid ending up with a dangerous vacuum of services, it is necessary to aim for a model of the welfare society made up of business, the public body and citizens with their organizations, all contributing according to their ability and giving what they are able to give according to well-defined partnership protocols.

Just to be precise here. I am talking about "circular subsidiarity," not horizontal subsidiarity, because the latter, while it integrates with welfare capitalism well, it is not capable of being universal. I was surprised when in 2001, Italy changed Title V of its Constitution. In the new Articles 118 and 119, the principles of vertical and horizontal subsidiarity were introduced. Even if they are important principles, they are unable to provide universal coverage. It is impossible not to see how crucial the contribution of the Italian Catholic movement is for implementing the model of a welfare society. We, therefore, need to be aware of this and start changing gears to move things along.

4. Conclusion

As people know, there are two distinct kinds of power that must be distinguished. The first is power as strength, that is, the power of power. The second is power as influence, which is the power to influence people's cognitive compasses and the decision-making processes of policy-makers. People often tend to assume that only the first kind of power is important and the one worth of fighting for. Without it, there is nothing left to do but give up and wait for better times. This is absolutely untrue. In many cases throughout history, power as influence can prove to be even more decisive than the other kind of power. So, when it comes to power as influence, Catholics today can express all of their full potential and make a vital contribution to shaping a new humanism.

On one condition, however. A lesson must be drawn from the myth of Antaeus, son of Poseidon and Gaia. In Greek mythology, Antaeus received an extraordinary gift from his mother – as long as he was touching the ground, he would have superhuman strength and could win every fight against any opponent. In fact, when Hercules discovers this secret, he comes up with a ruse to get Antaeus off the ground to strike him dead. The metaphor's meaning is quite clear. When Catholics have "their feet on the ground," that is, when they look at the real problems people and communities are having, they "win." But when they are scattered or dawdle for too long on cultural projects that – no matter how interesting – are purely intellectual expressions, they are defeated and accomplish nothing. I believe that the current situation does not allow religious any "luxuries" of this kind. The betrayal would be far too serious.

STEFANO ZAMAGNI
Professor of Political Economy
University of Bologna,
Adjunct Professor Johns Hopkins University (USA)

ROUNDTABLE

TOWARD A PROPHETIC, CARING ECONOMY OF COMMUNION

Chair

SISTER EVELINE FRANC, DC
Superior General of the Daughters of Charity

PROCLAMATION OF THE GOSPEL AND SOUND ECONOMY

Enrique Sánchez González, mccj

Prophecy of the mission

I have been invited to share with you our experience as missionaries who currently live in many parts of the world where our apostolate is proclaiming the Word of God and the Gospel, and working to transform the world. Evangelization includes an economic aspect that is not to be ignored. We tackle this issue starting from lived experience, that is, by living every day as a challenge and an opportunity to contribute to building a humanity that is in harmony with the dream or plan of God. I think it is necessary to say right from the start that today the mission is going through great changes and profound transformations.

The changes, challenges and opportunities we encounter in so-called "missions" oblige us to be aware of the fact that the criteria for carrying out our works of charity or human development – implicit in missionary action – cannot be the same as they were thirty or forty years ago. The mission is changing and we missionaries find ourselves facing realities that, until a short time ago, did not exist. Suffice it to mention the young local churches, with their leaders, their communities, their priests, with their lay members taking on ever increasing responsibilities – something that was impossible in the past.

To put it briefly, it seems to me that missionary work – considered from an economic perspective – is letting go of having the missionary play the protagonist. This role meant taking on for oneself the task of human development, which highlighted the figure of the benefactor, who generously gave charity to the most needy, but which risked creating dependencies that have not always led to sound development and the promotion of the human person. It seems to me that today we feel more "at ease" and aligned with a concept of mission in which we are seen as part of an experience which leads us to share what we are, which is not limited to offering or promoting an action, and tries to do good by involving all parties.

In some missionary experiences we have seen that it has not always been easy in certain environments to give the kind of charity that spontaneously springs from the Gospel. It has also become a huge challenge to set up a sound economy that can defend the identity of Christian charity from the trap of confusing it with the work of any other non-governmental organization involved in development. Just mentioning these few things, I wanted to highlight an aspect which seems fundamental to me: within the missionary experience, it is not possible to separate the proclamation of the Gospel from a sound economy. A sound economy is understood as a concrete expression of the charity which is asked of us in our encounter with the person of Jesus – a charity which He left us as an inheritance for the continued building up of the kingdom.

How do we live the prophetic aspect of the economy within the mission? In sacred Scripture the prophet is always the one who serves as an instrument for the manifestation of the Lord; it is the person who speaks in God's name and the person of whom God makes use of in order to manifest himself to those He loves. We missionaries are fortunate enough to have this experience constantly because the mission brings us in contact with the poorest and the most marginalized. Therefore, because we are with those who are privileged by God, the wealth of God passes through us.

You will ask yourselves: but what does this have to do with the economy? A lot, I think. The first experience we missionaries have is that of making sure that the mission's works are supported by divine providence in an extraordinary way. We are the first witnesses of God's goodness; He does not abandon his people and we are witnesses of a logic which does not follow the criteria of power and possession that govern an economy based on money. A lot of money passes through our hands, a lot of assets and a lot of resources that become projects and works in the places where we are present. And the beautiful thing is that all of this is possible thanks to the charity of many Christians, who in many cases are poor themselves, because they are the most generous and what they have received through God's goodness, they make available to others.

I say poor Christians because the great benefactors of the missions are not the immensely rich, among whom we can also find Christians today. I do not think I am mistaken in affirming that the mission's great works, even today, are advanced thanks to the small, meager coins of so many poor people who remain anonymous. And they give them with joy to the missionary, trusting he or she will give them to those who need them even more. I can say with great simplicity that the mission's economy keeps going thanks to the generosity of many poor people who know how to give despite their poverty and, fortunately, the mission is not supported by major industries, business deals or stock market investments. It is an economy which seems not to take into account the forecasts of losses or gains in the stock market or financial markets.

In considering this aspect of the economy, I think missionary institutes could be listed or classified among the mendicant orders, since we live off what the people provide for us with much simplicity and enthusiasm in order to advance the missionary project of the Church. And I can humbly affirm that our secret lies in this: the more we depend financially on charity, the better our service will be and the more we will be free to dedicate ourselves completely to the mission. The problem arises when we hoard or we don't have faith in God's continual providence. I think all of us missionaries have often had, on an economic level, the experience that has led us to observe that as we give more, the more we receive. Great missionary works have never arisen from the support of big capital, even though in reality it is easier to sleep knowing that tomorrow we will be able to pay the people we owe. I think good economic management, which permits putting to good use the means the Lord has provided us, becomes a concrete way of showing just what this charity and love are that we preach about in proclaiming the Gospel.

An economy of solidarity

With regard to the aspect of solidarity in the way an economy is lived within the mission, it seems to me that, many times, we missionaries have fostered and promoted solidarity among people. By being the voice of those who don't have a voice, many times we missionaries have been instrumental in raising awareness about the responsibility our contemporaries have and we have collaborated in building consciences that do not let us remain indifferent before the suffering and pain of our brothers and sisters. Often we are witnesses to the suffering and pain of the people with whom we walk on the frontiers of the world, and many times we are seen as people who stir people's consciences and remind people of the responsibility we all have in confronting the misery present in the human race.

In this sense, mission is a "mediation" which helps people understand that talking about an economy of solidarity does not mean just stripping ourselves of something that ultimately does not affect our wealth, but rather it has to do with something more profound, which goes beyond the money or the material goods we may philanthropically share with others. Solidarity lived through the missionary action of the Church is a very concrete way to tell our brothers and sisters most in need that they are close to our heart and we cannot abandon them or allow them to be left to their fate. And it could also be seen as an opportunity to help people, whom luck has treated kindly, recognize there is within their brother and sister a hidden treasure that they need to grow as a Christian and as a person.

In the vision of the economy like the one Pope Francis is now reminding us of, solidarity is not limited to being just a simple gesture of goodwill towards another whom we discover to be more fragile and in need. Rather it is the obligation we each have to respond to the other person's misery because it pains me and it does not allow me to be what God always dreamed for me. In this sense, all those who have been fortunate enough to share the life of the poor in the mission – even if only for a short time – have always said they received more than they gave. And, because it is a matter of giving and receiving, I do not think I have strayed off topic, since those who are experts in accounting talk about income and expenditure as being a basic rule of finance.

An economy of communion

Today the experience of mission is teaching us that the days of economic paternalism and major works being funded by resources coming from afar are over. The mission in which some played the role of benefactors and others played the beneficiaries, with all the dependencies this might entail, that kind of mission is ending and is making way for a mission in which we value collaboration, defending a common cause and walking the journey at a different pace. We are close to an important change, particularly if we consider the new foundations the mission is based upon. Many of us could not carry on with a model of mission founded on consistent economic support because we are children of churches that are poor from a material standpoint. The wealth of the mission will be made up more and more by the people who are willing to give everything to share the faith, to meet others halfway and to discover together with the Father, who wants to make us one human family.

The new face of the mission will let us have a deeper experience of communion, in which the values of collaboration, of recognizing the other as a treasure, of being for others, will matter much more than just doing things for others. This new image of the mission is showing us that the economic model most focus more on sharing and mutual enrichment.

Concretely, how do we live out these aspects within the mission today?

Many structures still exist today that try to respond to the need to exercise that charity implicit in missionary service. This is why we concern ourselves with creating structures which help with or respond to the needs that are most urgent in the field of education, in particular schools and institutes for professional and technical training. We must be concerned with and interested in a formation that helps people become capable of taking on their own responsibilities and become protagonists of their own formation. And we realize that good administration must form people to be able to keep the works going, otherwise those resources will be wasted.

Experience in this field allows us to appreciate projects that range from a small school with a straw roof in the forest to a university campus with a strong level of professionalism. Certainly major investments are currently being made in training and educating new generations. Intense work is also being done in medical services and healthcare. We are present in many places where the mission is the only structure that works, where many people travel hundreds of kilometers to be seen by a doctor. There are dispensaries, often precarious, in many places that work more like "emergency rooms," being the only place to go to avoid dying. We are trying to invest in training leaders who will be capable of working in different fields that offer the greatest number of people the chance to use to full advantage the qualities and human richness they hold. I think awareness about promoting women is constantly increasing, particularly because we see how, in our society, they are very much exposed to vulnerability.

We try to involve people as much as possible in all of this work so they may become protagonists and builders of their own futures. In many places today we don't start our work unless we can count on the availability and collaboration of people in the area or in the local institutions, including the local Church. In this sense I can say that today we missionaries are called to carry out an increasingly clearer role of being witnesses and collaborators, and less as being the protagonists. Undoubtedly this is a source of profound happiness.

ENRIQUE SÁNCHEZ GONZÁLEZ, MCCJ
Superior General
Comboni Missionaries of the Heart of Jesus

NEIGHBORHOOD NETWORKS

Marco Impagliazzo

I want to begin my reflection by starting with the crisis. It has been more than five years since the Western economic system was put on the ropes by a financial collapse that has dragged down – in a chain reaction – the real economy, production and employment. Pope Francis clarified its nature during a Pentecost vigil with Catholic lay movements: "This time of crisis, beware, is not merely an economic crisis. It is not a crisis of culture. It is a human crisis: it is the human person that is in crisis! Man himself is in danger of being destroyed! But man is the image of God! This is why it is a profound crisis! At this time of crisis we cannot be concerned solely with ourselves, withdrawing into loneliness, discouragement and a sense of powerlessness in the face of problems. Please do not withdraw into yourselves!"

What has the crisis highlighted? What emerges from observing what is going on around us? Let me try to try to sketch something out.

The idea of the "common good" is fading. The great social achievements, at least until the end of the 1970s, were collective and required very broad and inclusive grassroots coalitions to achieve them: political parties, unions, associations and groups. At some point a fracture was created. It went from what was in the best interest of all people to the interests of each individual. This cultural shift has caused great damage. One such loss is the perception that human ties are an obstacle to personal realization. To build relationships responsibly takes time and space away from myself, who goes first all the time and in everything. It is an expression of a sort of "fundamentalism of self."

One of the most evident consequences is the crisis of the family. Today, this crisis has roots that go deeper than those of the economic crisis. Certainly, there has been a lack of adequate support for the family lately, particularly in encouraging birthrates. But it is the essence of the family that somehow has been undermined: planning the future together, sharing each other's space together, making room for others in my life.

"Save your own self" has been the most widespread and practiced message these past decades. To quote Zygmunt Bauman, "nobody or almost nobody continues to believe that changing the lives of others may have some use for his or her own life" and, therefore, it is normal that every individual should be left to themselves. But changing other people's lives was for a long time the great dream of politics, of the ideals of the 20th century, was the driving force that gave voice, courage, relevance to the humble, to the masses on the margins of history, to the excluded. Today the paradigm has profoundly changed, and the pope, in *Evangelii gaudium* (53), grasped the sense of it with deep intuition: "We have created a 'throw-away' culture which is now spreading. It is no longer simply about exploitation and oppression, but something new. Exclusion ultimately has to do with what it means to be a part of the society in which we live; those excluded are no longer society's underside or its fringes or its disenfranchised – they are no longer even a part of it. The excluded are not the 'exploited' but the outcast, the 'leftovers.' " In the individualization of society, whoever has a problem, a handicap, a stigma, is cast out. There is not even room for savage utilitarianism or for exploitation. That's why the true pathology – the great disease – of our time is solitude.

Today the social problem is shifting from being the world of the exploited to the world of the excluded. The exploited protest and rebel because, paradoxically, they do matter in a world of inequality and slavery since their exploiters cannot go on without them. Instead, the excluded are those who really do not matter anymore to anyone. The unemployed, especially those who are no longer young, are no longer able to find work because they have left the market, they are not needed anymore, they have been made obsolete by others who are younger, more efficient, more capable. But above all, this can be seen in the world of the elderly. Today, science and medicine let us live longer, and often with better health, but then, after a certain age, people no longer know for whom and for what purpose to spend their life: they have become useless.

The Community of Sant'Egidio always asks itself how it can be close to the elderly. For more than 40 years, we have been visiting so many elderly people who have been left on their own – those who are home-bound and especially those in nursing homes. This experience, which has always been founded on a strong spiritual experience in fidelity to Scripture and prayer, has led us to come together and develop new models to propose. The program, *Long Live the Elderly*, started in 2004 as one of a number of experiments the Italian Ministry of Health launched in four Italian cities in response to the emergency heat wave of the summer of 2003.

The program developed in Rome by the Community of Sant'Egidio focuses in particular on the neighborhoods in the historical center: Trastevere, Testaccio and Esquilino. It consists of actively monitoring residents who are older than 75. The basic idea is to connect traditional services (home care, semi-residential facilities, etc.) with an alternative initiative whose primary purpose is preventing the negative effects of critical events, in particular, summer heat waves, flu epidemics, cold winters, falling down, etc. It is done with a "light" and "active" monitoring system and with the support and cooperation of social networks. Through this program we have so far made contact with more than 9,000 seniors, who are accompanied and helped so they can stay in their own homes. The real strength of this model is that, when fully operational, it costs 75 Euro cents (€ 0.75) per elderly person, against the more than 3,000 Euros (€ 3,000) that is paid for each bed in a nursing home – of that sum, about 1,600 Euros (€ 1,600) is paid for by the individual and 1,600 Euros (€ 1,600) is paid for by the government's health program.

We have reached our goal of proposing a more economical and efficient model of "welfare" than the one that now exists, which is no longer sustainable, and we have worked towards repairing the social fabric. In fact, we have worked on neighborhood networks, contacting almost 8,000 people who are active in their communities and who are now fully involved as unpaid volunteers in the program: volunteers, doctors, doorkeepers, business owners, neighbors, family caregivers. With their help and availability and by building a network and coordination that work, we are able to be near so many elderly, reducing not only the number of deaths of those older than 75, but also reducing the number of people being admitted to nursing homes and requests for emergency hospital assistance. This is how we have realized that the more equality there is, the more a collective social fabric is created and the more people help others be better off, the more development is fostered because it is helping all of society live better.

There are interesting studies showing how the "wealth of nations" does not coincide with the flow of created economic goods and services, but with the "stock" of spiritual, cultural, relational, natural and economic goods or assets that belong to a community and territory. For example, the GPI (*Genuine Progress Index*) starts with the GDP and corrects it, adding or subtracting the monetary estimate of other variables that are considered important in the measurement of "authentic" progress. For example, housekeeping and volunteer work are included. The monetary value of social costs (like crime and unemployment) and environmental costs (water and air pollution, climate change, etc.) are also subtracted from the GDP. In the United States, starting in the 1970s, one sees how a strong growth in GDP is linked with a substantial stagnation of progress as measured by GPI. This is one of the reasons that explains the crisis of 2007, which was economic in nature, but had some deep cultural and social causes in its distant origin.

The Community of Sant'Egidio is dedicated to giving dignity and enormous recognition to everyone who works in the world of serving the human person, which is an immense field for the future. We do this with *Long Live the Elderly*, because helping the elderly in their homes is a job that requires great expertise and professionalism. However, we also do the same thing with people with disabilities. Some years ago, we created a social cooperative in which members were people with mental disabilities, and, together with them, we opened a restaurant that today is a beautiful establishment in the heart of Rome; it does good business, even in these years of crisis. The youth that work there, with their seriousness and passion, have turned *Gli Amici* [Friends] restaurant into a place where people eat well and may spend a pleasant evening. They are always cordial with the clients, they know how to joke around, create a nice atmosphere, and they help each other because they do not have that exasperated spirit of competition that so often exists in workplaces and ruins human relationships. All this means that, for the past five years, this cooperative has made a profit and, up until today, it has been able to take on 20 people with disabilities. The experience of *Gli Amici* restaurant has clearly shown that the disabled, who are excluded most of the time, are instead a resource in our society. These people are able to work professionally, with motivation and productivity, and to offer their contribution to the building of a society that made for the human person.

In our opinion, this means working towards a new view or culture of disability, and also entrepreneurship. In fact, as Luigi Zoja explains well in his book *The Death of the Neighbor*, alienation – which essentially struck the worker, who was alienated from what he produced and from the world that product helped create – also strikes the capitalists today, alienating them from the production process as well. Businesses are financed and controlled by very long chains of command and often they are made up of shell companies, as the situation with Telecom Italia demonstrates.

Inside the "shell" there are neither products nor people, which is substantially different compared to the entrepreneur who directly controlled the production process of goods and services. The financialization of the economy and the world has removed value from manual work. The Community, in this sense, helps give value to labor.

Thus, creating a new developed economy also starts with the concrete experience of working for and together with others for the building of a society that may be not only more just, but in which human beings are able to live better, happier lives. Some great economists have already examined in depth this link between development, solidarity and personal happiness. John Stuart Mill, for example, declared that "Those only are happy... who have their minds fixed on some object other than their own happiness: on the happiness of others, on the improvement of mankind." In this respect, there is economic development insofar as prosperity is redistributed. When there is this redistribution and people help each other be a little better off, society profits. Our constant work towards the social inclusion of the "discarded" and the "excluded" boosts growth and development. And in our own city, the presence of the Community, along with the many religious congregations and orders, is a guarantee that there may always be room for freedom, prayer and concrete solidarity, in which the value of giving freely and the culture of gift are able to transform our society and make it more human. As Pope Francis has explained on many occasions, giving freely is really a revolutionary act that supports social development.

I would like to conclude with the words from Pope Francis' exhortation that I think clarifies this urgency very well: "The need to resolve the structural causes of poverty cannot be delayed, not only for the pragmatic reason of its urgency for the good order of society, but because society needs to be cured of a sickness which is weakening and frustrating it, and which can only lead to new crises" (*Evangelii gaudium*, 202). "None of us can think we are exempt from concern for the poor and for social justice: 'Spiritual conversion, the intensity of the love of God and neighbor, zeal for justice and peace, the Gospel meaning of the poor and of poverty, are required of everyone.' [...] I trust in the openness and readiness of all Christians, and I ask you to seek, as a community, creative ways of accepting this renewed call" (*Evangelii gaudium*, 201).

MARCO IMPAGLIAZZO

President of the Community of Sant'Egidio
Professor of contemporary history
at the University for Foreigners – Perugia

NATIONAL LEADERSHIP ROUNDTABLE ON CHURCH MANAGEMENT

KERRY A. ROBINSON

New managerial challenges

It is a very special honor to be with you. My name is Kerry Robinson and I am the executive director of the National Leadership Roundtable on Church Management that promotes excellence and best practices in the management, finances and human resource development of the Catholic Church in the U.S. through the greater incorporation of the expertise of the laity. The Leadership Roundtable is a network of ordained, religious and senior level lay executives from every sector and industry – CEOs, university presidents, philanthropists and chairs of boards of corporate and nonprofit organizations. We harness the collective expertise and managerial experience, financial acumen, and problem solving capability of hundreds of top leaders to strengthen the temporal affairs of the Church. We bring a collaborative style to address increasingly complex managerial challenges facing church leaders and foster social entrepreneurially approaches to solving those challenges. All who comprise this network of leaders care deeply about the Church and want to lend what they know and what they do best to help call the Church to greater levels of managerial excellence, accountability, transparency, ethics and openness.

The Roundtable was created during difficult days for our Church, in the wake of the sexual abuse crisis. At that time many lay leaders, anguished by the crisis who might otherwise have opted to abandon the Church, became even more deliberatively engaged in the Church in order to call it to greater holiness, to help restore trust, to solve the managerial crisis, to be part of the solution. Our own founder, financier and philanthropist, Geoff Boisi, said, "To do nothing is to be complicit." And "When your family is in crisis you do everything possible to help effect reconciliation and healing." We were a heartfelt, hopeful experiment in July 2005 when we convened our board for the first time. A star studded cast of famous ordained, religious and lay leaders, these men and women agreed to serve as trustees of the Leadership Roundtable because each one of them owed a personal debt of gratitude to the Church – to a priest or nun or lay pastoral associate – who had played an important and life-giving role in their lives. And those that were married with children worried deeply that the Church was becoming less and less relevant to their children and grandchildren and were deeply saddened at the thought of how impoverished their lives would be without recourse to the rich sustenance of our faith.

What we were proposing to do had never been done before and few believed we would have much of an impact. And yet we had so much collective expertise in management and finance and problem solving to offer the Church. To fail to bring those intellectual resources to bear when the Church needed them the most would be to fail at an important responsibility of stewardship. Now almost a decade later we have earned the trust and respect of bishops and provincials of men's and women's communities in the United States. We have developed an entire menu of resources and services for the Church. We work at the parish, diocesan, regional and national and international levels. We work with religious communities, Catholic schools, and Catholic nonprofits. We are entirely focused on management and do not delve into any doctrinal matters. We are intentionally laudatory and positive. We know that there already exist many examples of best managerial practice in the Church and when we find an example we elevate it, celebrate it and share it as widely as possible the better to be emulated.

Let me be clear. We understand that the Church is not a corporation in the way that McDonald's or Microsoft or Coca Cola is a corporation. It is *sui generis*, with a divine mission. Nevertheless the Church is comprised of people, finances and facilities and they deserve to be cared for with the highest levels of ethics, accountability and excellence. It should be the Church that is the gold standard for the rest of the world in how it cares for its most valuable assets. And the reason it is important to insist on such levels of excellence and accountability in the care of the Church's temporal goods is that it directly affects and impacts the Church's ability to carry out its mission. And the mission of the Church is that much more important than the bottom line of a company.

Let me offer three concrete, practical examples of how we are positively impacting the Church.

Standards for excellence

Many provincials and pastors said to us, "We want to ensure that the way we are stewarding our finances and caring for our employees reflects contemporary best managerial practices, but how do we know that we are in fact doing so?" Our Catholic Standards for Excellence is a comprehensive set of 55 best management practices compiled from the various areas of temporal life relevant to the good stewardship of Catholic religious communities, parishes, dioceses, and nonprofits. The program includes a cohesive set of downloadable resources corresponding to each of the 55 standards providing essential information and tools helpful in implementing each of the management practices.

The Catholic parishes, dioceses, religious communities, schools, universities, and organizations which are implementing the Catholic Standards for Excellence, experience greater impact from their ministerial efforts, more engagement by the laity, and more human and financial resources to serve the mission of the Church. Trust is restored and nurtured. Systems of checks and balances, and accountability are put in place.

Toolbox for management

The second resource I bring to your attention can be easily adapted and replicated for religious communities. In the United States we created it first for new pastors. We created a six-day intensive retreat allowing pastors to reap measurable benefits from strengthening critical skill sets in the areas of administration, finance, and personnel management.

A dozen experts in various fields give presentations on such topics as a theology of management, stewardship, internal financial controls, risk management, building finance and pastoral councils, as well as standards for excellence from which every parish, and its pastor, can benefit. These important, if brief, courses in temporal management in many cases provide the only managerial pedagogy in the pastor's experience. This program is being adapted for specific utility in religious communities, preparing ordained, religious and lay leaders in the managerial basics, while incorporating the particular charisms of each religious community into the framework.

Pooled investment initiative

The third concrete example I offer today is the creation of a pooled investment initiative that allows the endowments of religious communities, dioceses, Catholic colleges and hospitals, etc., to come together to form one large client in order to access the best investment opportunities and investors and have a far more consequential return on investment. Undergirding this opportunity is a strong and contemporary commitment to socially responsible investment, which ensures to the fullest extent possible that positive screens are in place to care for the social responsibility of investment and to positively influence secular investors.

Thank you for the opportunity to be with you today and to share in our Holy Father's call for positive managerial reform and stewardship of Church assets, both human, physical and financial in service to the Church's mission and the Gospel. Let me leave you with one important note from our experience. There is an elegant byproduct of Church leaders, provincials and treasurers of religious communities, for example, availing themselves of the intellectual, problem solving capability of the laity. And that is evangelization. One is far more likely to become fully immersed and invested in the very life of the Church if one is recognized for what she or he does best and is invited to lend that in service to the Church.

Thank you.

KERRY A. ROBINSON
Executive director of the National Leadership Roundtable on Church Management (USA)

THE CAMALDOLESE AND THEIR EVANGELICAL WITNESS

Alessandro Barban, osb.cam

Ever since its founding, the Camaldolese community, which celebrated its millennium in 2012, has described its life with two explicit purposes:

– the first as an eremitical order, giving priority in the Hermitage to contemplative prayer, silence, personal and community conversion and fraternal life between communion and solitude, marked by a life of concrete sobriety;

– the second, promoting the cenobitic life at the Monastery ever since its beginnings and managing a hospital, that, for the most part, gave free treatment, both to pilgrims and to residents in nearby towns. In the 1900s the historic hospital was turned into a guesthouse.

This model of hermitage-monastery-hospital was established in a wholly unique way at Camaldoli. On the one hand, it emerged as an original indication from the Romualdian spirituality, and on the other, it came to specify the Camaldolese spirituality increasingly well. The monastery housed a community living a cenobitic life dedicated to serving guests, and, next to that, a hospital served those most in need. In fact, having the spiritual heart of the search for God in the Hermitage, and near the Hermitage, was the Camaldolese monastic way of being present in the church and of evangelizing the poorest – the evangelical witness that has been pursued for centuries by the monks of Camaldoli. However, not being able to re-establish the same monastic project in the different places the Camaldolese were called to, our presence was limited to having just the monastery with the annexed hospital, as was seen in many cities in Tuscany and Umbria. This special way of life has permitted the Camaldolese to draw close to the needs, expectations and questions of faith of entire generations over different eras. In other situations – for example in Sardinia – the Camaldolese monastery's presence was largely pastoral with a strong focus on evangelization, going from the teaching of the Christian faith to direct involvement in reclamation and, in the same vein, working farm land.

Because it was diligently recorded in accounting books, historians have confirmed that the Camaldolese community not only redistributed its wealth to the poor, but, together with almsgiving, the community had developed a sustainable economy over the centuries for the people who lived close by or on the monastery's property. In fact, in Camaldoli, they plant the forest, which is still a real jewel of nature and of the economy today. The first forestry law was devised and written right in Camaldoli, detailing when and how to harvest and plant the trees. The forest has provided jobs for many families, who are paid every month, and the proceeds from the sale of wood go for:

– the support of the monastic community, the advancement of the library and culture in general;

– the upkeep of the forest itself;

– assistance to farming families (for example, the construction of homes that are more comfortable and safer; the distribution of food and clothing during the year, especially during periods of economic crises; dowries for the daughters; healthcare and economic assistance that today we can define as welfare and microcredit).

There were farm fields in addition to the forest. Historians of Camaldolese monasticism inform us that Camaldoli had set up a unique farm economy for the land; its strong point was letting the farmers themselves share in the production of the agricultural fields with *ante litteram* tenant farming contracts or cropland rental contracts. By seeking to remain faithful to the Gospel and give witness to the simplicity and poverty both lived and proposed by Saint Romualdo, Camaldoli's past has been full of fruitful and diverse experiences of welcoming, helping the poor, and economic-social support and promotion. I've cited some aspects of this millennia-long history only in order to highlight how what we are doing today is in continuity with a longstanding style and purpose.

Turning to the present day, I cannot present here each one of our community's initiatives for the poor and the lifestyle of sobriety each community seeks, but I wish to turn your attention to just two projects that are especially close to my heart.

The first was established in Camaldoli in the 1970s in the wake of the Second Vatican Council and was spurred on by Pope Paul VI's *Populorum Progressio.* This project began after becoming acquainted with and promoting *fair and ethical trade* and opening a retail shop with products from farmers and artisans from southern countries of the world. We were among the first in Italy to believe in fair and ethical trade. This project inspired people within the monastic community – the oblates of the monastery and the many guests – to become more involved and take a direct interest in the poorest people of Latin America, Africa and Asia. This interest and involvement gave life to a dedicated non-profit organization whose purpose is helping children from birth to ten years of age through thousands of long-distance adoptions, which focus on the economic condition of their family, and above all, guarantee their schooling. We can say that having the Camaldolese monks return to Brazil in the 1980s to the State of Sao Paulo was born not only out of the desire to restore our presence in that great country, which had been interrupted in the years 1924-1925, but above all, out of our great stirring interest in the experience of sharing in the listening of the word of God with the poorest and in being able to help them economically and with their scholastic education. In the last two years we have been able to give back 250,000 Euro (two hundred fifty thousand Euro) each year:

through other religious congregations that operate directly in the field of education; through the community-families who adopt and put themselves at the service of street children or children who cannot rely on their own parents; or through associations that promote direct action towards the development of the world's neediest people. The requests for help are many and on the rise. We try to give a concrete response to the majority of the requests with the amount of money we earmark. Nevertheless, what matters to me is that we are still who we are, a monastic community in the northern hemisphere that distributes money to projects that – we hope – go beyond almsgiving and pave the way for long lasting structures of development.

The second project is – in my opinion – more significant, in that it was coordinated by our Ashram in India in the State of Tamil Nadu. It is a poor community that lives off of its own earnings. Therefore, it follows in the wake of our monastic tradition, their projects of sharing are run directly by the Indian monks with very little help from Italy. In this context, the monks are poor men who help other people who are even poorer than they are. As many will know, it is unthinkable that an Ashram in India be just a place of silence, prayer and meditation, but this one is truly authentic, according to Hindu religious culture, as it opens up to helping mendicants and those most in need. The project, therefore, began as early as the end of the 1970s with the construction of a hospice for the elderly who – being on their own with no family – would have had to try to survive on the street. This hospice is directly supported by the Saccidananda Ashram, which provides for the maintenance of the building, supplying the beds, mattresses and sheets, cleaning services, medicine for those who are ill and daily meals. Furthermore, a sewing school for young girls was established. At the end of the course, they not only have learned a skill that will let them be able to make a secure living, but they receive as a gift the same sewing machine they learned to sew on. Finally, everything that is needed for elementary school is supplied to the children of the poorest families in the nearby village. It's true that the Ashram also receives assistance from the foreign guests who take part in the courses they offer. But the thing I want to underline is the evangelical and prophetic approach that I was able to observe often in India or other parts of the world, especially where many missionaries work: that many situations of poverty can be faced not so much and not only because there are contributions from the rich, but because a continual exchange of assistance is created among the poor themselves.

I cannot end my talk without recalling what the Camaldolese monks here in Rome do in the Abbey of Saint Anthony, where they distribute more than 100 meals every day to the poor and immigrants (many of whom are Muslim). At one of their monasteries in Tanzania in Mafinga, they have a nursery school where residents of the village nearby can bring all their children from three to six years of age for free. Here they are washed, receive clean clothes, play, get a bit of schooling by learning to read and write, and they can receive a meal each day.

Pope Francis envisions a poor church for the poor, a church that wants to share its own goods and redistribute its own wealth. His invitation is meant for every member of the church, but he particularly points to religious orders that serve God with the vow of poverty. Now, no one can ignore how many of them were founded precisely on the desire to come to the aid of the poorest of men and women. But throughout every moment in history, all religious families have always been committed to assessing and facing different forms of poverty – from healthcare to social needs, from economic to cultural poverty, anticipating the profound changes within different human societies. The vow of poverty asks us to be detached from goods and money, it invites us to become *poor in spirit* by entrusting ourselves wholly to God and depending on him, and to have enthusiasm for gift, and it asks us to intervene and heal situations of inequity. We know that not only must we stay poor with a simple, frugal and sober life, and that we must also commit ourselves *for* the poor who face many forms of human poverty today, but even more so we have learned to live *with* the poor. And this living with the poor has been the experience that has converted many religious men and women even more deeply to God during these last 50 years after the Council.

ALESSANDRO BARBAN, OSB.CAM.
Prior General of the Camaldolese Congregation of the Order of Saint Benedict

ECONOMY OF COMMUNION

OLGA MARÍA RODRÍGUEZ CORREA - MARCO AQUINI

The Focolare Movement was inspired by Chiara Lubich in Trento in 1943, during the Second World War. It rose, therefore, within the Church during a period marked by the pain and destruction caused by the war and marked by the presence of ideologies which pushed people towards hatred and to banish God from society. In this context, God revealed himself to Chiara Lubich and to her first companions as what he really is: Love. Their great discovery was: "God loves us immensely," "God loves you immensely." God is no longer far away, but incredibly close, present in all circumstances of life, whether they be painful, joyous or indifferent. This was the first proclamation they made to anyone they met: God is here, He loves you, He died for you. In the face of this rediscovery, it came spontaneously to respond with love, which is not empty sentimentality. The Gospel – that small book they took with them into the shelters when the sirens went off, marked their life with its words, transforming it and revolutionizing it.

Chiara remembered that period this way: "Within the fascination emanated by the whole Gospel, we were struck above all by some of Jesus' words and by the realities which highlighted love itself: loving God, loving our neighbor, loving each other, welcoming the spiritual presence of Christ among us, as He has promised, where two or more people unite in his name (cf. *Mt* 18:20), that is to say in his love; following love most manifested – in crucified Jesus; creating unity, an effect of mutually fulfilled love, and not just with those who are part of the Church, but with everyone ('that they all may be one' [*Jn* 17:21]) – that unity we are called upon to live as Christians, modeled on the Most Holy Trinity."

They lived in wonder and astonishment, seeing evangelical promises realized every day: the "give and it shall be given unto you" (*Lk* 6:38); "the overflowing" which unfailingly arrived for having sought his kingdom; the "hundredfold" experienced by those who had left everything for God. The words of the Gospel revealed themselves as guidelines for the development of a spirituality of union that was personal and communal at the same time. Thus the communion of goods was born in the first community in Trento, made up of some 500 people of different ages and vocations, a communion of spiritual goods and what little material goods there were. It should be highlighted that the communion of goods is ordered by the love each person gives: those with their availability, those with their needs. One of the first effects is equality among all. This making concrete, which sought to emulate the life of the early Christians, was perhaps the first sign that the Movement would have a social dimension. That first period is filled with infinite experiences. They asked on behalf of the poor and unfailingly they received bread, powdered milk, potatoes, preserves, clothes... which they took to those in need.

How is the communion of goods lived out today in the Focolare Movement, which includes people of every language, race, people and religion, spread across the entire world in more than 180 nations?

As far as economic life is concerned, a phrase from the Gospel is key, "seek ye first the kingdom of God, and his righteousness; and all these things shall be added unto you" (*Mt* 6:33). In order to provide for ourselves, we are committed to working and trusting in the providence of God.[1] When called upon to live a communal life, consecrated *focolarini* bring only one dowry with them when they enter into a "focolare" community: knowing how to work and make a living. They fully live a communion of goods: they give their wages, they hand over whatever other earnings they have and they

[1] Cf. *General Statutes of the Work of Mary – Focolare Movement*, artt. 24 et seq.

give witness helping the poor, particularly through the educational, apostolic, charitable and social activities of the Movement. All the others – young people, families, adults engaged in the working world, etc. – freely give whatever they consider, before God, as not essential. The Movement as such only possesses goods that are used directly towards its purposes. We are witnesses that today, just like in the early days, Providence continues to arrive unfailingly and abundantly and makes it possible to carry out the various initiatives which the Movement undertakes in order to achieve its purposes. There is extensive community action which is expressed in concrete works set up by members of the Movement as an expression of love and which respond to the specific needs of each nation or region of the world. There are about one thousand (more or less) major social works.

Young people in particular support micro-projects and fund-raising in response to the consequences of natural disasters. Typical of our Movement is the Economy of Communion (EoC), lived out naturally in freedom. On receiving her honorary doctorate in Lublin (Poland), Chiara Lubich presented this project like this: "From the start of the Movement we tried to offer a solution to economic problems emerging in our work, and this through the communion of goods. But some years ago, precisely because of the growth of the Movement, I realized that this was not enough. This happened on one of my visits to Brazil in 1991. I have travelled to that country a number of times and have had occasion to observe the enormous contrasts which plague it: development and underdevelopment, wastefulness and destitution, abundance and misery.

"With a presence there since 1958, the Movement has spread to every quarter, attracting people of all social classes. Social initiatives of every kind have developed there, too. Furthermore, the Mariapolis of Araceli has been there since the 1970s, acting as reference point for our activities. And it is in this little city that the idea for an economy of communion developed. It seemed to me that God called upon our Movement in Brazil – some 200,000 people – to achieve a more extensive communion of goods that would involve the Movement as a whole. While being not at all informed on economic matters, I thought it was a case there of creating some businesses, some enterprises. Their management would have to be entrusted to capable and competent people, who would be able to run them effectively and make a profit. These profits – and herein lies the novelty – would be shared communally."

To what ends? For those of the early Christian community it was: to help those who are in need, providing for them until they are able to find work; then, naturally, to build up businesses; and, finally, to develop structures of formation for "new men and women", animated by Christian love. Without these "new men and women," there can be no new society. The idea was greeted with enthusiasm not only in Brazil, but also in Europe and other parts of the world. Many businesses were established and many were "transformed" in accordance with the criteria of the Economy of Communion. But this requires an economic culture and practice that – while embedded within the dominant economic system – go in the opposite direction from the fundamental criteria driving the kind of economy that is widely considered today. It goes, in short, against the current, avoiding behaviors contrary to evangelic love, adopting attitudes inspired by our spirituality, based precisely on mutual love and unity.

In 2011, after 20 years' experience, the International Assembly of the Economy of Communion was held in Brazil itself. It was an occasion to reflect on its implementation and what possibilities are open for the future.

The following points can be highlighted:

– Chiara's initial invitation to the Movement's community in Brazil in 1991 unexpectedly resonated on an international level;

– the entrepreneurs who take part in the project have tried to base their business management on the logic of communion. There are some 700 businesses taking part;

– the commitment to the poor – whom we try to turn into protagonists and not people receiving assistance – has been constant and is given priority. It is supported by the businesses' profits and by an extraordinary communion of goods earmarked precisely for this purpose. The annual business profits earmarked for this project vary between 700,000 and 800,000 Euro;

– scientific and cultural reflection has deepened, both because of the involvement of teachers and students and because of so many university theses being written on this topic – more than 400 as of now. Thus new avenues open up in universities in various countries for teaching economic views and theories that are different from those dominant today. The Sophia University Institute, which is located in the Movement's international Mariapolis of Loppiano (Florence, Italy), includes in its educational curriculum a specialized degree in economics, based on the Economy of Communion in a broader context of civil economy.

The Economy of Communion, therefore, is a small seed, which nonetheless is bearing fruit both it its specific purposes and it its collaboration with other older and more recent economic initiatives centered on the human person.

We hope to have given you a brief picture and some points for reflection derived from our experience, which is aware of including ourselves with humility in the rich history of the charisms of the Church, but aware that the communion between ancient and new charisms enriches the Church and contributes to witnessing its beauty and its unity.

Olga María Rodríguez Correa
Focolare Movement, "Communion of goods, economy and work"

Marco Aquini
Focolare Movement, "Communion of goods, economy and work"
Professor of International Cooperation for Development
Pontifical University of St. Thomas "Angelicum" – Rome

FOURTH SESSION

Moderator

FATHER ADOLFO NICOLÁS PACHÓN, SJ

Superior General of the Society of Jesus

DEBTS AND OBLIGATIONS:
THE RESPONSIBILITIES OF INSTITUTES AND MEMBERS
(Can. 639)

JESU PUDUMAI DOSS, SDB

"Pay what you owe" (*Mt* 18:28), says Jesus in one of his parables. He spoke at different times about debts and debtors (especially *Mt* 18:21-35; *Lk* 7:36-50). To pay a debt is "an elementary truth of justice" [1] and an essential principle of human coexistence, as exemplified by the parables of Jesus.

When it comes to the responsibility towards contracted debts (and regarding the administration of goods in general), religious life also must bear in mind the rules of human coexistence in every part of the world where religious life is present, not just the universal ecclesiastical norms and proper law, as it seeks with the evangelical counsels "the most radical way of living the Gospel *on this Earth.*" [2] Beginning with some premises in order to understand the meaning of can. 639, this essay wishes to individuate the different levels of responsibility of religious institutes, of the juridic persons present in them and of their members regarding contracted debts and obligations (can. 639 §§ 1-3). Furthermore, this essay seeks to comment on the actions to consider against the person who has profited from these financial activities (can. 639 § 4) and the essential elements that superiors must be aware of when they authorize these contracts (can. 639 § 5). It concludes with some suggestions regarding the authorization and the management of these contracted debts.

[1] D. ANDRÉS, *Le forme di vita consacrata*, Rome 2008, 279.

[2] JOHN PAUL II, Post-Synodal Ap. Exhort., *Vita consecrata*, 18.

1. Premises

To comment on can. 639 requires a few premises about the differences of legal systems to bear in mind, the variety of juridic persons, which have a wide range of asset management abilities, and the meaning of the expression "contracting debts and obligations."

1.1. Diversity of juridical sources

In order to properly comprehend the administration of goods – in our case, contracted debts and obligations, one must distinguish the various regulations that affect their realization by indicating the conditions and the effects. The first thing to keep in mind is canon law because "the temporal goods of religious institutes are ecclesiastical, (and) they *are governed by the prescripts of Book V, The Temporal Goods of the Church*, unless other provision is expressly made" (cann. 635 § 1 and 1257 § 1). Therefore, the general dispositions of Book V of the Code of Canon Law become the legal framework within which must be inserted the specific dispositions of canon law established for religious regarding the administration of goods, especially contracted debts. This is the sole object of our commentary, regarding can. 639.

There is another level of specific provisions governing public juridic persons in the church. They are found in the norms deriving from "their own statutes" (can. 1257 § 1), and in our case, the norms of religious institutes, which are held to establish "suitable norms concerning the use and the administration of goods" (cann. 634 § 1 and 635 § 2) and to "determine acts which exceed the limit and manner of ordinary administration and to establish what is necessary to place an act of extraordinary administration validly" (can. 638 § 1). This determination in proper law must make the norms conform to the specific poverty of the institute. Again applying the principle of subsidiarity, canon law permits the ordinaries (can. 134 § 1) and the major religious superiors (can. 34 § 1) to "take care of the ordering of the entire matter of the administration of ecclesiastical goods by issuing special instructions" (can. 1276 § 2), in order to "to clarify and specify the ways and times of implementing the appropriate laws concerning ecclesiastical goods, in the spirit and within the limits of universal, supplementary and particular law, complementary and particular" (*Note* 5a).[3]

One cannot forget that the complexity of financial matters and the various laws that regulate them, both on the civil and fiscal levels, influence everything about the administration of goods. In fact, the situation in different countries and their aims can lead to a great variety of solutions[4] concerning the administration of goods, and can involve the civil constitution, the type of juridic persons, their capacity in managing assets, their way of contracting debts and their eventual responsibilities, etc. The observance of civil laws, which canon law calls for, is based first of all on the "canonization"[5] of civil laws rendering them "ecclesial" (cann. 22 and 197), especially in the cases of contracts (can. 1290), precaution (cann. 668 § 4, 1274 § 5 and 1284 § 2), and obligations in the labor-social sphere (can. 1286).[6]

[3] Cf. PONTIFICAL COUNCIL FOR THE INTERPRETATION OF LEGISLATIVE TEXTS, *Explanatory Note. La funzione dell'autorità ecclesiastica sui beni ecclesiastici*, February 12, 2004, in *Communicationes* 36 (2004) 24-32 (= *Note*). (Editor's translation).

[4] Cf. ITALIAN CONFERENCE OF MAJOR SUPERIORS - LEGAL SECTION (ed.), *Atti Contrari al voto di povertà e illeciti di carattere amministrativo ed economico*, Rome 2010, 10; cf. V. MOSCA, Povertà e amministrazione dei beni negli Istituti religiosi, in *Quaderni di Diritto Ecclesiale* 3 (1990) 242-243.

[5] "If it is true then that the Church, in the administration of temporal goods, resorts, for the most part, to the canonization of civil laws for perfectly reasonable motives, it must also be recalled that such canonization always has the clause 'insofar as they are not contrary to divine law and unless canon law provides otherwise.' This clause demonstrates well the significance of law in the church. It is legal only if it remains in line with divine law and enters into the divine plan of salvation. But, above all it should be noted that in the few norms universal law offers, it is in order to protect the identity of the temporal goods of the church in general, and the particular or proper law, and for the sake of the meaning and characteristics of the public juridic person that it intends to regulate." V. DE PAOLIS, La rilevanza dell'economia nella vita religiosa, in *Angelicum* 85 (2008) 256.

[6] Cf. V. DE PAOLIS, *La rilevanza*, cit., 247-266.

1.2. The different patrimonial powers of juridic persons in religious institutes

From the canonical point of view, can. 634 § 1 recognizes as juridic persons (can. 113 § 2), by the law itself, religious institutes, provinces, and houses. This juridic personality is the foundation upon which the legal-economic capacities to acquire, possess, administer, and alienate temporal goods (can. 1255) are rooted. These capacities for managing assets are meant to sustain the life and accomplish the works of the religious institute, always in a way that is in harmony with the proper purposes of the church (can. 1254 § 2).[7] Only the constitutions (can. 634 § 1) can determine the exclusion or the restriction of the capacities[8] of these juridic persons (religious institutes, provinces, houses), thus becoming their "collective witness of charity and poverty" (can. 640). In fact, one can imagine a variety of asset management capacities of the juridic persons. "Much depends on the fact of whether the institute possesses everything or possesses nothing, or whether the holders are the provinces and not the houses or if only the houses have the capacity to possess, acquire, and alienate. The variety of systems that are adopted requires a diversity of methods, time periods, revisions, and dependence, according to the spirit and the custom of each institute."[9]

[7] Cf. Y. SUGAWARA, La povertà evangelica nel Codice: applicazione collettiva (cann. 634-640), in *Periodica* 89 (2000) 269-270; cf. V. MOSCA, Povertà e amministrazione, cit., 241; cf. CISM *Atti contrari al voto di povertà*, cit., 8-9.

[8] "Such exclusion or restriction would seem to regard just the capacity to act and not the legal capacity as such. In other words; the juridic person (institute, province, house) has the entire legal capacity, with its added capacity concerning the patrimony, but this last one is excluded or restricted, that is (simply) it cannot be exercised or it can, but not fully. If not, it must be concluded that in the cases of exclusion or restriction, it would be attributed to a juridical personality that is, so to speak, incomplete. This, however, does not appear to hold." A. PERLASCA, La capacità patrimoniale degli istituti religiosi, in *Quaderni di Diritto Ecclesiale* 22 (2009) 121; cf. Y. SUGAWARA, La povertà evangelica nel Codice, cit., 270.

[9] ITALIAN CONFERENCE OF MAJOR SUPERIORS (CISM), *Atti contrari al voto di povertà*, cit., 11; V. MOSCA, Povertà e amministrazione, cit., 243-244; cf. A. PERLASCA, La capacità patrimoniale, cit., 127.

1.3. The meaning of "contracted debts and obligations"

First, it is necessary to understand the meaning of "contracted debts and obligations," which is repeatedly found in can. 639 in the definition of individual terms. A debt can be defined as "the legal obligation that binds a person [...] to some economic benefit, in a continuous and burdensome manner on all their assets, present and future, as long as the legal bond lasts." [10] With obligation, what is intended is "every type of contract, quasi-contract, deal, legal act, through which the entitlement to a proper benefit is conceded to another, by action or omission, and with an economic burden that comes with it.[11] When one speaks about "contracted debts and obligations," one must interpret "*contracting* [...] in a broad sense that includes all the possible ways, licit and illicit, and all the proper and improper contractual legal arrangements." [12] In fact, "to obtain a certain legal uniformity in every single territory, all legislation concerning contractual matters is deferred to civil law (can. 1290) with the consequence that the civil or commercial laws become 'canonical,' [13] with the sole limitations that civil laws not be 'contrary to divine law or canon law provides otherwise' " (can. 1290).

Second, can debts and obligations be considered acts of extraordinary administration? In fact, "The notions of ordinary and extraordinary administration do not correspond only to technical-legal criteria, but they also are determined on the basis of economic criteria – that is, by the greater or lesser degree of the patrimonial importance of the acts in relation to the size and significance of the patrimony of the subject who must place those acts." [14] Leaving

[10] D. ANDRÉS, *Le forme di vita consacrata*, cit. 281.

[11] *Ibid.*

[12] *Ibid.*

[13] J. MIÑAMBRES, La responsabilità nella gestione dei beni ecclesiastici dell'ente diocese, in J.I. ARRIETA (ed.), *Enti ecclesiastici e controllo dello Stato. Studi sull'Istruzione CEI in material amministrativa*, Venice 2007, 84-85.

[14] CISM, *Atti contrari al voto di povertà*, cit., 12.

their determination to proper and particular law, canonical legislation generally considers the following to be acts of extraordinary administration:[15] "Acts which exceed the limit and manner of ordinary administration" (cann. 638 § 1 and 1281 § 1); and "any other affair in which the patrimonial condition of a juridic person can worsen" (cann. 638 § 3 and 1295).

One can consider the "contracted debts and obligations" as an act of extraordinary administration, because in some sense it "exceeds the limit and manner of ordinary administration" (cann. 638 § 1 and 1281 § 1), since such an act is not indicated among the ordinary acts of administration of 1284 § 2. This seems to be the reason why the Italian Bishops' Conference, in its *Decreto di determinazione degli atti di straordinaria amministrazione per le persone giuridiche soggette al Vescovo diocesano* [*Decree for the determination of acts of extraordinary administration for juridic persons subject to the diocesan bishop*], added this among other things: "The contraction of any kind of debt with credit institutions, juridic persons, *de facto* entities, physical persons,"[16] as being an act of extraordinary administration! It is also to be noted that canonical doctrine counts among the second category of extraordinary administrative acts (cann. 638 § 3 and 1295) certain grave types of debts: "In addition to alienation, also mortgages, bonds, holdings, and stocks can lead to damage or diminish the stable patrimony of the institute."[17] Considering therefore,

[15] Cf. V. Mosca, Povertà e amministrazione, cit., 246-247; cf. CISM, *Atti contrari al voto di povertà*, cit., 13; cf. V. De Paolis, *La vita consecrata nella Chiesa*, Bologna 1991, 254.

[16] N. 13 in *Allegato C. Decreto di determinazione degli atti straordinaria amministrazione per le persone giuridiche soggette al Vescovo diocesano (cf. can. 1281 § 2) [Facsimile]*, in Conferenza Episcopale Italiana, *L'istruzione in materia amministrativa*, 2005, [*IMA*] in http://www.chiesacattolica.it/cci_new/documenti_cei/2005-11/02-26/Testo%20Istruzione.pdf (accessed February 24, 2014).

[17] V. Mosca, Povertà e amministrazione, cit., 248; CISM, *Atti contrari al voto di povertà*, cit., 14; cf. J. Beyer, *Il diritto della vita consecrata*, Milan 1989, 285. "Generally, one can say that extraordinary acts of administration are

"debts and obligations" as extraordinary acts of administration (can. 638 §§ 1 and 3), one cannot forget that "in the procedure for placing acts of extraordinary administration, the Code gives a general norm that must always be preserved: permission from the competent authority is required; without it, the act is invalid" (can. 1281 § 1).[18] The requested permission, therefore, is for the validity of the act itself.[19]

2. Responsibility towards contracted debts and obligations

Can. 639 determines, in its first three paragraphs, the different levels of responsibility of religious institutes and their members towards contracted debts and obligations.[20] Responsibility will depend on various factors: who has contracted the debts and obligations, what goods have been contracted (or for whom), what were the canonical prerequisites to fulfill and have they been fulfilled or not, etc.

those that have the potential to change the patrimonial significance of an entity (for example, acts of alienation, contraction of debts, etc.)," L. CHIAPPETTA, *Il Codice di diritto canonico. Commento giuridico-pastorale*, edd. F. Catozzella, A. Catta, C. Izzi, and L. Sabbarese, Bologna 2011 3rd ed., vol. I, 762; cf. ID., vol. II, 570.

[18] V. DE PAOLIS, *La vita consacrata nella Chiesa*, cit., 255; cf. Y. SUGAWARA, Amministrazione e alienazione dei beni temporali degli Istituti religiosi nel Codice (can. 638), in *Periodica* 97 (2008) 254-255.

[19] "In canon law there are different normative sources that determine the acts whose validity requires permission; Hence, acts of extraordinary administration can be separated into two categories: *a*) acts determined by the code for all public juridic persons" (*IMA* 2005, 61), including "other transactions that may worsen the patrimonial condition of a juridic person (can. 1295)" (*IMA* 2005, 62). "Can. 1281 § 1 affirms the general principle whereby every act of extraordinary administration requires the written permission of the local ordinary for its validity" (*IMA* 2005, 66).

[20] Cf. CISM, *Atti contrari al voto di povertà*, cit., 17; cf. J. BEYER, *Il diritto della Vita Consacrata*, cit., 288.

2.1. Responsibility of juridic persons or religious who act for themselves (can. 639 §§ 1-3)

All three paragraphs of can. 639 speak about debts contracted by or for the juridic person and the permission of the superior, but from two very different points of view. On the one hand, § 1 indicates, *above all*, the relationship between the debts of the juridic person and the person who gives the authorization and has higher authority over the juridic person. On the other hand, the first three paragraphs (§§ 1-3) also speak about the relationship between the debts of the juridic person and the persons who act "by mandate" in view of the authorization that they have received or not.

a) *The basis of accountability: ecclesial nature of the goods of the institute*

Being juridic persons (institutes, provinces, religious houses), "all the goods belonging to any institute of consecrated life or society of apostolic life are legally considered 'ecclesiastical goods.' For that reason, the administration of these goods must abide by the principles and the objectives set out in can. 1254 § 2 (cf. cann. 634 § 2 and 635 § 2) in order to ensure a fundamental spirit of poverty be safeguarded and witnessed."[21] In fact "the ecclesiality" or ecclesial nature of these goods, which "stems from the destination for the proper ends of the Church" (*Note* 1), requires that they be governed by canonical provisions (cann. 635 § 1 and 1257 § 1; *Note* 3).[22] One can also "affirm that the unity of the church's patrimony is guaranteed not only by the purposes, but

[21] Congregation for Institutes of Consecrated Life and Societies of Apostolic Life, from a letter to men and women superiors general from some years ago about the documentation to be submitted to the above-mentioned congregation in view of obtaining the authorization for handling some legal transactions concerning the administration of temporal goods, December 21, 2004, in *Enchiridion Vaticanum*, vol. XXII, nn. 2003-2004.

[22] Cf. V. De Paolis, La rilevanza, cit., 251-252.

also by the power of the Roman Pontiff – in virtue of his supreme governance and representation in the Church – and not by ownership, which remains with the juridic person who made the acquisition" (*Note* 7, 2, 4, and 10; cann. 1256 and 1273). Therefore, the different aspects of the legal-financial responsibility of contracted debts by or for juridic persons are based upon the ecclesial aspect of the goods of the institute.

b) *Scope of the permission of the superiors (can. 639 § 1)*

The Pontifical Council for Legislative Texts, in its *Note* of 2004, indicates the proper meaning of the word "permission:"[23] "In canon law, permission means the concession made by the competent authority to a subject to exercise a faculty or right in its possession, but the exercise of which, for reasons of public interest, is conditioned by an 'external control' of law itself. In reality, granting permission and other administrative acts of this type do not imply undertaking what makes up the project that the permission or the *nulla osta* has been given for. [...] Permission [...] is not an act of patrimonial control, but rather an act of administrative power aimed at guaranteeing the proper use of goods of public juridic persons in the church" (*Note* 12).

Therefore, according to can. 639 § 1, the superior's permission[24] does not transfer the responsibility of contracted debts from

[23] The *Note* of the PCLT explains the consequences of permission, applying it to alienation: "Can. 1292 establishes the requirement *ad validitatem*, that is, for the validity (with respect to the canonical effects) of the permission of the Holy See for the alienation of ecclesiastical goods, when the value exceeds the maximum amount established by the conference of bishops (can. 1292 § 1). [...] When the Holy See gives permission for the alienation of ecclesiastical goods, it does not assume for itself the eventual economic responsibilities related to the alienation, but it only guarantees that the alienation is consistent with the purposes of the ecclesiastical patrimony. The responsibility stemming from its contribution refers exclusively to the correct exercise of the Church's power" (*Note* 12) (Editor's translation).

[24] Permission of the superiors according to Andrés, "is not an *avocatio obligationis*, but an *ablatio impedimenti*, so that a juridic person may carry out its

the juridic person to the authority who grants the permission, but only indicates the control[25] of the validity and the legitimacy of the acts (debitory) made by the juridic person. "The superior who grants permission is not properly responsible for the administrative act; he or she does not give a mandate, but simply authorizes an act, giving the go ahead, without assuming for herself or himself the responsibility. It comes under the power of supervision, not of administration." [26] Regarding who is ultimately responsible for contracted debts, the canon establishes that if a juridic person has contracted debts or obligations, *that* juridic person must answer, not the juridic or physical person who is under or over that person.[27]

In fact, *only this* juridic person who has contracted debts must respond both canonically and civilly to any consequence subsequent to the action taken,[28] such as: when debts are exhausted, not just the interest; judicial or extrajudicial consequences; penal or administrative consequences of the contracted debts; and eventu-

economic standing, and as a result, respond responsibly to all of the outcomes put in place. The *avocatio obligationis* brings with it the responsibility for the contracted debt or obligation." D. ANDRÉS, *Le forme di vita consacrata*, cit., 281; cf. CISM, *Atti contrari al voto di povertà*, cit., 17; cf. V. MOSCA, Povertà e amministrazione, cit., 250; cf. J. BEYER, *Il diritto della vita consacrata*, cit., 288.

[25] "Prior checks by the superior must be seen as a form of fraternal collaboration within the framework of a community that is arranged hierarchically: one acts on decisions that have already been adopted, before and in view of their implementation, at the request made by the administrator to the competent authority" (*IMA* 2005, 60).

[26] V. DE PAOLIS, La rilevanza, cit., 265.

[27] In fact, in their *Note* of 2004 the PCLT explains this distinction: "For this reason, canonical laws provide a clear distinction and autonomy of the various ecclesiastical entities relative to each other. Hence, according to canon law, for example, the 'bankruptcy' of a parish does not mean that it falls to the diocese and must be repaid with the assets of the diocese or of another parish. Even in civil law the 'bankruptcy' of an inferior entity does not mean the intervention of a superior entity to recuperate assets" (*Note* 3). This same line of reasoning can be applied also to "contracted debts and obligations" of a juridic person in religious institutes, as it is discussed in can. 639 § 1.

[28] Cf. D. ANDRÉS, *Le forme di vita consacrata*, cit., 281-282.

ally the declaration of bankruptcy by the juridic person with the seizure of goods, even being deprived of his patrimonial capacity and/or of the liberty of his representatives.

c) *"Validity" that depends on the permission of the superior (can. 639 §§ 1 and 3)*

Based on this "permission of the superior"[29] that is requested for validity (can. 1281 § 1) in the contraction of debts and obligations (*as we have already seen*) as an act of extraordinary administration, there is another very important aspect to emphasize in can. 639 § 1 (reading it together with § 3) from the perspective of "persons who act on behalf of the juridic person," regarding the permission that they have received or not. Therefore, when the persons, who can act legitimately on behalf of the juridic person,[30] have contracted debts and obligations for the juridic person, which has been "rendered valid," in fact, by the "permission of the superior" (cann. 639 § 1, 1281 § 1, and 1304 § 1), it will be the juridic person who is "bound to answer for them" (can. 639 § 1). On the contrary, when one of these (or also any religious person) has contracted debts and obligations for the juridic person "without any permission of the superior," thereby in absence of the validity

[29] Cf. V. De Paolis, *La vita consacrata nella chiesa*, cit. 255.

[30] When it comes to the juridic person, those who "represent the public juridic person and act on its behalf, are the ones to whom such competence is recognized by universal or particular law or by their own statutes" (can. 118). Applying can. 1279 § 1, it is possible to identify various persons who can act validly and legitimately on behalf of the juridic persons of the religious institutes in the area of administration, like in the contraction of debts and obligations: superiors, who can perform all the administrative acts, both ordinary and extraordinary (can. 622); according to the determination of proper law, even finance officers (can. 636 § 1) and "other officials designated by proper law, within the limits of their office" (can. 638 § 2), as administrators or legal representatives. Cf. S. Recchi, L'economo degli istituti religiosi, in *Quaderni di Diritto Ecclesiale* 22 (2009) 133-134; cf. V. De Paolis, La rilevanza, cit., 264; cf. Y. Sugawara, Amministrazione e alienazione, cit., 256; cf. CISM, *Atti contrari al voto di povertà*, cit., 14-16.

of the act, "he or she must answer, but not the juridic person" (can. 639 § 3).[31]

Therefore, the responsibility of the juridic person towards contracted debts and obligations depends on the "permission of the superior" for the validity of the act. In this way, if the juridic person acts (or someone on behalf of it) with the permission of the superior, the juridic person who acts validly "is bound to answer to them" (can. 639 § 1), but whoever acts for the juridic person "without any permission of the superior," "he or she must answer, and not the juridic person" (can. 639 § 3), because a necessary prerequisite *ad validitatem* (for validity) would have been missing.[32]

d) *A religious who acts "by mandate" for juridic persons (can. 639 § 2)*

In contrast to the "permission of the superior" that is necessary to render the act valid and legitimate when the debts are contracted by the person who can act legitimately on behalf of the juridic person in religious institutes, "a *mandate* [...] is an assignment expressed by the superior, who, by making the member an authorized representative of the institute of consecrated life, grants him or her the faculty to manage the business on behalf of the institute itself."[33] The mandate, therefore, becomes the essential and validating element for conducting business "on behalf of the

[31] Can. 639 § 3 states a principle of justice: a religious who acts without the permission of the superior must answer for his or her acts. Cf. J. BEYER, *Il diritto della vita consacrata*, cit., 288. This "personal responsibility" of the person who contracts debts and obligations invalidly (that is, *without permission*), seems more binding (interpreted within the meaning of can. 635 § 1) than the general provision of can. 1281 § 3, that sets out the responsibility of the juridic person when "and to the extent that [the act] is to its own advantage" also when it is a matter of "acts illegitimately placed by its administrators."

[32] Cf. V. MOSCA, Povertà e amministrazione, cit., 251; cf. CISM, *Atti contrari al voto di povertà*, cit., 18; cf. V. DE PAOLIS, *La vita consacrata nella Chiesa*, cit., 255.

[33] D. ANDRÉS, *Le forme di vita consacrata*, cit., 283; cf. CISM, *Atti contrari al voto di povertà*, cit., 17; cf. V. MOSCA, Povertà e amministrazione, cit., 251-252.

juridic person" by a religious, insofar as he or she does not have the capacity to act either for the juridic person or on behalf of the juridic person.

All of the responsibility regarding contracted debts and obligations by a religious person for the juridic person, because of the mandate of the superior, falls only to the juridic person: "The institute must answer" (can. 639 § 2), acting as a principal. Thus, one may conclude that the responsibility concerning debts contracted for the juridic person would fall on the religious and not on the juridic person, if he or she has acted without the expressed mandate of the superior. However, in the case of the religious entrusted as an authorized representative, whose acts are illegitimately but validly placed, the juridic person will be responsible for the contracted debts, but the juridic person may bring action against the religious as set by by canon. 639 § 4.[34]

2.2. Debts of members concerning their own goods (can. 639 §§ 2-3) and the goods of others (cann. 672 and 285 § 4)

Can. 639 §§ 2-3, further indicates the responsibility regarding debts contracted by religious concerning their own goods. Below are comments about their responsibility when they act with the goods of others (cann. 672 and 285 § 4).

a) *Basis of responsibility: dependence and limitation in the use and disposition of goods*

As a necessary consequence of "dependence and limitation in the use and disposition of goods"[35] required by the evangelical counsel of poverty professed by religious persons (can. 600),

[34] Cf. D. ANDRÉS, *Le forme di vita consacrata*, cit., 283-284.

[35] In fact, "dependence and limitation mean that consecrated persons do not enjoy the disposition of goods even when they are their own. They are necessary for an effective exercise of the profession of poverty and constitute [...] a minimum request for the counsel of poverty." Y. SUGAWARA, La povertà evangelica nel Codice: norma commune (can. 600) e applicazione individuale

canonical norm holds that all religious must "cede the administration of their goods to whomever they prefer" (can. 668 § 1). Therefore, it is very clear that "to place any act regarding temporal goods" (including in our case contracting debts and obligations regarding one's own goods and the goods of others) religious persons "need the permission of the competent superior" (can. 668 § 2).

Even if, through the vow of poverty one does not normally lose the ownership of goods, it is necessary to keep in mind particular cases in which some religious "due to the nature of the institute" must "renounce fully his or her goods [...] as far as possible, even in civil law; it is to take effect from the day of profession" (can. 668 § 4). In this case, "A professed religious who has renounced his or her goods fully due to the nature of the institute loses the capacity of acquiring and possessing and therefore invalidly places acts contrary to the vow of poverty" (can. 668 § 5). Therefore, in these cases, he or she would be unable to contract debts! Also a perpetually professed religious can "renounce his or her goods either partially or totally," but only "with the permission of the supreme moderator" and "according to the norms of proper law" (can. 668 § 4). How this second case affects the validity or legitimacy of acts contrary to the vow of poverty will depend on the extent of the renunciation and of the dispositions of proper law.

b) *Responsibility of members regarding contracted debts with their own goods (can. 639 §§ 2-3)*

Speaking about contracted debts by religious regarding their own goods, can. 639 § 2 notes: "If a member has entered into a contract concerning his or her own goods with the permission of the superior, the member must answer for it." There are two

(can. 668), in *Periodica* 89 (2000) 57. Furthermore "religious persons, with the vow of poverty, renounce their independence in the sphere of temporal goods. Appropriation, independent use of goods, or free administration of their own goods is incompatible with their vow" (63).

aspects to be emphasized when identifying the responsibility of the members toward contracted debts regarding their own goods. On the one hand, the *personal* responsibility of the religious for debts and obligations contracted regarding their own goods is clear, insofar as he or she is able to place validly and legitimately the acts of administration (applying also can. 668 §§ 4-5). As such, when it comes to contracted debts regarding his or her own goods, even with the permission of the superior, the religious person "must answer for it" personally (can. 639 § 2). Such personal responsibility becomes more serious when the religious has contracted debts and obligations without the permission of superiors as "he or she must answer" (can. 639 § 3).[36]

On the other hand, *as has already been seen* (cf. can. 639 § 1), the "permission of the superior," which concerns only the *juridical nature and legitimacy* of the completed act (in this case, debts contracted by religious regarding their own goods), does not result in making the superior or the juridic person to which the religious belongs: houses, provinces, and institutes, responsible for the debts contracted by the member. This is the sense of can. 639 § 3, which indicates explicitly the responsibility of the religious regarding contracted debts: "He or she must answer, but not the juridic person." Therefore, in no way can the superior or the juridic persons of the religious institutes be involved, civilly or canonically, in repaying debts and obligations contracted by a religious regarding his or her own goods.

One must also remember the canonical norm that advises religious superiors not to admit to the novitiate persons "burdened by debts" and unable to pay them (can. 644). The admission of these persons could be interpreted by a third party as a willingness on the part of the institute or of superiors to help these individuals overcome their economic problems with the goods of the institute.

[36] Cf. V. MOSCA, Povertà e amministrazione, cit., 251; cf. CISM, *Atti contrari al voto di povertà*, cit., 17.

c) *Debts of members concerning the property of others (cann. 672 and 285 § 4)*

Regarding debts contracted by a religious concerning another's goods, there is an indirect reference in can. 672, which applies one of the obligations of clerics specified in can. 285 § 4 to all religious: "Without the permission of their ordinary, they are not to take on the management of goods belonging to lay persons or secular offices [...]; They are prohibited from giving surety even with their own goods without consultation with their proper ordinary. They also are to refrain from signing promissory notes, namely, those through which they assume an obligation to make payment on demand" without a specific reason. It is possible to distinguish three areas of application: the administration of the goods of lay people, guarantees, and promissory notes.

Religious should not administer the goods of laypersons, nor contract debts concerning their goods "without the permission of their ordinary, "due to the risk of having to respond with their own goods or with their liberty."[37] Furthermore, the canon prohibits that, "without consultation with their proper ordinary," religious cannot "become guarantors of credit on any occasion and condition, with any type of person, with the goods of others and also his or her own. In this way, he or she avoids complications and difficulties that would be detrimental to his or her life, spirit, and ministry."[38] Because of the negative effects it also can have on the institute itself, the law strongly prohibits the so-called "IOU": "They also are to refrain from signing promissory notes, namely, those through which they assume an obligation to make payment on demand" without a precision reason (can. 285 § 4). In fact, canonical law has not prescribed the responsibility for debts contracted by a religious regarding the goods of a third party; however, it is clear that the sole person responsible is the religious who carried out the acts, applying can. 639 § 2-3.

[37] D. ANDRÉS, *Le forme di vita consacrata*, cit., 524.

[38] *Ibid., 525.*

3. Right to compensation

The principle of justice upon which this section is based (can. 639 § 4) is found in can. 128: "Whoever illegitimately inflicts damage upon someone by a juridic act or by any other act placed with malice or negligence is obliged to repair the damage inflicted." It is clear that "the person whose patrimony is benefited to some degree following that contract" has removed that advantage from the juridic person, also creating damage to the patrimony of the juridic person. As such, on the one hand, whoever receives benefit has the obligation to repair the damage caused by his actions (can. 128). On the other hand, whoever feels compromised as a result of "that contract" (can. 639 § 4), having experienced harm (or lost a benefit), can always bring legal action (canonical or civil) against the person who has wrongfully profited,[39] because he or she "has the right to compensatory payments, restitution or redress proportional to the benefit drawn by whomever is responsible."[40]

In fact, the following canonical actions are possible. One can begin the penal process (cann. 1717-1731) to ask just penalty against the person who prevented the legitimate use of ecclesiastical goods (can. 1375) or persistently disobeys (can. 1371) or acted with culpable negligence of office (can. 1389 § 2) or to ask for privation against the person who has acted with an abuse of office (can. 1389 § 1). Together with this penal process, one can bring "a *contentious* action to repair damages" (cann. 1729-1731). For dam-

[39] "The three factors are included in the Latin phrase '*contra eum in cuius rem aliquid ex inito contractu versum est:*' The action is aimed against whomever receives financial gain because of or following a contract. It hinges upon a *cause and/or license* that is immediate and visibly illegitimate; and to another that is *mediated and substantive*, which is the legal certitude that the person who acted in that way appropriated something that was owed to one of the parties to the contract, to whom it must be returned." D. ANDRÉS, *Le forme di vita consacrata*, cit., 285.

[40] J. BEYER, *Il diritto della vita consacrata*, cit., 290; cf. CISM, *Atti contrari al voto di povertà*, cit., 18; cf. V. MOSCA, Povertà e amministrazione, cit., 251.

age caused to the institute and juridic persons, one can also initiate "optional" dismissal against the religious provided that the conduct is among those causes that are "grave, external, imputable, and juridically proven" (can. 696 § 1). Regarding possible civil action, one can apply can. 1296 on alienation: "It is for the competent authority, after having considered everything thoroughly, to decide whether and what type of action, namely, personal or real, is to be instituted by whom and against whom in order to vindicate the rights of the Church."

4. Authorization for contracting debts

Can. 639 § 5 states some conditions just for the authorization of contracting of debts, not obligations. First of all, canonical law advises superiors against permitting debts to be contracted. Such a prudent call is based on the foundation of the goods of the institute, which always remain ecclesiastical goods with particular reference to the Roman pontiff, who "by virtue of his primacy of governance [...] is the supreme administrator and steward of all ecclesiastical goods" (can. 1273).

The canon permits superiors to give authorization only in the case in which it is possible to guarantee with moral certainty the fulfillment of two conditions on the part of the requesting parties. The first condition concerns the debt interest that one must cover with the ordinary income of the juridic person who is requesting the authorization, such as "paid work, their own holdings, their own capital with interest income, alms and regular and periodic donations." [41] The second condition that must be ensured regards the restitution of all the capital within a period of time that is not too long with a legitimate amortization. This requires that the entire burden of debt or mortgage be payable "in installments" by the superior, who is backing the juridic person making the request, within the term of his or her office.

[41] Cf. D. ANDRÉS, *Le forme di vita consacrata*, cit., 287.

5. Some practical conclusions

It seems opportune to suggest some practical conclusions to keep in mind both in economic management – most of all concerning debts – and in the specification of proper law regarding the responsibilities of the superiors and others involved in administration.

a) When a superior grants permission for debts or obligations following the request of a juridic person, it is better to specify clearly in the permission granted that this in no way entails any "economic responsibility" of the superior towards contracted debts and obligations. In fact for "the Congregation for Institutes of Consecrated Life and Societies of Apostolic Life, in the rescripts with which the permission is granted, it is customary to add a clause in which they decline assuming any responsibility." [42]

b) If necessary, however, other juridic persons can always intervene using "the principles of charity, the common good, fraternity and the best practical usefulness." [43]

c) Following this very prudent canonical law in cases of debts and obligations, it is better that the proper law (and/or the statutes of juridic persons with civil recognition) not create subsidiary and/or 'binding' ancillary responsibilities for other juridic persons (superior or inferior), so as not to put the entire religious institute into difficulty.[44]

d) Also when a superior grants permission requested by a religious to contract debts regarding his or her own goods (or another's goods), it is better to clearly specify in the permission granted that the permission in no way entails that the superiors or the

[42] V. MOSCA, Povertà e amministrazione, cit., 250; CISM, *Atti contrari al voto di povertà*, cit., 17; cf. J. BEYER, *Il diritto della vita consacrata*, cit., 288.

[43] Cf. D. ANDRÉS, *Le forme di vita consacrata*, cit., 282; cf. CISM, *Atti contrari al voto di povertà*, cit., 17; cf. V. MOSCA, Povertà e amministrazione, cit., 250; cf. J. BEYER, *Il diritto della vita consacrata*, cit., 288.

[44] Cf. D. ANDRÉS, *Le forme di vita consacrata*, cit., 282.

juridic persons of the institute the religious is a member of (the house, province, or institute) have any "economic responsibilities" towards the contracted debts.

e) It is good for proper law to specify better: the type of authorization necessary in order to contract debts; the conditions for it to be valid and licit; the persons (such as superiors, finance officers, administrators, special delegates, etc.) that can carry out the business of the juridic person (above all debts and obligations); the minimum and maximum limit for all the acts of extraordinary administration, etc. Like the *Italian Bishops' Conference* has done, it would be better to place the "contraction of debts of any sort with any physical and juridic persons" among acts of extraordinary administration.

As with every aspect of religious life, the administration of goods – in particular the contraction of debts – also must be lived in the light of the three evangelical counsels: "It is opportune to remember that economic management does not concern just poverty, but that it also has to do with obedience since there are laws of the church, the institute, and governments that have to be followed. It also has to do with chastity since it is indispensable the heart be free so that goods might be put at the service of the human person." [45]

JESU PUDUMAI DOSS, SDB
Professor of Canon Law
former Dean of the Faculty of Canon Law
Salesian Pontifical University – Rome

[45] V. DE PAOLIS, La rilevanza, cit., 242-243. De Paolis takes these words from: the UNION OF SUPERIORS GENERAL, *Economia e missione nella vita consacrata oggi*, Rome 2002.

PUBLIC JURIDIC PERSONS: ADVANTAGES AND DRAWBACKS

Peggy Ann Martin, OP

Buongiorno, Good afternoon

I am Peggy Ann Martin, a Dominican Sister of Peace, from the United States. Presently, I am the senior vice president for sponsorship and governance at Catholic Health Initiatives in Denver, Colorado. Catholic Health Initiatives is a large Catholic health system which operates in 18 states within the United States. This health system is sponsored by Catholic Health Care Federation, a public juridic person of pontifical rite. Part of my responsibilities is to manage the public juridic person, Catholic Health Care Federation.

Today the Congregation for Institutes of Consecrated Life and Societies of Apostolic Life has been referring to the public juridic persons, such as Catholic Health Care Federation, as ministerial public juridic persons. This is to distinguish them from public juridic persons established by law, such as, religious institutes and dioceses. Throughout this presentation I will use the term "Congregation for Religious" to refer to the Congregation for Institutes of Consecrated Life and Societies of Apostolic Life.

Catholic Health Care Federation was established by the Congregation for Religious in 1991. It was at the request of Catholic Health Corporation, a Catholic health system in Omaha, Nebraska, that Catholic Health Care Federation came into being. At that time, it was the Catholic sponsor for a few health care entities, but not all of the health care entities which participated in Catholic Health Corporation. Most of the congregations of women religious kept their canonical rights even though Catholic Health Care Federation had been established. In 1996, three Catholic health systems came together to form Catholic Health Initiatives, Catholic Health Corporation out of Omaha, Nebraska being one of them, and at that time we petitioned the Congregation for Religious to have Catholic Health Care Federation became the Catholic sponsor for all of the ministries of Catholic Health Initiatives. Ultimately, this included the health-care ministries of twelve institutes of women religious. It was understood at that time that the twelve congregations of women religious would alienate their health care assets to Catholic Health Care Federation. Since this was the first of its kind, the Congregation for Religious asked the religious institutes not to alienate all at once, but instead to alienate their health care assets over a five year period. Today when a ministerial public juridic person is established, alienation takes place at the same time.

I have been asked to address the advantages and the drawbacks of having a ministerial public juridic person, such as Catholic Health Care Federation. I am personally a member of one of the congregations of women religious participating in Catholic Health Initiatives and I was in leadership of my congregation at the time it was formed. I have to say that it was a wonderful experience to come together with other congregations for the healing mission of the Church.

Advantages of a ministerial public juridic person are many depending upon the particular congregation of religious. First and foremost, it has allowed the ministries of the individual congregations to continue as a Catholic ministry. The witness value of the congregations working together speaks volumes. The individual congregations have also been able to reflect upon their charisms to see where they are being called in the world today. They are able to be true to their charisms in responding to these new calls because the ministerial public juridic persons are maintaining their former health care ministries.

It has allowed both vowed religious and lay persons together to be involved in sponsorship. Prior to this, lay-persons were only involved in governance. The sponsorship oversight for the ministry needs people, both vowed religious and lay, who are experienced and knowledgeable of the Catholic Church and the industry. Health care has become quite complicated in the United States and the religious need experienced persons to help them continue the ministry. This is in both governance and sponsorship. The ministerial public juridic persons have allowed for greater flexibility in recruiting persons as members of the juridic persons. Vowed religious today see great value in the collaboration between themselves and the laity for the continuation of the healing ministries of the Church.

The ministerial public juridic persons allow for greater stability in the oversight of the ministry. Prior to this, it could be that changes in oversight, requirements, and processes might be different every time a new leadership team was elected. Also, there was a risk that no one on the new leadership team would have the experience, knowledge and/or care about the ministry. With the ministerial public juridic persons, both the persons in the ministry and those responsible for sponsorship oversight do not need to be concerned about new leadership in the individual congregations. Plus the congregations are then free to elect leadership for their future not necessarily because a person was/is a nurse or lawyer or whatever their expertise might be.

Formation of sponsors is a highlight advantage for me. Early on after the establishment of Catholic Health Care Federation, we began talking about the necessary formation for the physical persons who represented the sponsor. Catholic Health Initiatives is part of a collaborative effort in the formation of sponsors for public juridic persons. People have said to me, the sisters received their formation when they entered the convent. I realize formation for religious has changed since I entered in 1962 but the formation needed for sponsors today is different from the formation for a religious. It is an amazing privilege to journey with people, both vowed religious and lay, through formation in Scripture, spirituality, theology, ethics, the social teachings of the Church and, yes, my favorite, canon law. It is the ministerial public juridic persons that have brought this forward. If we were still religious institute public juridic persons, we probably would not even think about needing formation as sponsors, plus we most likely would not have laypersons as sponsors with us. In the formation journey for public juridic person sponsors, we are forming people for life. Once people understand what sponsorship is all about, they have a difficult time when their term is over, they feel so committed to the ministries and want to continue. It is so life giving and such a privilege to be part of this.

Another advantage on the side of the congregations is that many more sisters can be involved. The sister does not have to be in leadership of her congregation. On the side of the laity, they feel called; they feel they are living out their baptismal call.

In some ministerial public juridic persons in the United States, the members of the public juridic person and the trustees of the civil corporation are the same physical persons. This can be a great advantage. It is an example of everything working together and one could say it is going back to the time of the religious congregations when their leadership teams did it all together. It does provide a clear picture for all, the mission questions are always in front of the entire group. Other ministerial public juridic persons make the choice to have two separate groups of people, those in sponsorship and those in governance. One way is not better than the other. It all depends upon the culture of those involved, what they feel works best for all involved to further the healing ministry of the Church.

Now, it is not all roses. I'm not sure I would call them drawbacks, but there are definitely challenges. It can be challenging when new leadership is elected in an individual congregation. For individual sisters who are not in leadership, it can be challenging to understand what actually happened to "their" ministries. Then if a former ministry is alienated or there are downsizing of employees, it comes back to the sisters – these are difficult situations. It really has nothing to do with the ministerial public juridic person, but that is where the blame goes.

It can be particularly challenging for the local bishop. The bishops were accustomed to working with the major superior of a particular congregation and now it is a ministerial public juridic person and probably someone like myself that they interact with on the major issues. Then the headquarters of the ministerial public juridic person are most likely located outside of their individual diocese and both vowed religious and lay are in the sponsorship role, no longer just the sisters. Especially difficult for the bishops has been the changing world of health care. For the most part, health care is not their field of expertise and yet they have oversight responsibilities for the Catholic ministries in their individual dioceses. Then add to that the fact that most of us have moved from individual health care facilities into health care systems and then joined health care systems together. It is difficult to keep up with all of this. It can become frustrating for the local bishops.

Prior to ministerial public juridic persons, the elected leadership of a congregation exercised all rights and responsibilities, both civil and canonical. For the most part it happened without even thinking what was civil/governance and what was canonical/sponsorship. With the coming of ministerial public juridic persons, those rights and responsibilities have needed to be separated. This is difficult no matter whether it is one congregation or five or twelve. Those are difficult questions to answer: is this really governance or is this necessary for oversight of the Catholic identity and mission? It brings out a lot of emotions and, of course, the phrase, "We've always done it this way" is bound to be heard. Or "Do the sisters really want this?" Or "Do the sisters know this is happening?" Then there can also be overlap between those persons exercising the governance and those exercising the sponsorship rights and responsibilities. This is a very delicate situation to work through.

As the ministerial public juridic persons of pontifical rite have evolved since 1991, the question of accountability is emerging for the Congregation for Religious. Since the assets of the ministerial public juridic persons were former assets of religious institutes, the ministerial public juridic persons of pontifical rite have been accountable to the Congregation for Religious. In some of the ministerial public juridic persons, the original religious institutes no longer have rights, be they civil or canonical; in others, the rights have always been on the civil side and not on the canonical side; in some there is a connection to the original congregations, but it is not through any legal civil or canonical rights and/or responsibilities; some are as they were when the leadership teams held all of the rights and responsibilities with the addition of lay persons. All of these evolutions are calling into question accountability for the ministerial public juridic persons of pontifical rite.

At this time, I do not know the answer to the accountability questions. I do know that my colleagues and I like reporting to the Congregation for Religious because they understand what we are about and our ministries. The Congregation for Religious has allowed the ministerial public juridic persons to evolve to meet the needs of the congregations of religious and the people of God.

Are ministerial public juridic persons, especially those in health care, a good way or the best way to sustain the Catholic ministries into the future? They appear to be at this moment in history and more and more congregations of religious are asking about the future possibilities for their ministries. Already some ministerial public juridic persons have more than just one type of ministry. Some have health care and education in the same juridic person. Others include all of the sponsored ministries of a particular congregation. There was a question whether one body of members could have sponsor oversight for more than one type of ministry, but it appears to be working. The members do not all need the same expertise, they need to bring different expertise which works for all.

I do not have a crystal ball so I cannot see into the future. I do know that the ministerial public juridic persons are working well at this time for those of us who have chosen this path for our ministries. They are not necessarily for everyone, not necessarily for every congregation of religious who sponsor Catholic ministries.

One of the great gifts of the Congregation for Religious is that it has allowed the public juridic persons by decree to be formed. It has allowed each one of them to have some individual characteristics within the formal structure. For us this is gift, for the Congregation for Religious I can imagine it becomes a challenge. I can definitely share with you that Catholic Health Care Federation has been a gift for the twelve congregations of women religious who participate in Catholic Health Initiatives. It continues to be a gift for two congregations of religious who are about to join us and for all of those who will come in the future.

I look forward to working with the Congregation for Religious and the local bishops in solving the challenges as we go forward committed to the mission of the Church.

PEGGY ANN MARTIN, OP

Senior vice-president of sponsorship and governance at Catholic Health Initiatives – Denver (Colorado)

INSTRUMENTS OF CIVIL LAW: FOUNDATIONS, REAL-ESTATE FUNDS, AND NON-PROFIT ORGANIZATIONS

Alberto Perlasca

I really hope I will not be telling you anything new with this presentation of mine. Its aim is very modest and is simply to recall the principles of canon law on the subject of temporal goods, and the particular precautions required when these interact with state law. In some cases, we are dealing with issues that have not been totally defined yet and, therefore, are open to everyone's reflection and contribution.

The concept of ecclesiastical goods is intimately tied to public juridic personality in the Church, that is, to those subjects of canonical juridic law which pursue, *nomine ecclesiae*, the institutional aims of the Church itself (can. 116 § 1). This deputation to the particular purposes the divine Founder assigned to his Church requires that the aforementioned goods must be primarily governed by the norms of canon law. With regard to this, can. 1257 § 1 establishes: "All temporal goods which belong to the universal Church, the Apostolic See or other public juridic persons in the Church are ecclesiastical goods and are governed by the following canons and their own statutes." As is well known, religious institutes, provinces and houses (can. 609 § 1) are precisely public juridic persons on the strength of the same law (can. 634 § 1).

Precisely because the Church's purposes are transcendent, the canonical legislator has concerned himself, throughout the centuries, with establishing norms intended to safeguard the goods necessary for the achievement of those purposes, and to make sure that these goods: would not be alienated without a highly justified reason; would not be put to use for purposes that are different from the Church's purposes; and, last but not least, would not be usurped, not only by men and women of the Church, but also by secular authorities, which had always wanted to appropriate the church's patrimony. As an example, think of the strict legislation on the matter of alienation of goods established under the pontificate of Leo IV (847-855), who was concerned that "*Ecclesia Dei ad nihilum non redigatur*", and of the even more rigid norms contained in the Apostolic Constitution *Ambitiosae* of Pope Paul II (1468).

This requirement gives rise to that whole system of canonical controls such as, for example: the obligation of accountability in administration; permission from the Holy See; the consensus required from the internal governing bodies in accordance with their constitutions; and the requirement that, at least on an institutional and provincial level, the administration of goods be entrusted to a finance officer, distinct from the respective major superior (can. 636 § 1). These are norms derived from the centuries-old wisdom of the Church. On the one hand, the Church knows well the weaknesses of humanity and its heart, and, on the other, feels the need to protect, through appropriate legal provisions, not only that set of instruments that allows it to pursue its proper institutional purposes, but also to protect the people themselves. It seeks to protect people from setting up operations which could lead to extremely serious consequences, not only for those who carry them out, but also for other members of the institute if they find themselves deprived of the means necessary for existence, which, in most cases, are the fruit of huge sacrifices and costly renunciations. So long as canonical controls concerning ecclesiastical goods are perceived as obstacles to be avoided, rather than a form of assistance to be sought, there can never be real progress in managing the goods of the Church.

All this, obviously, must not lead us to think that in the administration of ecclesiastical goods we should disregard the civil legislation enforced in different countries. Civil law, together with canon law, must be recognized, respected and, where appropriate, appreciated. One of the obligations imposed on the administrator of ecclesiastical goods is precisely to be on guard so that no damage comes to the Church from the non-observance of civil laws (can. 1284 § 2, 3°). And the same may also be said concerning employment contracts, as recalled in can. 1286, 1°, and contracts in general (can. 1290).

Today, however, there is a tendency to uncritically employ secular law in managing the goods of the Church as well. The reasons are varied. Sometimes laudable, such as, for example, wanting to distinguish, appropriately – from a juridical point of view as well – between the different activities of an institute, above all when it comes to commercial activities. Other times, however, the reasons are rooted in an insufficient knowledge of canon law, both by clergy and religious, and laypeople, who increasingly have to take care of the administration of ecclesiastical goods. Lay jurists may know civil law well, but if they do not know equally well canon law – and, above all, the reasons behind it, there is truly a risk that the goods of the Church may be managed like any other worldly good, and that the Church may become a business to be run according to criteria whose only aim is profit.

An expression of this can be found, first of all, in the ever increasing number of civil foundations being set up and in the resulting transferral of the institute's goods and activities to these juridical subjects – sometimes to a large degree. In light of everything we have said up until now, the danger of this happening cannot be ignored, as much as it may appear relatively easy. In effect, goods which are transferred from the institute, which is a public juridic person, to this civil foundation are no longer ecclesiastical goods and, as such, are no longer governed and protected by canon law. These goods are subject exclusively to civil legislation, over which the Church can do very little. And this can be said particularly of those countries in which democracies are fragile and changes in government are sudden and violent. All this without mentioning the moral significance when a similar operation might be carried out as a way to deliberately elude canonical controls.

Therefore, it is possible, that the surest road, although often the longest and hardest, is where the canonical entity is recognized in civil law. Even more so since canon law recognizes the juridic institute of the foundation both when it is as an autonomous foundation, that is, with its own juridical personality, and if it is a non-autonomous foundation, that is, a foundation which, so to speak, refers to a previously existing canonical juridical person (can. 1303 § 1, 1°-2°). Since juridical recognition from the state changes nothing in the juridical nature of the canonical entity and its goods – that is, a canonical entity recognized in civil law remains a canonical entity and its goods remain ecclesiastic goods, and therefore, subject to the laws of the Church – this would seem the best way to adequately safeguard goods which are transferred to a foundation from the religious institute or one of its branches that are granted public juridic personality.

Here, however, we face a problem which, while it has already been studied,[1] may require further detail, since it seems the religious superior, even if an ordinary (can. 134 § 1), does not have the faculty to establish juridic persons, either public or private, but can only do so by virtue of apostolic privilege or on the basis of specific norms approved by the Holy See.[2] In fact, authorities who are able to set up juridical persons within the Church would be the Holy See, the episcopal conference and the diocesan bishop. The diocesan ordinary could only do so because of a special mandate from the bishop – his superior. Moreover, if the religious institutes do not belong to the hierarchical structure of the Church (can. 207 § 2), it is difficult to understand how a religious superior, even if ordinary, could set up a juridical person which instead belongs to the said structure. Religious institutes and their respec-

[1] V. De Paolis, L'autorità competente ad erigere una persona giuridica nella Chiesa, in *Periodica* 92 (2003) 3-20 and 223-255. The study is also reprinted in its entirety in Id., *La vita consacrata nella Chiesa*, Venice 2010², 103-144.

[2] The Code of 1917 reserved this prerogative to the local ordinary (can. 1489). Currently the only competent authorities as regards legal jurisdiction are the Holy See, the episcopal conference and the diocesan bishop.

tive branches, in fact, receive juridical personality *ipso iure* (can. 634 § 1) and not as a result of an act by the competent superior. In any case, it is a problem which requires further reflection.

If the recognition of a canonical body in civil law is not possible, or the authority does not have the faculty needed to establish a juridical person, and if establishing a civil entity is, therefore, in some way unavoidable, it is necessary at least to be a little prudent and insert specific precautions in its statutes such as, for example: reserving to the ecclesiastical authority the appointment of the institution's leadership positions or at least most of them; the same should be done with members of the administrative board; establishing the obligation of handing in to the competent ecclesiastical authority periodic accountability reports of the entity's administrative management; also, a major rule of caution is ensuring that the goods of the entity, while they are not ecclesiastical in a technical sense, ought to be equally governed, nonetheless, by the Church's norms on these matters. In fact, since the statute is the proper law of the entity, inserting this last specification can sometimes be the only and final defense for protecting goods, which, in themselves, are at the mercy of civil legislation. This, moreover, is expressly required by can. 1295. Finally, it must not be forgotten to establish precisely and clearly the allocation of goods in case the entity is extinguished or suppressed. Unfortunately, these aspects very often are overlooked in statutes.

All of this also pertains to the various associations of lay faithful who, by sharing the charism of a religious institute, align themselves with it, so to speak. They often even involve the name of the institute itself, but without the institute then being able to effectively verify their work and, if necessary, intervene in the case of improper conduct which, sometimes, can even compromise the good name of the institute.

There is then another legal and financial instrument, which, as of late, has interested some religious institutes that are no longer able to manage their own facilities for a number of different reasons. These are real estate investment funds. There is no shortage of risks in this matter, too. First of all because these financial operations cover a long timeframe: 10, 20 or 30 years. Secondly, because during that period, ownership of the goods passes to the fund. The fund, therefore, is not just the manager of goods, which stay with the institute, but it becomes the owner. Therefore, for the duration of the fund, the religious institute loses ownership of the goods conferred to the fund. A third open question is the market value of the real estate when the fund expires. If the real estate market is high, then there could be real income. But if the real estate market is down, as it is at this time, there is the risk that the institute may have to further supplement its shares in order to reclaim ownership of the goods which, at the time, it had conferred to the fund as inalienable. It seems possible to say that the real estate investment fund is an instrument geared more for the divestment of real estate, rather than for its preservation. Wherever possible, it seems that the preservation of assets is better guaranteed by granting the management of the property in exchange for an annual fee from the manager – possibly compensated by renovation work. Indeed, in this case, there is the advantage – and not a minor one at that – that the ownership of the real estate remains with the institute.

The brief time available does not allow me to take on the complex issue of societies of apostolic life, as per the program. Therefore, I have opted to discuss a legal entity, which is increasingly being adopted by religious institutes as well, and that is the creation of a non-profit organization. In Italian, the acronym for an NGO is "ONLUS," which means "non-lucrative organization of societal utility." It comes under a particular fiscal regime, which is open to associations, foundations, committees, cooperatives and ecclesiastical bodies as long as they belong to a religion the state has stipulated a pact, accord or agreement with. First of all, it must be said that the religious institute itself never takes on the status of an "ONLUS"; it can only set up within itself an "ONLUS" branch that is limited to carrying out one of the activities of social benefit provided for in Article 10 of the Italian legislative decree No. 460

of December 4th, 1997. Among those activities are: social and social-health assistance; charity; and education or training etc., if offered to people who are disadvantaged because of their physical, psychological, economic, social or family conditions or to members of a foreign community, which is then limited to humanitarian assistance. It must be remembered then that the creation of an "ONLUS" branch is not an obligation, and it is not – if I may be forgiven the expression – a fad, since the institute can just as well carry out (or continue to carry out) the same social activity under its own fiscal regime. This needs to be said because in exchange for the fiscal advantages that are granted, there are precise rules: 1. There are precise limitations on the activities carried out, which is why it is not then possible to bring into the "ONLUS" branch the institute's other activities which have nothing to do with the ones that have been declared. 2. The income derived from the activities declared must not exceed 66% of the organization's total expenditure. 3. It is forbidden during the life of the organization, unless the allocation or distribution is imposed by law or is made to another "ONLUS," to distribute profits and compensation payments as well as funds, reserves or capital, even in an indirect way (for example: payment of fees, wages and salaries exceeding certain parameters). 4. There is an obligation to use profits or remainders of management for carrying out institutional activities and activities that are directly connected to them. 5. There is the obligation to cede the organization's assets, in the case of its dissolution for whatever reason, to other "non-lucrative organizations of social utility" or community service organizations. Therefore, in the event that the "ONLUS" ceases to exist, the residual assets – both liquid assets and property – are not at the disposal of the entity, but shall be reserved for the decision of the authorities of the "ONLUS." In addition to all of this, there are a number of strict requirements regarding transparency in accounting and administration.

Therefore, it is not necessarily the case that setting up an NGO branch is always the best choice. Before making this decision it is necessary to critically consider all the elements at play. Proof of this is the fact that setting up an NGO branch is considered a potentially prejudicial act and, therefore, subject to specific authorization. Fundamentally there are advantages on three levels with an NGO: 1. It is not considered to be a commercial activity and, therefore, any income is tax exempt. However, this is hardly significant when the entity regularly breaks even – indeed, if it doesn't make a loss, or if it is only a case of offering services (for example, a soup kitchen for the poor). 2. Donations are deductible. 3. There are tax benefits with the acquisition of property. As previously stated, since the assets that went into the "ONLUS" must be ceded to another "ONLUS" or to a community service (according to the decisions made by the agency for the "ONLUS") when the ONLUS' activities are discontinued, it is advisable to keep real estate out of the "ONLUS," so that if its activities are discontinued, there should be no particular problems in making the property be fully available to the institute once again.

ALBERTO PERLASCA
Official at the Vatican's Secretariat of State Administration office

STABLE PATRIMONY

Sebastiano Paciolla, O.Cist.

This paper should be seen as a synthesis of a more extensive doctrinal reflection[1] that was made to introduce the subject that is under study, namely, the *stable patrimony* of a public canonical juridical person. Found under this latter category are: public associations of the faithful *in itinere* – namely, those with the intention of becoming an institute of consecrated life or a society of apostolic life; institutes of consecrated life and societies of apostolic life; provinces or parts of the institute deemed equivalent; and autonomous monasteries.[2] As has already been made clear in the other presentations by previous speakers, temporal goods belonging to public canonical juridical persons are ecclesiastical goods and are governed by universal law as well as by their own statutes.[3]

[1] For a broader treatment of the subject see, cf. V. Rovera, I beni temporali della Chiesa, in Aa.Vv., *La normativa del nuovo codice*, Brescia 1983, 261-283; M. López Alarcón, Can. 1285, in Aa.Vv., *Código de Derecho Canónico*, Pamplona 1983, 769; F.R. Aznar Gil, *La administración de los bienes temporales de la Iglesia*, Salamanca 1993, 407-408; V. De Paolis, Alienazione, in *Nuovo Dizionario di Diritto Canonico*, Milan 1993, 8-13; Id., *I beni temporali della Chiesa* (Il Codice del Vaticano II, 10), ed. A. Perlasca, Bologna 2011, 244-247; J.-C. Périsset, *Les biens temporels de l'Église: commentaire des canons 1254-1310*, Paris 1996, 199-200; J.P. Schouppe, *Elementi di diritto patrimoniale canonico*, Milan 1997, 130-132; F. Grazian, Patrimonio stabile: istituto dimenticato?, in *Quaderni di Diritto Ecclesiale* 16 (2003) 282-296; A. Perlasca, *I beni temporali della Chiesa*, Milan 2005, 468; C. Begus, *Diritto patrimoniale canonico*, Vatican City 2007, 222; L. Simonelli, L'alienazione dei beni ecclesiastici e i cosiddetti "atti peggiorativi," in *Ex Lege* 2 (2013) 17-22. The Italian Conference of Major Superiors held a study seminar January 25, 2014, on the theme: *Il patrimonio stabile: novità, significato, ricezione di un istituto a tutela e garanzia dei beni ecclesiastici*, of which the publication of the proceedings is expected.

[2] Cf. can. 634 § 1.

[3] Cf. can. 1257 § 1.

The *stable patrimony* of a public canonical juridical person is an aggregate of goods determined by the competent ecclesiastical authority and is subject to a particular legal framework.

The concept of *stable patrimony*, introduced in the 1983 Code of Canon Law, falls within the framework of systematic and material innovations regarding temporal goods.

However, it had already been an institution that was noted in previous doctrine and was incorporated in the current legislation. In fact, even if the Pio-Benedictine Code did not speak of *stable patrimony*, can. 1530 § 1 had the expression "*Res ecclesiasticae immobiles aut mobiles, quae servando servasi possunt.*"

Catholic doctrine sought to give legal substance to the new expression of *stable patrimony* by turning, above all, to can. 1530 of the abrogated Code because it recognizes a parallel there. While admitting with De Paolis that "in order to specify the object of the goods that are, in and of themselves, inalienable and thus alienable only according to a certain procedure and, in particular, with the permission of the competent authority, can. 1530 § 1 uses a rather difficult phrase for the translation,"[4] it ought to be recognized that the parallel is not extrinsic.

Starting from this premise, it is possible to affirm that all immovable property and all those movable goods that can be conserved – and thus ought to be, constitute a specially protected category, according to their nature or function or destination. Perlasca also goes along the same lines when he translates the expression of can. 1530 from the 1917 Code as meaning "permanent endowment of immovable and movable property, which constitutes the economic capital necessary for remaining viable and operative."[5]

The introduction of this concept in the current Code, as it was described in *Communicationes*, did not happen without difficulty since some consultors believed that the expression *stable patrimony* was not relevant to the dynamics of the modern economy. In the

[4] V. DE PAOLIS, *I beni temporali*, cit., 245.

[5] A. PERLASCA, *I beni temporali della Chiesa*, cit., 468.

report, in fact, one can read: "Nonnulli crisim fecerunt de locutione 'patrimonium stabile,' quae apta erat condicionibus rerum praeteritorum, sed nostris temporibus non idonea videtur, attenta mobilitate et ozioneate oeconomiae hodiernae. Consultores autem concordant circa necessitatem ponendi aliqeum limitem [...], quod fieri ozion nisi sumendo ozione aliquam conventionalem per verba 'patrimonium stabile' indicatam." [6]

After considering the economic reality today, which recognizes movable property that can to be invested in a stable and permanent way, and noting how immovable property no longer has the importance it had in the past, and bearing in mind that the distinction between movable and immovable property today is not determined easily just on the basis of the criteria of Roman law, the formulation of can. 1530 of the 1917 Code was replaced with the expression *stable patrimony*.

If the concept is present in the Code of Canon Law, the basics of *stable patrimony* are not explicitly defined in the current Code, which presupposes a confirmation of the classical understanding, which is developed by the canonical doctrine of goods legitimately assigned to the juridical person as being a permanent endowment to facilitate the realization of the institute's purposes and ensure financial self-sufficiency.

Doctrine prior to the 1983 Code already spoke about stable patrimony, for example, Arturo Tabera defines it in the following terms: "Stable patrimony may be understood as those assets that almost make up the foundation of the existence of the person, such as earnings from capital one must live on. And accordingly, they are considered to have relative immutability. They are, in a certain way, intangible, they cannot be consumed, and one seeks to keep it far from the danger of loss or diminution."[7]

In more recent times, some authors, in our humble opinion, have stood out for having offered a useful description – not defi-

[6] *Communicationes* 12 (1980) 420.

[7] A. TABERA, *Il Diritto dei Religiosi*, Rome 1961, 101.

nition – for a greater understanding of the notion of stable patrimony.

For Rovera, a stable patrimony is made up of "the goods that [...] are destined to constitute the permanent endowment of the entity, which, directly or indirectly, allows the entity to realize its proper purposes." [8]

Commenting on can. 1285, López Alarcón has outlined the concept of stable patrimony in the following way: "Stable patrimony ought to be understood to mean the set of assets, which constitute the minimum and secure financial foundation from which the juridic person might be able to exist in an autonomous way, and carry out its proper purposes and services. There are not, however, absolute rules for nailing down the notion of the stability of an asset because this is defined by taking into account not only the nature and quantity of the goods, but also the economic requirements needed for fulfilling the purposes as well as the steady and expanding economic situation of the entity as it carries out its mission." [9]

Along the same lines, Jean-Pierre Schouppe emphasizes that "the stable patrimony is a collection of goods that enjoy a certain immutability, in such a way that any act that would modify it would be considered to be extraordinary administration. The rationale for these goods, legitimately assigned as a permanent endowment, is to ensure stable financial support in order to guarantee the entity's economic self-sufficiency and future viability as well as to facilitate the achievement of its proper purposes." [10]

On this subject, Christian Begus believes that "if something can be deduced from the letter of the canons, it is that the adjective 'stable' makes clear that this is a set of assets not intended for the ordinary operations of the juridic person. It involves, however, the presence of movable and immovable goods that not only constitute

[8] V. Rovera, *I beni temporali della Chiesa*, cit., 277.

[9] M. López Alarcón, Can. 1285, cit., 759.

[10] J.P. Schouppe, *Elementi di diritto patrimoniale canonico*, cit., 131.

the minimum financial and economic foundation for the autonomous existence of the ecclesiastical juridic person, but that also allow the person to carry out its proper purposes and services."[11]

There are two canons of the current Code of Canon Law – can. 1285 and can. 1291 – that use the term *stable patrimony.*

Such an expression appears, almost in passing, in can. 1285, which says: "Within the limits of ordinary administration only, administrators are permitted to make donations for purposes of piety or Christian charity from movable goods which do not belong to the stable patrimony." This is a canon, present in Book V of the Code, which is directly addressed to the administrators of ecclesiastical goods, authorizing them, on the one hand, to make donations, but limiting these acts of donation just for the purposes of Christian piety or charity, and only involving those movable goods that do not belong to the *stable patrimony.*

This first canon, without defining the criteria for identifying the stable patrimony, is limited to offering an indication of the goods that make up part of it, in that it states that it concerns goods which the administrator cannot dispose of, not even for the purpose of donations. In this canon, however, a clarification is introduced that is not present in can. 1291, which also talks about stable patrimony – that movable goods can also be among the patrimonial assets.

Can. 1291 explicitly speaks about *stable patrimony*, in reference to acts of alienation: "The permission of the authority competent according to the norm of law is required for the valid alienation of goods which constitute by legitimate designation the stable patrimony of a public juridic person and whose value exceeds the sum defined by law."

Can. 1291 also does not give a definition of stable patrimony, but the terminology is used to specify the goods for which alienation is being requested, for the validity of the act and the permission of the competent authority. Assuming the existence of this stable patrimony, the canon is concerned with specifying that this

[11] C. BEGUS, *Diritto patrimoniale canonico*, cit., 222.

consists of those goods that ought to be assigned to the stable patrimony with a specific act. We are speaking, in fact, of the constitution of goods in a stable patrimony *ex legitima assignatione*, an act posited in accordance with the norm of law, universal and/or particular.

While there are no absolute indications concerning the extent and the type of goods attributed to the stable patrimony, the innovation of the current Code is in expressing the need for an act of designation according to the law. It has been pointed out that "for public canonical juridical persons, then, there ought to be an act which determines which goods should constitute this patrimony. It is, therefore, a true and proper category of goods, that ought to be specified by the competent ecclesiastical authority. These goods belonging to the stable patrimony depend, then, on a precise legal act." [12]

All of the movable and immovable goods, the rights and debt/asset ratios of the juridic person, considered as a whole, make up the patrimony. The notion of *stable patrimony*, however, is not the same as the patrimony of the juridic person; in other words, not all the goods of a juridic person are goods belonging to the stable patrimony, nor are they presumed to be.

Indeed, the opposite presumption is the case, namely that all the goods of a juridic person are not goods belonging to the *stable patrimony*, since that requires a specific juridical act that removes such goods from being freely disposed of to being given to the stable patrimony. For public canonical juridical persons, then, there ought to be an act of legitimate designation that determines which goods ought to constitute such patrimony.

From what has been said, and keeping in mind the norms of the Code of Canon Law, the stable patrimony can be defined as that portion of goods of the total patrimony of a public juridic person that, following a legitimate designation, constitutes the minimum necessary for the financial survival of the person and for the fulfill-

[12] F. Grazian, Patrimonio stabile: istituto dimenticato?, cit., 283.

ment of its purposes, taking into account its particular circumstances, and precisely for these reasons it enjoys special protection at the time of its eventual alienation.

Can. 1291 also indicates that for every public canonical juridical person, one ought to specify, with its establishment or by means of a specific act at a later time, the set of goods that constitutes the stable patrimony. In this second case, when the legitimate designation happens after the person's establishment – since it is an act of special importance for the purposes of administration – this act ought to be considered an act of extraordinary administration and therefore fall under the norm of can. 1281.

Concerning the designation of certain goods to the stable patrimony, De Paolis writes: "If it is true that it is the act of legitimate designation which assigns the goods to the stable patrimony, one ought not to forget to point out: 1) that every juridic person has a stable patrimony and that certain goods are this way by nature because without them, the juridic person would absolutely not have the means to carry out its proper purposes; 2) that the extent of such goods needs to be appropriate to the nature, purposes and requirements of the juridic person; 3) that certain goods are, by their nature, non-disposable, so as not to risk the demise of the juridic person itself and that, therefore, they are, by nature, part of the stable patrimony and that, therefore, the legitimate designation is the implicit result of other acts; 4) that it is not licit to neglect making such a designation for the sole purpose of evading the requirements of canon law regarding alienation. Such laws, in fact, are for the protection of the goods themselves and, therefore, to guarantee ecclesiastical goods." [13]

That citation certainly deserves further consideration [14] we will want to consider elsewhere. However, now we turn our attention to the statement that there are goods that, by their very nature, belong to the stable patrimony. Those goods constitute the means

[13] V. DE PAOLIS, Alienazione, cit., 247.

[14] Cf. F. GRAZIAN, Patrimonio stabile: istituto dimenticato?, cit., 288-289.

necessary for the juridical subject to realize the institution's proper purposes.

It is easily understood then that the question of *stable patrimony* is not about assuring, through a certain amount of goods, that the public juridic person can provide for its own subsistence, but rather it is how the goods relate to the institutional purposes of the juridic person. Or, in other words, it is about guaranteeing that the public juridic person has the concrete possibility to pursue the purposes for which it was formed.

The public juridic person is entitled to the goods insofar as it has ecclesial purposes to achieve.[15] Therefore, it ought to ensure it has the necessary and sufficient means in order to be able to carry them out.

Although there is no explicit obligation of a stable patrimony, implicitly such an obligation derives from other canonical norms.

Can. 114 § 3 is extremely clear on this point: "The competent authority of the Church is not to confer juridic personality except on those aggregates of persons or things which pursue a truly useful purpose and, all things considered, possess the means which are foreseen to be efficient to achieve their designated purpose." Precisely due to the fact that its purpose is useful for the Church, this purpose ought to be supported by being able to provide the adequate means.

Because the legislator was limited just to envisaging the existence of a stable patrimony and avoided more detailed requirements, one might well wonder how the public juridic person may and should identify the extent and type of assets to designate to the stable patrimony.

From the above and with current doctrine, we believe that the goods that are designated as the stable patrimony must be deduced from the nature of the goods, and from the purposes that the juridical subject intends to achieve, and by the needs of the juridic person itself.

[15] Cf. can. 1254.

Just by way of some examples, the following are generally considered stable patrimony:

– the goods making up part of the foundational endowment of the entity;

– those received by the entity itself, if the source of the donation has so decided;

– those designated as stable patrimony by the governing body of the entity;

– movable goods given *ex voto* to the juridic person.

From what has been said, one finds "that the stable patrimony of a juridic person ought not to be set up in an arbitrary manner, but ought to be made up of a set of goods that, in some way, represent the entity itself, its official purposes, its current needs, the extent and nature of its activities, and the number of people that are part of it." [16]

We can say that these are goods that, due to their nature or function or destination, are connected to the purposes of the entity and, therefore, must be preserved.

In church doctrine, there are authors who invite us also to keep in mind historical-cultural factors that demand a particular juridical subject bind itself not only to those goods that are immediately instrumental for sustaining or pursuing its proper purposes, but also to goods that are a part of its history and related situation.

As has been rightly pointed out, the legitimate designation of an asset to the *stable patrimony* can have legal effects: "If, for example, the designation to the stable patrimony is done with the act of establishing the juridic person, it may also be the case that a change in the assets' ownership occurs by way of the designation to the new juridic person. In such a case, some provision should also be made so that the formalities required by the local civil law in force can be strictly observed. Sometimes, however, the competent

[16] F. GRAZIAN, Patrimonio stabile: istituto dimenticato?, cit., 289.

authority simply ascribes to the stable patrimony a good or set of goods that already belongs to the juridic person. In both cases the goods take on a special *stabilitas*,"[17] which does not mean inalienability in an absolute sense.

Back at the time of the Pio-Benedictine Code, the legislator did not use the term "inalienability". If one finds the heading, *De bonis eccelsiasticis non alienandis*, in old codifications and in the commentaries before the 1917 Code, the question of alienation is found in the Code of Canon Law of 1917 among sections dealing with contracts, indicating the cases in which alienation is possible.

Stable patrimony, however, does not mean assets that are permanently fixed, since the same law provides for possible modifications and even alienation under certain conditions and with certain precautions. While not being immovable in absolute terms, that *patrimony* is in fact, however, *stable* because it is stabilized. That is to say, it is clearly identified and protected, and thus, in some way fixed, even if such a situation is not necessarily absolute or irreversible. The law foresees, in fact, that in the presence of a proportionate reason and under precise rules, an asset belonging to the stable patrimony may be alienated.

A further point to consider is whether the designation of a particular good or a set of goods to the stable patrimony is a binding act, given that there is no unanimous consensus among the authors.

De Paolis and Schouppe, for example, pose two distinct positions. De Paolis maintains that: "There is no explicit obligation for a stable patrimony. But implicitly, such an obligation derives from other canonical norms. Therefore, can. 114 [...]. Can. 319 takes it as a given that the public juridic person has goods that do not cover the expenses of ordinary day-to-day life. But above all, the right for every juridic person to have goods for pursuing its purposes (which are always ecclesial purposes, cf. cann. 1254-1255) is rec-

[17] Ibid., 292.

ognized,"[18] while Schouppe does not insist on the obligatory nature of the designation.[19]

By virtue of that obligation – even if it is implicit, part of the doctrine holds that *stable patrimony* must be made for each public canonical juridical person, so that, if it has not been established, it will be necessary to provide it.

In order to delineate and identify the stable patrimony, it is useful to know which goods of the public juridic person should be specially protected so as to facilitate the job of the administrator and the person charged with oversight; it helps them understand what kind of authorization to ask for or to grant.

"The primary effect of designating the stable patrimony is not just formal. It allows for identifying what goods need to be preserved with special care and for having a clear idea about the size of the patrimony to be administered. It is necessary to be very clear that temporal goods are not part of the stable patrimony just because they are being given special attention, but that they ought to be given special attention precisely because they are part of the stable patrimony."[20]

Since can. 1291 emphasizes the importance of legitimate assignment so that a good may become part of a juridic person's *stable patrimony*, it therefore becomes opportune that every public juridic person in the church provide an inventory of goods that are part of its *stable patrimony* and make public, with acts that are equally valid in civil law, the act of legitimate assignment and the goods that are legitimately assigned.

Therefore, the principle of a good or a set of goods implicitly belonging to the stable patrimony because of its very nature, as suggested by parts of doctrine, cannot represent the rule in this area but, at best, an exception.

[18] V. De Paolis, Alienazione, cit., 10.

[19] Cf. J.P. Schouppe, *Elementi di diritto patrimoniale canonico*, cit., 13-132.

[20] F. Grazian, Patrimonio stabile: istituto dimenticato?, cit., 293.

With the institution of *stable patrimony*, the legislator tried to ensure not only the preservation of the means needed to support the existence of the public canonical juridical person, but also to ensure the effective pursuit of its institutional purposes.

Public associations of the faithful *in itinere*, institutes of consecrated life and societies of apostolic life are urged to implement these intentions of the law, interpreting them on the basis of the concrete situations of each public canonical juridical person, identifying the stable patrimony in accordance with its particular economic, financial and pastoral situation.

The legitimate assignment of specific goods – movable and immovable – to the *stable patrimony*; the effective legal protection of such patrimony; and the conditions for eventual alienation ought to be governed by proper norms, which are established by the competent authority within the institute and which also take universal norms into account.

SEBASTIANO PACIOLLA, O.CIST.
Under-secretary CICLSAL

A SUMMARY OUTLINE

✠ José Rodríguez Carballo, OFM

While I'd like to thank the commission that worked with me on drafting the guidelines that I am proposing, I'll begin with two brief comments:

a) These guidelines are intended to be finalized with a *Circular Letter* from the dicastery on "Guidelines for the Administration of the Assets in Institutes of Consecrated life and Societies of Apostolic Life";

b) These guidelines, in principle addressed to treasurers, must reach the major superiors and their councils.

Premise

Over the centuries, the choices made by consecrated persons in the field of economics have been significant, innovative and prophetic for all of humanity. The great innovations in history, even financial innovations, have been the fruit of gratuitousness and abundance; they are more than something anthropological, and they have made it possible for humanity to move forward. In this regard, religious charisms have often blazed new trails. Our founders have made innovations in the economic and social fields: management found its start in Benedictine abbeys; the first forms of microcredit came from the Franciscans; hospitals and schools were begun by religious congregations in the 1600s and in the 1800s, as were the first universities. In the current socio-economic context, humanity needs a prophetic presence in this field more than ever. Which new frontiers await us?

In an economic system where the maximization of profit and income seems to be the sole criterion for decisions made by corporations, our works must shine forth just like those places that are animated by the spirit of our founders, by the values of the Gospel and by other high ideals, without sacrificing the creation of economic value in order to be able to sustain them.[1] In an economic system that often – too often – generates inequity and exclusion,[2] we consecrated men and women, who follow a poor Christ, are called to offer witness that only through fraternity, sharing, solidarity and a wise use of resources is it possible to remedy the thousand forms of misery and poverty that people experience. We, consecrated persons, are convinced that the economic dimension is not an optional in our consecrated life but is fundamental because of how it is connected to the mission and to our following Christ. Fundamental choices in our lives have to do with the economy and when we make these choices, our choice to live the vow of poverty, have a sober lifestyle and be attentive to others must come through.

This particular moment in history we are going through is seeing consecrated men and women experiencing certain difficulties in the financial field. Institutes find themselves managing large properties and complex works at a time when, in many parts of the world, vocations are diminishing, lay personnel is increasing and budgetary constraints are increasingly tighter. In more complex situations, we sometimes lose control of the works and these, because of concrete choices being made, move further and further away from our charism. Sometimes consecrated persons' management styles are self-centered, and they are not aware that if things are badly administered or are administered for one's own self, the problems that follow stain the Church's image. On the contrary, good management leads to trust in the Church. The need to live out a sound and wise management of goods and money also con-

[1] BENEDICT XVI, Encycl. Lett. *Caritas in veritate*, 37.

[2] FRANCIS, Ap. Exhort. *Evangelii gaudium*, 53.

cerns institutes that do not operate works as well as secular institutes; in this field our witness is fundamental.

Another difficulty is linked to the sound administration and management of the institute's patrimony, which is fruit of the work and resourcefulness of our predecessors and fruit of God's charity through donations and wills. This cannot be put at risk. Consecrated men and women are just the guardians. Nevertheless, many times, part of the patrimony may have high operating costs and then, with prudence, we must also know how to free ourselves from it, keeping in mind that, first of all, works of charity and prayer may continue. But according to what criteria? The exact opposite problem presents itself in places were consecrated life is experiencing expansion: there we run the risk of acquiring property or constructing buildings without sufficient planning and without a project.

Given the current situation and the difficulties that we live today, we as communities of consecrated life are called to express our discipleship of Christ in a new way, to lift our gaze, to give concrete witness that our goods are at the service of humanity.

Given the current complexities tied to the globalization of the economy and the management of goods, today more than ever, it is important that the figure of the treasurer or finance officer is not simply that of an executor or an accountant, but of a person who is prepared, who knows how to provide the general council with all of the necessary information and means for discernment and making decisions. While it is true that the economic dimension stands alongside all the others, it is equally important that the treasurer contribute to the discernment regarding any apostolic decision by providing his or her own point of view. The service of the general treasurer includes management, oversight, assistance and counsel, formation and information. Given the current circumstances and the new way of understanding economics, it would be good to have the treasurer at least participate in the council's meetings concerning economic matters if he or she is not part of the council.

Poverty

Our following Christ asks us first of all to be witnesses to justice, transparency and dependence on God. We want to say, with our personal and communal lives, that goods have been entrusted to us in order to open us up to charity and to serve the Church. This frees us from the desire to possess; indeed, it makes us evangelically free to live "without anything of our own." To live the vow of poverty today demands that we make choices expressing communion and solidarity: solidarity and communion among us and with the poor, *in imitation of the first Christian community, where no one was in need because everyone shared.* Nothing belongs to us, everything is given by the grace and love of God. Our task is to safeguard it, administer it with competence and "give it back" with generosity to the poor. In an age of globalization, to live in evangelical poverty means to feel how we are mutually dependent on each other. Prophetic gestures of interdependence for the institutes would be helping each other in the management of their goods and sharing goods among themselves for the service of humanity.

Following Christ also implies industriousness and labor. Sacred Scripture, particularly St. Paul (*1 Thes* 4:11; *2 Thes* 3:6-12), calls us to the commitment to work with our hands and to not waste time, which is a precious and free gift from God, who calls us to account. It's about living off our work and, therefore, paying attention to certain investments that, beyond the risk they may involve, might be used as a way "to spare" the person making the investment from his or her duty to work.

St. Francis, the founder of the first school of economics, writes in his Testament: "I worked with my own hands and I am still determined to work; and with all my heart I want all the other friars to be busy with some kind of work that can be carried on without scandal. Those who do not know how to work should learn [...]. When we receive no recompense for our work, we can turn to God's table and beg alms from door to door."[3] It can be seen from this that St. Francis places the grace of work in first place and in second place is the scenario of asking for alms, which today we call "fundraising." We are called to share life, to listen, to welcome, to proclaim, to give one's life for the kingdom of God and for the community that has been given to us, to get our hands dirty with the least among us, to generously give our time and energies to others. Only in this way can we count on the generosity of divine providence. Only the person who works is entitled to speak about the vow of poverty and true solidarity.

Finally, the communal witness of our vow of poverty depends on a transparent, innovative, prudent and wise management of goods and works: waste and losses resulting from bad management deprive us of resources to share in the mission; goods that we do not share cannot be the means and place for proclaiming God's love because they do not comply with Gospel values, to the *koinonia* of the Church or to the social doctrine of the Church.

The greatest challenge that we have before us is to show with our works and with our goods that God bends down to the men and women of our time to console them, particularly to the poor, to help them, support them and love them. The following words are meant to be a guide and a help in responding to this challenge.

Formation

Formation in respect to economic issues, so they are seen with the logic of the Gospel and in accord with the social teachings of the Church and one's own charism, is fundamental so that choices for the mission can be innovative and prophetic.

LIGHTS: Institutes are investing a lot in formation, above all in permanent and continuing formation; treasurers' associations and groups exist so information and best practices can be exchanged. These are experiences of interdependence and communion.

[3] *FF* 119-120.

SHADOWS: General formation in economic matters, which is not only for treasurers, is missing in institutes. This creates a dichotomy between finances and mission. Furthermore, formation for treasurers is not always adequate given the new trends and changing role of the treasurer, which is shifting from a perspective of financial reporting to one of management.

SUGGESTIONS: The financial sphere touches many aspects of our life and formation must take this into account at all levels.

– Initial formation must include programs on finances and management, the costs of community life and the missions, and accountability in living the vow of poverty today. This formation must help with developing a clear and courageous reading of reality in order to then offer adequate responses based in the Gospel.

– Formation in financial matters must be included in formation programs in pontifical universities – the majority of which are managed by religious, and in centers of study and centers of formation for consecrated persons.

– Formation for treasurers must increase the brothers' and sisters' awareness of the evangelical principles on which financial transactions are based and also provide them with the skills so that the treasurer's task is carried out with competence in line with sound management; treasurers must also be helped and accompanied so they can carry out their role as being one of service – and not a position of control, of being generous and proactive in ensuring the availability of assets for the apostolate and the mission.

– Formation of local, provincial and general councils must keep these matters in mind along with the governing body's responsibility regarding financial choices, which are to be made for the development of the mission and in accordance with the goods that have been entrusted to us.

– The study of finances and management must be "new," even in seeking new models and paradigms. We must have the courage to think of different ways of managing and not to believe that approaches are neutral in relation to the goals that we want to reach. Formation in financial matters will not change so long as we continue to believe that principles are on one side and skills we get from books on management are separate and somewhere else. We must have the courage to invent new approaches that correspond to our principles. For this reason, we also need people who are serious and high-level scholars of economics and management to develop new theories, methods and tools.

Mission and works

Works are the expression of the mission. Historically, works change in response to the needs of the times and take on different expressions, according to social and cultural contexts. It may happen, then, that we find ourselves with works that are no longer in accordance with the current expression of the mission and with properties that no longer serve the works as an expression of the charism.

LIGHTS: There is a variety of very comprehensive works that respond to multiple expressions of need. Often these works become well-established and developed, and sometimes they are ahead of the times and are a beacon for human and social development. In some cases, they are the only response to needs that other institutions have not succeeded in giving a response and solution to.

SHADOWS: It can happen that an institute, which in the past had given life to a work that was a response in accordance with its mission, finds itself today keeping these works alive just to keep them going and not so much as a way to express the mission. Or, moreover, it happens that it loses control of certain works that are no longer a sign of the original mission. Or, it happens that, after seeking help from outside institutions, a work is created that is different from the founding mission. For example, the founder had a charism of nursing, but always refused to work in hospitals, preferring to help people abandoned on the margins. Meanwhile, today the institute owns hospitals that are only accessible to people who can pay for treatment. Or the founder of an institute had an educational charism exclusively aimed at poor and marginalized youth in the peripheries and today the institute owns schools in the heart of the city and where only children whose parents have high incomes can attend.

SUGGESTIONS: Undertake a re-reading of the mission according to the charism, focusing on the founding vision and identifying characteristics of the works set up as a response. Through this re-reading, one can determine what to continue, what to shut down, what to modify and, above all, which new frontiers to strike paths of development and witness to the mission in response to the needs of today, in harmony with the vision of the founders.

In this redefinition, done in dialogue with the particular Church, there is a need to draw attention to the sustainability of the works and the properties assigned to them. It is a re-reading a property's opportunities, too, not just in light of a patrimony to preserve and bear fruit, but also as an occasion of service for works that perhaps are no longer relevant to the mission of the institute which owns the property, but might be for other institutes or organizations that want to contribute with their efforts to the development and realization of works that are in keeping with their founding values and mission. Whenever there is need to build new structures, experience tells us that they need to be structures that are versatile and easy to manage, less burdensome over time and, in moments of vocational difficulty, easily transferable or partially usable without high management costs. We think it is *necessary* to be careful not to export structures that are already unmanageable in richer countries to countries that have fewer economic resources.

Relationship with the Bishops and the local Church

Our mission is universal and the mission of many institutes embraces the whole world. Nonetheless, it is also incarnated in specific local situations.

LIGHTS: In some dioceses, dialogue and good relationships between the bishops and major superiors have allowed for some property or works to be transformed to serve the mission in a new way; many times the institutes respond with generosity to bishops who call them to different dioceses.

SHADOWS: Often it happens that the institutes transform or alienate their goods without sufficiently informing the dioceses, and sometimes they leave an entire territory without the presence of Catholics and religious; other times, dioceses "appropriate" the institute's goods without recognizing their fair value.

SUGGESTIONS: It is important to create conditions for regular dialogue between the bishop and the major superiors of institutes in the diocese, and not to leave this dialogue up to the goodwill of individuals or only when goods are being alienated or acquired. When dialogue is regular and consistent, even extraordinary decisions are made with mutual respect, in a way that is not impulsive and does not make mistakes. Consistent dialogue can, furthermore, help bishops better understand the importance and significance of religious life in a diocese. It is also important, before making significant decisions regarding a specific territory, that institutes share their intentions with other institutes, so as not to leave and entire territory without the presence of religious.

Planning

To think in terms of prevention helps mobilize all the resources for the mission and not waste resources – even this is a way to live the vow of poverty today.

LIGHTS: Some institutes have done budgeting and planning by seeking to create project plans for their works, and the results show.

SHADOWS: Many times instruments, such as budget plans, project planning and operating budgets, are experienced as a burden, and how they can be used to their full potential is not understood. Many times these instruments are not used at all and, along the way, one keeps running into problems, which in time increasingly get bigger.

SUGGESTIONS: Every institute should put procedures in place that allow for sound planning. Planning that is done well helps achieve the mission and it is indispensable when starting up new works. It is useful for making informed decisions, even in the process of disposing of or alienating property. Good planning foresees the use of budgets and balance sheets, the flagging and verification of budget variances, the oversight of management, the cautious reading of balance sheets, and the assessment and adjustment of steps to be taken. Everything is based on multi-year plans and projections in a way that preempts problems rather than chases after them. Works incurring losses are to be monitored and followed up on, seeking, even with the help of qualified experts, to implement deficit reduction plans. In these cases, a dependency culture must be overcome. Trying to cover the operational losses of a work that has management problems without resolving those problems means wasting money that could be used for the mission differently.

Budgeting tools also should be used in communities as a means of formation and education in the area of finance and as a way to share in what many families experience – the need to plan their spending properly in order to make it through to the end of the month.

Transparency

The world today does not ask us not to have any goods, but rather to manage them in full transparency, in compliance with the laws and while addressing countless forms of poverty.

LIGHTS: Some congregations have annual audits and they have the budgets of their works certified; financial decisions are shared within many congregations and people participate in defining the financial goals at the service of the mission.

SHADOWS: However, there remain cases of a lack of clarity, of not sharing the budgets, of personalizing works in a way that there seems to be no need for sharing information about how works are progressing. Clear processes of delegation and accountability for the person who is delegated are missing. Many times, budgets presented to the council are not clear and are sometimes incomprehensible.

SUGGESTIONS: Transparency is critical for the efficiency and effectiveness of the mission and it is needed in order to have a clear reading of how works are going. Transparent procedures are a sign of love for the work, but also a sign of the necessary objectivity the person must have in order to manage the work well. One also teaches transparency by forming people to share and to make choices in communion. With this line of thinking, oversight must not be understood as a lack of trust, but as an expression of service to communion and transparency, as well as a way to protect those who carry out the delicate task of administration. To be transparent and share with others implies that the superiors have a clear picture of how all the works in a province are to be managed, whether they are owned by the institute, are promoted by the institute or are an extension of the institute (associations, for example). Finally, and always with the goal of transparency in mind, it is very important that there be a clear distinction between the budgets of the works and budgets of the communities.

Management of goods

The institute's goods and the money it manages belong to the Church and they are to be used for works of charity. Therefore, they should not be put at risk and their management must be transparent.

LIGHTS: Many institutes have sound procedures for protecting the goods of the institute; over the years, attention to money management has increased with particular awareness about ethical investments.

SHADOWS: Sometimes money is wasted with bad or hasty management that is carried out superficially and without considering all of the possible consequences. It should also be taken into account that investments are always at risk due to the fragility of the economic system.

SUGGESTIONS: Make simple and ethical investments where the capital may always be guaranteed and written in the contracts that are drawn up with companies and banks. We must be very careful about promises of really high gains because this means putting the capital at risk. It is necessary that institutes are aware of the risks and are prepared to take them because every investment involves risk. Plans for money investments must be shared with the major superiors.

Relationships with collaborators and consultants

It is impossible today go without the collaboration of the laity, qualified experts and members of other institutes when it comes to the financial management of goods and works.

LIGHTS: It is important to collaborate with laypeople and experts, who can help treasurers and councils with the complex situations of financial management. It is a sign of hope that there are so many reliable people who collaborate with us, often as volunteers, in advisory commissions and study groups.

SHADOWS: Two extremes exist. On the one hand there are those who do not make use of consultants to avoid spending money, thereby taking the risk of running into legal, financial or tax problems. On the other hand, there are those who squander the institute's money on consultants, who have been hired without discernment or who do not always end up being effective. Sometimes institutes are preyed on by unscrupulous consultants, who squander the institute's patrimony or who use the good faith of treasurers in order to render favors or help friends.

SUGGESTIONS: Professional consultants are necessary in tax, legal, administrative and management matters, and they are essential when it is not possible to find the needed professional skills within the institute. Prior to choosing a consultant, information must be requested and the required evaluations must be made – never just go by the first impression. Consultants and employees must not be chosen from among benefactors, relatives and friends; in the same vein, relationships must be professional and not overly friendly. A good practice for an institute that has different provinces and uses different consultants is to have the consultants meet periodically and get equal compensation. Collaboration among institutes could also build up a sort of roster of trustworthy consultants.

Good management, planning and prevention, lived in the communion of goods, are the key to sustainability, not only financial sustainability, but also relational and spiritual. When financial problems gnaw at communities, relationships become more difficult and spiritual life can be affected. And then vice versa: bad financial management also can be the consequence of a superficial spiritual and community life. May our communities know how to find the way for a prophetic evangelical witness in every area of human life.

Changes to structures

I want to conclude with an invitation to change the structures of the current economic system that is "unjust at its root" because it gives precedence to "the survival of the fittest, where the powerful feed upon the powerless" (Pope Francis). The economic crisis that we are living through will be resolved not with a "superficial solidarity" of occasional assistance, even if this is necessary. Rather, it will need the creation of structures that are in line with the values that give meaning to our consecrated life, beginning with the internal structures of our institutes – local, provincial, general – and with economic structures that respond to what here was called a "civic economy" and that are created with the values of justice, fraternity and gratuitousness. It is not enough to intervene in the distribution of benefits in an economic structure, which is, at times, the fruit of a "structure of sin" (Paul VI). It is necessary to lay the foundations for an economy, which in this symposium we called "spiritual" or "ecological." It is this kind of economy, with rules that are very different from the free-market economy, which must take on "flesh and thought" in our institutions. Just as our fellow brothers and sisters who preceded us did, we consecrated persons today are called to create new economic structures that respond to the new situations we are living in.

The first words in this symposium were those of the Holy Father. I would like to conclude these guidelines by making reference to the message that Pope Francis benevolently sent us. From this message, I would like to underline 10 commandments as a kind of mandate for us consecrated men and women:

1. Let yourselves question the economy of inequality and exclusion.

2. Be protagonists and active in living and witnessing the principle of gratuitousness and the logic of gift.

3. Give a real contribution to economic, social and political development.

4. Make fidelity to the founding path and the consequent spiritual patrimony, as well as the purposes of each institute, remain the primary criteria for evaluating the management of goods.

5. Pay close attention so that your goods may be administered with prudence and transparency.

6. In such a time as ours, so absorbed with conquering, possessing and prestige, be prophetic voices and witnesses; build a new and authentic Christian way of thinking and a new style of church life.

7. Live a loving poverty, which creates solidarity, sharing and charity and which is expressed in sobriety, the search for justice and joy in the essential.

8. Touch the body of Christ in the poor.

9. Be the outposts of attention to all the poor and all forms of poverty – material, moral and spiritual – in the logic of the Gospel, which teaches to trust in Providence.

10. Wake up the world with a prophetic administration of goods, too.

✠ JOSÉ RODRÍGUEZ CARBALLO, OFM
Archbishop Secretary CICLSAL

Congregation for Institutes of Consecrated Life and Societies of Apostolic Life

De Aviz, Cardinal João Braz
Prefect of the Congregation for Institutes of Consecrated Life and Societies of Apostolic Life

Carballo, José Rodríguez, OFM
Archbishop Secretary of the Congregation for Institutes of Consecrated Life and Societies of Apostolic Life

Paciolla, Sebastiano, O.CIST.
Under-secretary of the Congregation for Institutes of Consecrated Life and Societies of Apostolic Life

Spezzati, Nicla, ASC
Under-secretary of the Congregation for Institutes of Consecrated Life and Societies of Apostolic Life

Speakers

Adam, Miroslav Konštanc, OP (Slovakia)
Professor of Canon Law, Rector of the Pontifical University "Angelicum," Rome

Aquini, Marco (Italy)
Focolare Movement, "Communion of goods, economy and work," professor of international cooperation for development at the Pontifical University of St. Thomas, "Angelicum," Rome

Barban, Alessandro, OSB.CAM (Italy)
Prior general of the Camaldolese Congregation of the Order of St. Benedict

Franc, Evelyne, DC (France)
Superior general of the Daughters of Charity

González Silva, Santiago Mª, CMF (Spain)
Professor of theology of apostolic life and social doctrine of the Church, dean of the Institute of the Theology of the Consecrated Life "Claretianum," Pontifical Lateran University, Rome

Impagliazzo, Marco (Italy)
President of the Community of Sant'Egidio, professor of contemporary history at the University for Foreigners, Perugia

MARTIN, PEGGY ANN, OP (USA)
Senior vice-president of sponsorship and governance at Catholic Health Initiatives, Denver, CO

MULLER, JEAN PAUL, SDB (Luxembourg)
Economer general of the Salesians of John Bosco

PACHÓN, ADOLFO NICOLÁS, SJ (Spain)
Superior General of the Society of Jesus, President of the USG

PERLASCA, ALBERTO (Italy)
Official at the Vatican's Secretariat of State, administration office

PUDUMAI DOSS, JESU, SDB (India)
Professor of Canon Law, former Dean of the Faculty of Canon Law at the Salesian Pontifical University, Rome

REUNGOAT, YVONNE, FMA (France)
Superior General of the Daughters of Mary Help of Christians

ROBINSON, KERRY A. (USA)
Executive director of the National Leadership Roundtable on Church Management

RODRÍGUEZ CORREA, OLGA MARÍA (Uruguay)
Focolare Movement, "Communion of goods, economy and work"

RODRÍGUEZ ECHEVERRÍA, ÁLVARO, FSC (Costa Rica)
Superior General of the Institute of the Brothers of the Christian Schools

SÁNCHEZ GONZÁLEZ, ENRIQUE, MCCJ (Mexico)
Superior General of the Comboni Missionaries of the Heart of Jesus

SUGAWARA, YUJI, SJ (Japan)
Professor of Canon Law, dean of the faculty of Canon Law at the Pontifical Gregorian University, Rome

TOBIN, JOSEPH W., CSsR (USA)
Archbishop of Indianapolis, former secretary of the Congregation for Institutes of Consecrated Life and Societies of Apostolic Life

ZAMAGNI, STEFANO (Italy)
Full Professor of political economy at the University of Bologna, adjunct professor at Johns Hopkins University (USA)

TABLE OF CONTENTS

SECOND SESSION

Moderator

Sister Nicla Spezzati, ASC

Under-secretary of the CICLSAL

PAPER

REPORTS

THIRD SESSION

Moderator

Brother Jean Paul Muller, SDB

General Econome of the Salesian Society of Saint John Bosco

PAPER

ROUNDTABLE

Toward a Prophetic, Caring Economy of Communion

Chair

Sister Evelyne Franc, DC

Superior General of the Daughters of Charity

FOURTH SESSION

Moderator

Father Adolfo Nicolás Pachón, SJ

Superior General of the Society of Jesus

QUAESTIONES

A SUMMARY OUTLINE

www.ingramcontent.com/pod-product-compliance
Ingram Content Group UK Ltd.
Pitfield, Milton Keynes, MK11 3LW, UK
UKHW052228270726
14060UKWH00004B/654